The Deception Planners

At the beginning of the Second World War Dennis Wheatley was an internationally famous, bestselling author. He was also 42 years old. He wanted passionately to get into the war but initially his efforts were unsuccessful. Then, through a series of introductions and as a result of putting forward some imaginative ideas on how Britain might resist invasion, he found himself – to his own astonishment – recruited into a small, highly secret department in the offices of the War Cabinet. On 31 December 1941 he became a Deception Planner.

The object of this department, working close to the control centre of Britain's strategy, was to divert the resources of the enemy away from the real Allied operations which were being planned and to direct them instead against imaginary operations devised by Dennis Wheatley and his handful of colleagues. Some of these deceptions – such as 'The Man Who Never Was' and 'Monty's Double' – have since become well known, but many have not been disclosed until now. The climax came over D-Day itself when it was vital that, with tens of thousands of lives at stake, the Germans should be deceived about the time and place of the Allied assault on Europe.

The Deception Planners is an almost day-to-day account of these men and their work – written from the inside. But it is far from being a dry historical record. Here is the war seen from a unique angle, and commented on vigorously and in a highly personal way. It is also the last of Dennis Wheatley's books to be published – not unfittingly, for he himself regarded the years which it describes as the most fascinating and valuable of his life.

Also by Dennis Wheatley

NOVELS

Duke de Richleau
The Prisoner in the Mask
The Second Seal
Vendetta in Spain
Three Inquisitive People
The Forbidden Territory
†The Devil Rides Out
The Golden Spaniard
†Strange Conflict
Codeword – Golden Fleece
Dangerous Inheritance
†Gateway to Hell

Gregory Sallust
Contraband
The Scarlet Impostor
Faked Passports
The Black Baroness
V for Vengeance
Come into My Parlour
Traitors' Gate
†They Used Dark Forces
Black August
The Island Where Time Stands Still
The White Witch of the South Seas

Julian Day
The Quest of Julian Day
The Sword of Fate
Bill for the Use of a Body

Roger Brook
The Launching of Roger Brook
The Shadow of Tyburn Tree
The Rising Storm
The Man Who Killed the King
The Dark Secret of Josephine
The Rape of Venice
The Sultan's Daughter
The Wanton Princess
Evil in a Mask
The Ravishing of Lady Mary Ware
†The Irish Witch*
Desperate Measures*

†To the Devil – a Daughter
†The Satanist

The Eunuch of Stamboul
The Secret War
The Fabulous Valley
Sixty Days to Live
Such Power is Dangerous
Uncharted Seas
The Man Who Missed the War
†The Haunting of Toby Jugg
Star of Ill-Omen
They Found Atlantis
†The Ka of Gifford Hillary
Curtain of Fear
Mayhem in Greece
Unholy Crusade
The Strange Story of Linda Lee*

SHORT STORIES
Mediterranean Nights
Gunmen, Gallants and Ghosts

HISTORICAL
'Old Rowley': A Private Life of Charles II (*Illustrated by Frank C. Papé*)
Red Eagle (*The Story of the Russian Revolution*)

AUTOBIOGRAPHICAL
Stranger than Fiction* (*War Papers for the Joint Planning Staff*)
Saturdays with Bricks*

MEMOIRS: THE TIME HAS COME...
The Young Man Said 1897–1914*
Officer and Temporary Gentleman 1914–1919*
Drink and Ink 1919–1977*

SATANISM
The Devil and All His Works*

All these books, with the exception of those marked*, are in The Lymington Edition
†Black magic stories

Dennis Wheatley

The Deception Planners

My Secret War

Hutchinson
London Melbourne Sydney Auckland Johannesburg

Hutchinson & Co (Publishers) Ltd
An imprint of the Hutchinson Publishing Group

3 Fitzroy Square, London W I P 6JD

Hutchinson Group (Australia) Pty Ltd
30–32 Cremorne Street, Richmond South, Victoria 3121
PO Box 151, Broadway, New South Wales 2007

Hutchinson Group (NZ) Ltd
32–34 View Road, PO Box 40–086, Glenfield, Auckland 10

Hutchinson Group (SA) (Pty) Ltd
PO Box 337, Bergvlei 2012, South Africa

First published 1980

© Dennis Wheatley Ltd 1980

Set in Monotype Baskerville

Printed in Great Britain by The Anchor Press Ltd
and bound by Wm Brendon & Son Ltd
both of Tiptree, Essex

British Library Cataloguing in Publication Data
Wheatley, Dennis
   The deception planners.
   1. World War 1939–45 – Secret service –
Great Britain
   2. World War, 1939–1945 – Personal narratives,
British
   I. Title
   940.54'86'410924   D810.S7

ISBN 0 09 141830 5

I dedicate this book
to my father, my grandfathers
and to my great friend in the First
World War, Gordon Eric Gordon-Tombe,
who, between them, made me
what I am

Contents

	EDITOR'S NOTE BY ANTHONY LEJEUNE	11
	LIST OF ABBREVIATIONS	14
	MEMBERS OF LONDON CONTROLLING SECTION	16
1	How It All Began	17
2	The Offices of the War Cabinet	23
3	First Faltering Footsteps	34
4	I Endeavour to Earn My Pay	44
5	Colonel Bevan Takes Over	58
6	We Move to the Basement	66
7	Preparations for Torch	77
8	Torch	88
9	After the Landings	102
10	The Casablanca Conference	112
11	The Completion of the Deception Section	126
12	'Nothing to Hide'	140
13	Operation Husky	149
14	Plan Bodyguard	159
15	The Americans Force Anvil on Us	165
16	Our Fake Army and Great *Coup* in Sweden	172
17	The Secret Weapon, Spies and the False Montgomery	183
18	D-Day	196
19	The Battle for France	210
20	Tribute and Departure	220
	GLOSSARY OF CODENAMES	230
	INDEX	231

Illustrations

Between pages 80 and 81

Dennis Wheatley as Squadron Leader
War Cabinet's underground headquarters,
near Whitehall
Colonel John Bevan
The London Controlling Section
General Lord Ismay
Joan Bright and Field Marshal Sir John Dill
Air Chief Marshal Sir William Elliot
Major-General Sir Leslie Hollis, RM
DW at his desk in the offices of
the War Cabinet

Editor's Note
Anthony Lejeune

When my old friend Dennis Wheatley died in November 1977, the obituary announcement in *The Times* said simply: 'Dennis Wheatley. Sailor, soldier, airman and author'. His own memoirs of a long and busy life were rather less succinct. They ran to five large volumes, of which only the first had been published and the second was in preparation at the time of his death. It was afterwards decided to combine the third and fifth volumes into a single book, *Drink and Ink*, which appeared in 1979, completing, in effect, his personal story. The fourth volume was distinct from the others. It dealt exclusively with his work during the Second World War as a Deception Planner in the offices of the War Cabinet.

Providing, as it does, an intimate picture of what went on in a small, highly secret, department close to the control-centre of Britain's strategy, it has some historical importance and will interest readers beyond the large circle of Dennis Wheatley's usual admirers.

Based on material actually put down on paper shortly after the war, it was supplemented but never fully revised. Since it describes, in close detail, events which occurred nearly forty years ago and many of its major characters – especially Colonel J. H. Bevan, who headed the Deception Unit – are now dead, checking facts and dates and names has been difficult. Mistakes, lapses of memory, may have slipped through. But this book (which was originally to have been called *Secrets of the War Cabinet*) is not, and does not purport to be, a detached historical record.* It is a unique, entirely individual, account of a little-known but not insignificant aspect of the war – as Dennis Wheatley experienced it, remembered it and reacted to it.

When the war began, Dennis was 42 years old and a very successful author. (In 1938 his books had earned him £12,647 – the equivalent of more than £200,000 today). He thought his services might be useful to the newly formed Ministry of Information: but his three applications were never even acknowledged. His elder stepson, William Younger, was already serving in MI5, having been recruited while still at Oxford. His wife, Joan, and her daughter, Diana, now also joined MI5. His second stepson, Jack, was a regular officer in the Coldstream Guards. Their pre-war servants were working in a munitions factory. But, to his chagrin, Dennis, who had fought in France during the First World War, could find no war-time job except as a group controller of Air Raid Wardens.

Having been bombed out of their house in St John's Wood during the winter of 1940, he and Joan took a flat in Earls Court, on the ground floor of a block called Chatsworth Court, which had a sizeable restaurant in the basement, where they could entertain. Diana and Bill took flats in the same block.

Then, in May 1940, Joan suggested to a colleague in MI5 that Dennis might be able to devise some useful and original ideas on home defence. He duly submitted a paper entitled *Resistance to Invasion*, copies of which went to the Joint Planning Staff of the War Cabinet, eventually to the Chiefs of Staff and even to the King. During the next eighteen months, he wrote nineteen other papers, with such titles as *Village Defence, Aerial Warfare, How to Keep Turkey Out of the War, Total War, After the Battle*, and so on.†

By now he had become friendly with a number of officers on the Joint Planning Staff. In November 1941 Group

---

* For that, readers are referred to Dr Charles Cruikshank's *Deception in World War II* (OUP 1979), which is based on official papers in the Public Record Office and the National Archives of the United States.

† These papers were published under the title of *Stranger than Fiction* (Hutchinson 1959).

Editor's Note

Captain William 'Dickie' Dickson (who afterwards became a Marshal of the Royal Air Force and Chairman of the Chiefs of Staff Committee) asked him to lunch to meet Colonel Oliver Stanley. Dickson had just been promoted Director of Plans (Air); Stanley was the Chief of Future Operations Planning Staff (FOPS).

Dennis was clearly being vetted for some kind of official job, probably, he thought, in a propaganda department. A few days later Stanley telephoned, summoned Dennis to his office and told him – to Dennis's surprise and delight – that he was to work under Stanley himself on the Joint Planning Staff. . . .

Abbreviations

AOC	Air Officer Commanding
CAS	Chief of Air Staff
CIGS	Chief of Imperial General Staff
CNS	Chief of Naval Staff
COSSAC	Chief of Staff to Supreme Allied Commander
DDSD	Deputy Director of Staff Duties
DMI	Director of Military Intelligence
DMO	Director of Military Operations
DNI	Director of Naval Intelligence
DPR	Director of Public Relations
EPS	Executive Planning Staff
FO	Foreign Office
FOPS	Future Operations Planning Staff
FUSAG	First US Army Group (fake)
GOC	General Officer Commanding
GSO1	General Staff Officer, Class 1
GSO2	General Staff Officer, Class 2
ISSB	Inter-Services Security Board
JIC	Joint Intelligence Committee
JPS	Joint Planning Staff
LCS	London Controlling Section
MEW	Ministry of Economic Warfare
MI(R)	Military Intelligence (Research)
MI5	Military Intelligence (Security Service)
MI6	Military Intelligence (Secret Intelligence Service)

Abbreviations

MI9	Military Intelligence (War Office branch responsible for escape and evasion of POWs)
OKW	*Oberkommando der Wehrmacht*
PAIFORCE	Persia and Iraq Force
PWE	Political Warfare Executive
SHAEF	Supreme Headquarters Allied Expeditionary Force
SIS	Secret Intelligence Service
SOE	Special Operations Executive
STRATS	Strategical Planning Staff
VCAS	Vice-Chief of Air Staff
VCIGS	Vice-Chief of Imperial General Staff

London Controlling Section and its predecessor
(in order of appointment)

Deception Section of Future Operations Planning Staff
(formed Dec 1941)
Lieutenant-Colonel A. F. R. Lumby, CIE, OBE (Dec 1941).
Pilot Officer D. Y. Wheatley, RAFVR (Jan 1942).

London Controlling Section
(detached from FOPS and renamed, Jun 1942).
Lieutenant-Colonel (later Colonel) J. H. Bevan, MC, Controlling Officer (Jun 1942).
Flight-Lieutenant (later Wing Commander) D. Y. Wheatley, RAFVR (Jun 1942).
Major (later Lieutenant-Colonel) Harold Peteval (Aug 1942).
Major (later Colonel) Ronald Wingate, CIE (Sept 1942); appointed Deputy Controlling Officer Dec 1942; appointed Controlling Officer, in succession to Colonel Bevan, Sept 1945.
Major Neil Gordon Clark (Mar 1943).
Major Derrick Morley (Mar 1943).

Attached:
Sir Reginald Hoare (Foreign Office representative).
Professor H. A. de C. Andrade, President of the Royal Society (part-time scientific adviser).

Chapter 1
How It All Began

Feints and cover plans designed to mislead the enemy are as old as the art of war itself. The beating of war drums, or the herding of cattle through bush, on one side of a village about to be attacked by a raiding tribe on the other, was practised before the dawn of history; and, if the truth be known, the successful blowing of trumpets under the walls of Jericho was, no doubt, a *ruse de guerre*.

There have been few great commanders who did not give much thought as to how best they could deceive the enemy about their intentions. But, until 1940, the employment of such stratagems and ruses depended solely upon the initiative of officers actively engaged in operations. No individual, or section, charged with the specific, whole-time duty of thinking out, proposing and implementing measures specifically designed to cause enemy Intelligence to make false appreciations, existed on the establishment of any headquarters staff.

There were, of course, departments in each of the British service ministries that concerned themselves with certain types of deception. A section of Naval Intelligence at the Admiralty used a variety of methods for misleading the enemy as to the whereabouts of HM ships, the sailing dates of convoys, etc.; while the Air Ministry appears to have gone much further than the other services in using wireless ruses to mislead the enemy about actual operations.

Each service ministry also had its department for using camouflage and dummies. Of these the redoubtable Air Ministry 'Star Fish' organization at Shepperton, under the extremely able direction of Colonel Sir John Turner, was by far the most advanced.

By comparison, the Army Camouflage Development Centre at Farnham, under Lieutenant-Colonel Baddington, was a very amateur affair; and no serious effort was made by the Admiralty to develop visual deception until Combined Operations Headquarters was formed in 1942 and Lieutenant the Earl of Antrim, RNR, was charged with creating dummy hards and landing-craft hides.

In addition, there existed at the War Office a section, having the free use of secret funds, called MI(R). This section consisted of four be-ribboned veterans and a girl: Colin Gubbins (later Major-General and head of SOE), Joe Holland (later Major-General), Norman Crockatt (later Brigadier MI9), Eddie Combe (later Lieutenant-Colonel and Military Member of the Inter-Services Security Board), and Joan Bright (later on the staff of General Sir Hastings Ismay).

It would have been difficult to find five people better qualified to run such a 'free-lance' department with vigour and imagination. But, unfortunately for our war effort, the uncompromising methods of these forceful personalities came into conflict with the policies of more orthodox and more powerful bodies. In consequence MI(R) was dissolved; its more spectacular activities were taken over by a new organization, named the Special Operations Executive, and the Inter-Services Security Board was formed to carry on certain other functions, including the making of cover plans.

However, cover plans are only the 'defensive' side of deception and it was no part of the Board's business to plan 'offensive' deception, such as threats to the enemy unrelated to any actual operation. Moreover, cover planning was only incidental to ISSB's charter. Its main concern was 'security' with all the innumerable problems that involves; the issue and registering of code words, the grading of documents, the marking of stores, the censorship of mails, cables, telegrams and telephones, visitor bans in certain districts, leakages of information, supervision of neutral journalists, indiscreet articles in the press, stoppages of leave, sealing of camps and marshalling areas, Irish labour, travel by civil airlines, security of ports and airfields, movements of troops, measures to deal with aliens, and so on. Little of the Board's time could be given to cover planning, and it was no part of its business to formulate proposals for overall strategic deception, or long-term policies to implement it.

Lastly there came into being the 'Twenty Committee', which consisted of the senior members of the ISSB, together with representatives of the three Directors of Intelligence, of MI5, of MI6, SOE and PWE. This Committee, the very existence of which was graded as *most secret*, met once a week on Wednesday afternoons to decide on what items of information should be passed by *most secret* channels to the enemy.

Such was the situation up to November 1940, in which month General Sir Archibald Wavell, C-in-C Middle East, had sent a signal to CIGS asking that a Lieutenant-Colonel Dudley Clarke should be sent out to join his staff.

Wavell had been on the staff of General Lord Allenby in 1918 and he had never forgotten how the final victory against the Turks had been achieved. A great number of camels had been assembled and ridden into the open desert beyond the Turkish flank, and the clouds of dust sent up by them had led the Turks to believe that their army was about to be encircled. When they had hastily redisposed their forces the British launched a full-scale frontal attack, taking them entirely by surprise. This deception plan foiled the enemy so completely that, on the morning of the breakthrough, the German C-in-C, General Leman von Sanders, had to quit his headquarters in pyjamas to escape capture.

When Dudley Clarke reached Cairo, General Wavell reminded him of this successful stratagem and charged him to set up a small section for the sole purpose of formulating and implementing plans to mislead the enemy.

Dudley Clarke was a regular Gunner and he had already seen considerable special service in the war, an account of which he published later in his fascinating book, *Seven Assignments*. He was the first officer to lead a reconnaissance party back to set foot on the Continent after the evacuation from Dunkirk; so he was, in a sense, the Father of Commando Raids as well as Father of Deception.

His mother was a Russian. He was a small man with fair

hair and merry blue eyes, an excellent raconteur and great company in a party, but with a strange quietness about his movements and an uncanny habit of suddenly appearing in a room without anyone having noticed him enter it. His great sense of humour must have contributed in no small measure to many of his successes in causing pain and grief to the enemy, while his military knowledge, combined with a most fertile imagination and tireless energy, made him the perfect deception planner. His ability to seize at once on the essentials of a problem and his facility at putting his thoughts clearly and briefly on paper led more than one of his staff officers to say that his gifts amounted to near genius.

From a few trusted subordinates his section soon grew into a private army, known as 'A' Force, consisting of a vast and tortuous network of deception personnel and secret agents throughout the whole of the Mediterranean, the Middle East, and Africa as far south as the Cape; in addition to which, in collaboration with Brigadier Crockatt of MI9 in London, he handled all measures in his theatre for assisting our prisoners of war to escape from enemy camps.

So successful was Dudley Clarke in his deception activities that in October 1941 General Wavell sent him home to give a personal account of his work to the Chiefs of Staff. This so impressed the Chiefs that they decided to create a similar body in their own organization to keep in touch with 'A' Force and to study the possibilities of applying organized deception in the European theatre. Such work fell into the category of future planning, rather than that of the Strategic Section of the JPS, which dealt with immediate matters; so Colonel Stanley was instructed to form a new team of three GSOIs as an addition to his FOPS.

The War Office nominated Lieutenant-Colonel A. F. R. Lumby, CIE, OBE, who duly reported for duty late in December 1941. The Admiralty nominated Captain Hallorhan, RN, who, after a tour of duty with ISSB, had been appointed British Naval Instructor at the Turkish Staff College; but with the proviso that, as he was already engaged on an important mission, they were reluctant to recall him until the deception set-up was really under way. The Air Ministry said bluntly that, as the RAF was fighting the war, they could not possibly spare a Group Captain for work of such problematic value. It was then that one of my friends, probably either Group Captain Roland Vintras or Air Commodore Dickie Dickson, had said 'What about Wheatley', and it was agreed to bring me in.

Here I should pay a tribute to Oliver Stanley's breadth of mind. Most writers are, in some way, connected with journalism, most soldiers would run a mile rather than confide even a minor secret to a journalist, and to do my job I should have to be given the whole works. Yet he paid me the compliment of taking me on.

After my interview with Stanley I was conducted through the endless corridors of the great building to Dickie Dickson's office in the Air Ministry, which occupied its western side. He told me considerably more about the work I was to do than I had gathered up to that moment, then, apologetically, that regulations made it necessary for me to attend a three-weeks' Intake Course at Uxbridge.

As we were talking, our voices were suddenly drowned by the hideous wail of near-by sirens. Dickie laughed and said, 'Don't worry, it's "Germans at the door". A practice alarm is always sounded on Saturdays at four o'clock in the afternoon.'

Henceforth I was to hear it every week, but it was not until long afterwards that the alarm was sounded just as I happened to enter the main door of the building. The offices of the War Cabinet were, of course, heavily guarded. A special troop of Home Guards, armed with revolvers, was always on duty to examine passes; there were sentries furnished by the Brigade of Guards inside all the entrances and armed Royal Marines who acted as officers' servants down in the basement; added to which there was a machine-gun post covering the broad stairs up to Mr Churchill's private apartments. At the sound of the alarm I halted in the hall to see the swift action that one would have expected to take place had German paratroops suddenly landed in St James's Park. But the great bronze doors remained open and not a thing happened.

On 2 December I received from the Ministry Form 1020, the application for a commission in the RAFVR, and my supporters were Dickie, Director of Plans (Air) and Sir Louis Greig, Private Assistant to the Secretary of State. I then went to Adastral House at the bottom of Kingsway, which housed the administrative staff of the Air Ministry, for my interview. A Group Captain gave one glance at the signatures, smiled at me and said, 'It doesn't seem that there's any point in my asking you any questions; you'd better ask me some.'

It then transpired that the next Intake Course for 600 new officers was already full and that there was a further waiting list of 700. But Oliver Stanley wanted me at once; so I was pushed in over the heads of the 700 as an extra on the Course at Uxbridge that started at the end of the week.

For me, Uxbridge was a waste of time, but it was so out of my world that it provided an interesting change. The many hours of square-bashing had an excellent effect on me physically, and I enjoyed mixing with the chaps in my barrack-room.

On 30 December 1941 the course ended, and I returned to the flat which my wife, Joan, and I had at Chatsworth Court in West London.

Next day I reported to take up my job.

Chapter 2
The Offices of the War Cabinet

The great block in which I was to work for the following three years lies at the extreme western end of Whitehall, and it housed many ministries. Its side facing Whitehall was the Home Office, that facing Parliament Square the Treasury – which had been bombed out of its own office on the far side of Downing Street – that facing on to King Charles Street the Operational Departments of the Air Ministry, and that facing on to St James's Park the offices of the War Cabinet. But on the third and fourth floors numerous sets of rooms were occupied by various Ministers of State whose work necessitated only a small staff.

To the right of the great bronze doors opening on to St James's Park the ground- and first-floor rooms had been given over to Mr Churchill and his personal entourage, because 10 Downing Street was 200 years old and, having no steel girders in it, very vulnerable to air attack. The PM lunched, dined and often held meetings at No. 10, but he slept and spent much of his time in this other accommodation, which was known as 10 Downing Street Annexe. Churchill's secretaries, Martin, Peck, Rowan and others, worked in the ground-floor rooms adjacent to his bedroom, and he also had a private map room run by Captain Pim, RNVR.

On the floor above were the offices of his personal assistant, Major Sir Desmond Morton, his ADC, Commander 'Tommy' Thompson, RN, and his scientific adviser, Professor Lindemann; there was also a mess for his entourage. Below the

PM's own rooms, and extending to the northwest corner of the building, lay the fortress basement in which worked and lived the Cabinet Secretariat and the Joint Planning Staff; so night or day he had only to telephone and any of his aides could be with him in two minutes.

The basement consisted of a warren of narrow passages and well over 100 rooms. It was also designed as a retreat for the War Cabinet in the event of a landing by enemy parachutists. There was an office, bedroom and small dining-room for the PM himself; bedrooms for Attlee, Beaverbrook, Eden, Bevin and the other members of the War Cabinet, who used them on nights of heavy raids, and bedrooms for Sir Edward Bridges, General Ismay, Brigadier Hollis, Colonel Jacob, Brendan Bracken, Harvey Wyatt and other members of the War Cabinet office.

There was also a big room in which the War Cabinet met on nights when there were air raids, a similar room for meetings of the Chiefs of Staff, accommodation for typists, a large map room staffed by twelve officers representing the three services, and a tiny mess. This last had originally been established only to provide the map-room officers with a snack; but by the time I arrived it had become customary for members of the JPS to lunch there if they were not going out to their clubs. Being under the northwest corner of the building, it formed the segment of a circle. Behind a curtain in one corner the Royal Marine orderlies could heat soup or knock up a dish of eggs and bacon but, in the main, we fed off cold food – hams, tongues, biscuits and cheese. The centre of the room was only large enough to take two card tables, which put together would seat six at one time. In the other corner there was a steel filing cabinet which held drinks.

This underground fortress resembled the lower deck of a battleship. It was white-painted and along the ceilings of its narrow passages ran a mass of cables carrying light, heat, telephone and air-conditioning to the many rooms, most of which were like ship's cabins. Down there was a small room that held the Atlantic telephone on which the PM talked almost daily to President Roosevelt. There was also a special telephone exchange, from which our skilful Post Office engineers had laid deep underground lines to the HQs of the various commands outside London, and to Edinburgh, Glasgow, Cardiff, Birmingham, etc., so that, should every telephone exchange in London be destroyed, communications with these centres would remain unaffected. The basement was gas-proof, flood-proof and had a four-foot-thick layer of concrete inserted between it and the ground floor of the building. It held an ample supply of medical stores and was provisioned for three months. So even had German parachutists temporarily seized central London, the fortress would have closed up like a clam and the PM and his advisers been able to continue to direct the war from it.

As is the case with all government offices, the principal floor is not the first but the second; perhaps to escape the noise and dust from the streets. The first floor was almost a mezzanine, with comparatively low ceilings, whereas the rooms on the second floor were spacious and lofty. It was there that Bridges (the Secretary of the War Cabinet), Ismay (the PM's principal Staff Officer), Hollis (his Deputy), and Jacob (responsible for communications), all had their offices. On that floor, too, was the room in which the Chiefs of Staff met every morning: and it always intrigued me that outside it in the corridor there stood a hat-stand – the only one in that whole vast building not inside a room. Why it should have been placed outside, I cannot think, but it always fascinated me to pass at about eleven o'clock in the morning. Only hats hung on it: that of Admiral Sir Dudley Pound, First Sea Lord and CNS, that of General Sir Alan Brooke, CIGS, that of Air Chief Marshal Sir Charles Portal, CAS, and, a few months after I joined, there was added to them that of Lord Louis Mountbatten as Chief of Combined Operations. No other hat-stand can ever have habitually carried such a weight of gold braid.

The third floor also had spacious rooms, if not quite so lofty. There the Minister without Portfolio and the FOPS had their offices.

As Director of Plans (Air), Dickie Dickson had one of the big second-floor rooms on the Air Ministry side of the building. Vintras had also been transferred from the JPS, and had become Dickson's senior Staff Officer. On arriving

I reported to him. Then he took me through the maze of corridors and up to the FOPS.

I was as nervous as a boy arriving on his first day at a public school. It was one thing to meet men like Darvall (later Air Marshal Sir Lawrence, who through Louis Greig had been my first contact with the JPS) and Dickson as a well-established author, but quite another to be taken into an organization consisting of the picked brains of the three Services and to make their acquaintance as a Pilot Officer RAFVR – the lowest form of commissioned life. I felt that my new colleagues would have good reason to look on me as an interloper who had been foisted on them by the whim of people much senior to themselves; since Commander Robertshaw was the only member of the FOPS to whom I had spoken, even for a minute, and it was quite possible that none of the others had ever read any of my papers, as these always went to the STRATS.

Added to this I was suffering at the time from an annoying disability. During my last week at Uxbridge I had caught a shocking cold which had gone to my throat. The trouble was greatly aggravated by the fact that I had had to continue to take my turn shouting orders at a squad on the barrack square. In consequence when I arrived at the Cabinet Offices I could talk only in a hoarse whisper.

My fears proved quite unjustified. Robertshaw welcomed me most kindly and introduced me to the others; then, as I was an airman, Group Captain Groom took me under his wing, and led me along to two rooms next door which had been allocated to the deception section. They looked out on St James's Park and in the past had usually been occupied by a Cabinet Minister. The larger one was at least twenty-five by thirty feet and the smaller only a few feet narrower. In the corners each side of the window were two large desks and at one of them sat the elderly and much-beribboned Lieutenant-Colonel Fritz Lumby. Standing up, he limped forward to shake hands and give me a smiling welcome.

He told me that the other big desk was to be mine; then we had a preliminary chat. It emerged that he had lost his leg at Loos in 1915 but remained in the Indian Army and spent the period between the wars in India as an Intelligence

The Offices of the War Cabinet

officer. He was a tall, thin, dark man with an exceptionally low voice, a shy manner and a bawdy sense of humour. He could not have been kinder to me and we got on excellently together.

At about half past ten Oliver Stanley strolled in, smiled at me, then had a few words about me with Lumby and ended by saying, 'Well, I think he had better make a start by reading his way into the war.'

Lumby then passed over to me several stiff-backed folders. When I looked at their contents I could hardly believe my eyes. They were the minutes of the recent meetings of the War Cabinet, the Defence Committee and the Chiefs of Staff.

Later I found that I had to spend many hours every day reading documents in order to have a knowledge of every aspect of the war. In addition to the above, there were the Joint Intelligence Summary, the separate Intelligence Summaries of the three services, the Political Warfare Summary, minutes from the PM, the Chiefs of Staff and the Directors of Plans, reports on the state of equipment of all divisions being formed, of the production of munitions, of our stocks of food and petrol, statements of manpower, aircraft, tanks, shipping and landing craft available, directives to force commanders, despatches from all C-in-Cs, draft plans under consideration by both the STRATS and FOPS, Foreign Office telegrams in and out, and numerous long papers put in from time to time independently by Cabinet Ministers, containing ideas on how we might better wage the war.

Lord Chandos (as Oliver Lyttelton he was our excellent Minister of Production) says in his memoirs that every day while he was in office he had to read papers which together would have exceeded in length a long novel. We all had to, and, as such material was already condensed, not much of it could be skipped.

That first day Lumby took me to lunch at the National Liberal Club. It was a kindly gesture.

That afternoon, while I was alone in our vast office, the door opened and a plump, fair-haired, red-faced Major, wearing the Glengarry and tartan trews of the Royal Scots, stood there giving me a smart salute. I at once jumped up and came to attention. He had brought a letter over from the War Office and, having introduced himself as Major Combe, asked me if I would lunch with him one day. Surprised but pleased, I accepted. When we'd fixed a date he said briskly, 'Right! One o'clock at Rules in Maiden Lane', then departed as quickly as he had arrived.

To deliver letters by hand in this way was quite unusual, and Eddie Combe told me afterwards that he had done so on this occasion only to have a look at me. Normally, all inter-departmental memos were sent from ministry to ministry, or from office to office in the building, in locked wooden boxes covered with black, grey or red leather, and stamped with the Royal Arms, the red ones containing documents of the highest secrecy. To them we carried keys according to our seniority.

Next day I lunched with Roly Vintras in the little basement mess, of which he told me that I was now entitled to become a member. While we were having drinks General Ismay came in. Roly introduced me to him. No man had more charm than dear 'Pug' and later he became one of my most treasured friends.

The day after, Victor Groom took me down to show me the RAF canteen on the ground floor. It catered for all ranks and both sexes, and by that stage of the war the food there was far from appetizing; so I never lunched there again.

The position of Lumby and myself was an unusual one. We were regarded as the most secret section in the whole building; kept absolutely incommunicado and not even allowed to tell the other members of the JPS what we were up to, although actually for several weeks we were not up to anything at all. The only communication allowed us was through the Inter-Service Security Board, since, before the creation of our special section, the Board had handled all cover plans and was now to act as our executive.

The ISSB met every morning at the War Office, and one day shortly after my arrival Lumby took me across with him to meet the officers who would implement the plans we might make.

The Chairman of the Board was a pleasant old man named Colonel Graham. The Naval member was Commander

'Ginger' Lewis, RN, a grand chap who had brought his destroyer back to port with the whole of her front half shot away. The Air Member was Wing Commander Byron. MI5 and MI6 were represented by Lieutenant-Colonel Gilbert Lennox, a fat and jovial man whom I already knew. I learned that it was he who had vouched for me from the security point of view to Oliver Stanley. The Home Office was represented by a Mr Buckley.

Their Deputies were Major E. P. Combe, Lieutenant-Commander the Hon. Ewen Montagu, RNR, Flight Lieutenant Tennant and Major Cass of MI5. The secretariat consisted of Combe, who was its senior member, and Majors Brunyate, Goudie and Moffat.

Montagu, Lord Swaythling's son, was nicknamed 'Scottish Ewen'. Tennant was a nice chap, one of the brewing family and a great philatelist. John Moffat was a self-made, very rich man and a clever stockbroker. Brunyate was a lawyer and rather pernickety about drafting documents. Under a carefree manner Eric Goudie concealed a first-class financial brain. After the war he became a property tycoon. He and Eddie Combe developed a friendship with me that continued for many years.

My reason for going so fully into the composition of the ISSB is because I was to have innumerable dealings with it. For the best part of two years I attended its daily meetings, and ceased to do so regularly only after our section was finally expanded, when Major Neil Gordon Clark was given the job.

The first meeting I attended happened to coincide with my lunch date with Major Combe, so after it we went off to Rules in a taxi. And what a lunch it was!

As a subaltern in the Royal Scots, Eddie had been at Mons. He had then become Adjutant to his battalion. From beginning to end he had spent the whole war on the Western Front, being one of the very few officers to have survived those four and a half terrible years without becoming a casualty. He had seen over twenty Colonels come and go, killed, wounded, promoted or sacked, and was a double MC.

After the war he had retired to become a stockbroker, and for a number of years past had been the London representative of the great New York firm, Clark, Dodge and Company. He was a bachelor, a wealthy man and a most generous host. At Rules a corner table for six was always kept for him and, unless he was lunching with someone else, he entertained a party there every day. His guests were from all three services, and there can hardly have been an officer playing any part that really mattered in the 'behind-the-scenes' side of the war who did not lunch at some time or other with Eddie Combe at Rules.

I did so innumerable times and, from the beginning, these lunches were invaluable to me; for I met at them every kind of 'cloak-and-dagger' man; and later, when I wanted the help of their departments, I had only to say over the telephone, 'You may remember we met a few weeks ago when lunching with Eddie Combe.'

The other thing that always made Eddie's lunches such happy occasions was that, in those days when good food and drink were difficult to come by, Rules was his 'oyster'. To start with we always had two or three Pimms at a table in the bar, then a so-called 'short one' well-laced with 'Chanel 5' as Eddie termed absinthe. Old Tommy Bell, who owned the place, or his top girl, Ivy, always took our order, first letting us know what special items were available. So there would be smoked salmon or potted shrimps, then a Dover sole, jugged hare, salmon or game, and a Welsh rarebit to wind up with. Good red or white wine washed this down and we ended with port or Kümmel.

Eddie, although fifty and fat, could, on returning to the War Office after these 'little' lunches, run up the three flights of stairs to his office; but it usually took me hours to recover. In fact, when I had been for some months down in the basement – to which my office was transferred later – I used to go into either Attlee's or Beaverbrook's bedroom to lie on the bed for an hour and sleep it off, having first arranged with my Naval colleague, James Arbuthnott, to wake me by a ring on the telephone if I was urgently needed. This may sound most reprehensible; but, in view of the thousands of hours of my time that I had given to writing papers for nothing, I did not regard it in that light.

The teams that worked in the FOPS under Oliver Stanley

consisted of three GSO 1s: Captain Buzzard, RN, Lieutenant-Colonel White and Group Captain Groom; and three GSO 2s: Commander Robertshaw, RN, Major Mann and Wing Commander Harvey.

I give these names because they are of historic interest. During 1943 and 1944, literally hundreds of officers worked on the preparations for our return to the Continent. But it was Oliver Stanley's FOPS who drew up the original appreciation in the spring of 1942. They made a study of the beaches from northern Norway to the Pyrenees, arguing the pros and cons of each. Eventually they decided that the Normandy beaches offered the best bet.

There was one very agreeable little custom that Stanley introduced into his section which took place in no other. This was that we should all meet in the GSO 2's room every afternoon for tea and a quarter of an hour's general chat.

For these parties our old office messenger, Baker, always brought in a box of cakes from a nearby shop. He did me a great service. After several days in my new job my voice had not come back, so he told me to boil up equal parts of turpentine and glycerine in a tin cup, soak a big pad of cotton wool in the mixture, put it on my throat as hot as I could bear and keep it there with a bandage all night.

Joan – my wife – was afraid that the turps would take all the skin from my neck. But I was desperate enough to try anything, and this remedy worked like a charm. Within twenty-four hours I was speaking normally; and it has had the same excellent results with many other people I have told about it.

Old Baker was quite a character. Tea was, of course, rationed, but the messengers who made it were allowed a little extra so that there would be enough to offer a cup to anyone who called on us. Ernie Bevin had his office just along the corridor from ours and in it he held a conference, one afternoon, of some twenty people. About half past four he rang the bell and, when Baker answered it, said, 'Bring tea, please, Baker.'

Baker gave one glance round, then looked the Minister of Labour straight in the eye, and replied, 'Wot! For this lot? Not likely!'

I soon learned more about Fritz Lumby's background. In India he had held a semi-political appointment as liaison officer between the Indian Political Security Department and Indian Military Intelligence, and, towards the end of his time in India, he'd been a member of the Legislative Assembly. He knew an immense amount about India but comparatively little about international politics and had never travelled extensively either in Europe or America. He also used to declare frequently that he knew nothing about soldiering as he had spent over twenty years peacefully oscillating with the changing seasons between Delhi and Simla in the train of the Viceroy.

He had retired in 1939 but been recalled just before the war and charged with the formation of the Military Intelligence College at Matlock, where he had remained as Commandant for two and a half years. In consequence, he had a vast acquaintance among war-time Intelligence officers but, having lived in India for the greater part of his adult life, knew very few of the key men engaged in the high direction of the war and this proved a considerable handicap in the new work he was to undertake.

This handicap was increased by the fact that, although he was a most lovable man, an amusing conversationalist with an astonishing memory for apt quotations, he was by nature shy and diffident and always spoke in an exceptionally low voice, which detracted from his getting over the points he wished to make when attending large conferences.

His mind was subtle, his decisions always sound; but he was extremely cautious and not particularly imaginative. His only real assets were his immense knowledge of Intelligence work and, from having a German mother, a valuable understanding of the enemy's mentality; but these qualifications were not enough to enable him to succeed in the very difficult task of 'selling' our new and, to most authorities, trouble-provoking baby – deception.

One had only to witness the enthusiasm with which his ex-students greeted him to realize what a successful 'father figure' this kindly man had made at Matlock; but on entering the offices of the War Cabinet he became just one more staff officer and his legion of admiring juniors was reduced to Pilot Officer Wheatley, who shared his palatial office. Added to this, after having for long held what amounted to an independent command, he was now himself under an extremely quick-minded and highly critical ex-Cabinet Minister. Not unnaturally, poor Lumby was most hesitant to initiate any positive action and looked to Stanley – who had been given the title of 'Controlling Officer' as a cover name for his activities as Deception Chief – for guidance in our new work. But Stanley was himself waiting for guidance on a Deception Policy from the Chiefs of Staff.

Technically my appointment was that of Secretary to our section. Vintras had suggested this because a secretary in that sense is not just a useful body to take notes but, like a Secretary of State, empowered to initiate activities of any kind that come within the sphere of his department.

A civilian disguised as a Pilot Officer was hardly in a position to chivvy the Chiefs of Staff into making up their minds about how his section should be employed. Nevertheless, I was desperately anxious to justify the position I had been given, so on realizing that no instructions were forthcoming, I set about writing a paper on *The Basic Principles of Enemy Deception*.

Chapter 3
First Faltering Footsteps

Although Colonel Dudley Clarke had been successfully practising military deception in the Middle East for over a year and had 'sold' the idea to the Chiefs of Staff, nobody apparently asked him before his return to Cairo for any information about how he carried out his task and, of course, no guidance could be obtained upon this new type of planning from any military manual. We had to start from scratch. That is why I wrote a paper embodying my ideas. I opened it more or less as follows about general principles:

1 Enemy deception falls under three heads;
(a) A long-term deception policy as to the manner in which we intend to bring the war to a victorious conclusion.
(b) A number of large-scale preparations for possible future operations calculated to mislead the enemy as to our future intentions in each separate theatre of war, or to induce him to believe that we have decided to open up new theatres in localities where we have no intention of attacking him.
(c) A week-to-week review of operations in all theatres with a view to disguising or implementing cover plans to mislead the enemy with regard to raids and troop or convoy movements.

The following few paragraphs dealt with the former responsibility of the ISSB for cover planning, the necessity for their continued assistance, the impossibility of formulating a long-term deception policy until the Chiefs of Staff took a definite

First Faltering Footsteps

decision on our future strategy, and a suggested policy to meet various possible alternatives.

Then I set out the following general principles which must be observed:

Wherever possible, deception plans should be tied up with forces and shipping already earmarked for despatch from one of our bases.

Our deception plans must be logical and therefore cause German Intelligence to take *serious notice* of them, otherwise our efforts would be a waste of time.

They should be within the scope of the resources that the enemy *believed* us to possess.

They should be plans which we should *actually carry out* if we had the shipping, trained personnel and materials at our disposal.

That no measure, short of definitely hampering our genuine war activities, should be neglected which would be taken were we actually going to carry out the deception plan.

That the fullest possible information should be made available to us of all enemy reactions to the deceptive material put out.

That as few people as possible, having regard to practical necessities, should be allowed into the secret of any deception plan.

I then listed every means I could think of to provide the enemy with material and mental evidence which would convince him that a deception plan was a genuine operation.

The paper concluded with several paragraphs on the importance of complete liaison with force commanders overseas, to ensure that their cover plans should not conflict with overall strategic deception policy, likewise with PWE and SOE for the same reason; the value of seeking the co-operation of the Foreign Office, and a list of the Chiefs of Departments, etc., who would have to be informed of our plans in order to implement them.

Six months later when Lieutenant-Colonel J. H. Bevan, MC, succeeded Lumby as the head of our section with the title of London Controlling Officer, he redrafted the major portion of my paper, putting it into approved staff form, and headed it *The Implementation of Military Deception*.

In view of the paper's new heading he did not include my paragraphs on general principles. His paper concerned only the measures by which a deception plan could be put over. I had listed forty-nine ways in which false information could be conveyed to the enemy. To these Bevan could think of only two to add, and no others were ever added subsequently.

This paper became the deception bible. Each officer who in due course joined our section had, as his first task, to master its contents. It was also sent to India, Australia and Washington.

By mid-January the Chiefs of Staff, having decided that an operation against Norway in the spring of 1942 was not possible, agreed that Stanley should produce a deception plan to persuade the Germans that we intended to land a force in the Stavanger area on about 1 May.

Lumby and I at once set to work, yet we did so under an extraordinary handicap. Both of us had for many years been used to having secretaries, but our deception activities were regarded as so super-secret that we were now denied this amenity.

When I had learned this it had filled me with consternation for, although my thrillers were said to keep people up at night in every part of the civilized world, I was a hopeless speller and knew nothing about grammar. I had always relied on my secretaries to interpret my writing. In fact I had been so ashamed of the exercise I had written for Stanley while at Uxbridge, about persuading the enemy that we were sending all our tanks overseas, that I could not bring myself to hand it to him as it stood.

Fortunately I had already met Joan Bright – at one time of MI(R) and now in General Ismay's office. This had been at a little dinner given by Roly Vintras at the RAC for her, my Joan and Peter Fleming, just before I went into uniform; and, although I did not know it at the time, Peter was about to be sent to the Far East as head of a deception section. Having learned from Vintras that Joan was one of the very few people who knew about the work I had been brought in to do, I got her to type my paper for me. But obviously we could not ask her to take on the work of our section; so Lumby and I were reduced to laboriously typing our own first thoughts about Norway with two fingers.

The handicap we suffered soon became apparent, but still for some days we were refused assistance because no one on the JPS, not even Stanley, had a private secretary. All the work was done by typists from a pool, and the machinations of Lumby and Wheatley were looked on as much too secret to be revealed to a number of young women, despite the fact that these same young women were entrusted with the typing of the plans for real operations.

Absurd as this was it eventually benefited us, for it was decided that we should be privileged even beyond the Directors of Plans and have a private secretary all to ourselves. To fill this post a pleasant and efficient girl named Joan Eden was brought in. She typed my forerunner of the deception bible, then our ideas for drawing German reinforcements up to kick their heels uselessly in southern Norway

When Stanley had passed our final draft we took it over to the ISSB. It was their business to provide a codeword for the operation, and Lumby very kindly suggested that I should choose it.

One might suppose that any word that springs to mind would do; but that is not at all the case, for in time of war every aircraft, ship and troop movement, and countless other undertakings, have to be concealed in this way; so between them the three services always have thousands of words in use. In fact, towards the end of the war it became difficult to find ones not in use, and to have used the same word for two different jobs might have had the most unhappy consequences. ISSB kept a register of all words in use, and a fat book was produced for me to choose from in which the words still free were not ticked.

I selected the word Hardboiled, and next day, when Stanley saw it on one of our memos, he remarked, 'Who was the bloody fool who chose such a silly codeword?'

His criticism displayed a curious blind spot in the minds of many men in high positions, Mr Churchill not excepted.

They, and he particularly, always wanted for major operations names that meant something. For example, after the invasion scare that came to nothing the codeword Cromwell had to be changed; so they chose Aflame. As in the old days beacons were always made ready for lighting should England be invaded, the choice could not have been more stupid; for, had any document so headed fallen into the hands of the enemy he would have needed little intelligence to guess that it referred to our plans for resistance to invasion. Overlord, for our return to the Continent, was not too bad, but the codeword for our initial landings on the Normandy beaches was a shocker – Neptune, if you please! But the German High Command was just as stupid, for they gave their plan for the invasion of England the codeword Sea Lion.

I admitted to Stanley that I had chosen Hardboiled and pointed out to him that the whole object of a codeword was to conceal the matter concerned; major operations ought to have codewords such as Table, Dress, Wedding Cake, from which the enemy could deduce nothing.

Having got our plan passed the next step was to arrange for such measures as were possible to implement it. For this purpose a meeting was called at the War Office by the Deputy Director of Staff Duties. It was attended by several Generals, a whole covey of Brigadiers, the members of the ISSB, Stanley, Lumby and myself, and the EPS. These last, the Executive Planning Section, were the third Section of the JPS, but unlike the STRATS and the FOPS its members worked in their respective ministries under their own Chiefs of Staff. They were not concerned with making plans, but when an operation had been approved it was passed to them. Their business was to report on the troops available, the shipping and supplies required, to make the operation a practical undertaking.

Stanley, having been Secretary of State for War, was always received at the War Office with considerable deference. The only open opposition offered was a certain amount of head-shaking about the practicability of actually getting done some of the measures for which he asked.

This, however, was the only meeting of its kind to which Stanley came, and the atmosphere at subsequent ones that

First Faltering Footsteps 39

Lumby and I attended proved definitely hostile. Few senior officers were gifted with imagination and the idea of a deception plan, as distinct from a cover plan for a real operation, was entirely new to them. To implement our plan sufficiently to get results meant taking troops off their normal training to practise mountain climbing, the diversion of shipping and aircraft, the issue of equipment that would never be used, the despatch of large quantities of stores that would not be used, special courses for officers about warfare in the sort of territory to which they were not to be sent, the printing of hundreds of maps that would be spoiled and wasted, the issue of special clothing and equipment suitable to a cold climate when the troops were really earmarked to be sent to a hot one, and of medical supplies against frostbite, instead of against malaria, and so on.

To get what we wanted done meant putting these people to a great deal of trouble, and very few of them could be persuaded that it was worth it. Some of them took no pains to hide their view that this newfangled business of strategic deception was a crack-brained idea upon which there was no justification for wasting the time of busy men like themselves; and unfortunately, kind, gentle, old Lumby had not a sufficiently forceful personality to convince them to the contrary.

At our first DDSD meeting, it was agreed that the Royal Marine Division should become the task force for Hardboiled, as such troops were particularly suited for a seaborne assault and they were conveniently stationed in Scotland; further, that, after they had done a period of training in mountain warfare, they should carry out an embarkation exercise.

After an hour or so Stanley and most of the big brass withdrew and a second meeting was held, the majority of those attending being Lieutenant-Colonels or Majors. These were 'below the salt' and not let into the secret that Hardboiled was only a deception plan. They were in turn instructed to provide Norwegian interpreters, have dual-language signposts made, issue maps of the Stavanger area, send Arctic clothing to the RM Division and in other ways implement the plan exactly as though it were to be a real operation.

These measures were to provide material evidence of preparation for an operation, which we hoped would be reported by enemy agents in this country who saw them, or came to hear of them through careless talk by the troops; the circumstantial evidence was to be conveyed by rumours put out abroad through various agencies.

It might be imagined that with Hardboiled actually in progress Lumby and I became fully occupied, but this proved far from the case. Only in one solitary instance were we called on to take any action. This concerned Norwegian sailors. From time to time a few of them in trawlers took a chance on breaking away from the German-supervised fishing fleet and escaped to Britain. They were temporarily interned at the 'Patriotic School' in South Kensington, where they were vetted to make sure they were not spies before being released by MI5.

In the hope that if a few of them got wind of our plan they would talk of it to other Norwegians and that among these there would be a Quisling who would pass on what they had heard to the Germans, it was decided that two of them should be brought to the Cabinet Offices and closely questioned about the Stavanger area with special regard to possible landing grounds for aircraft.

As it was an air matter I was selected to do the questioning, and in order to impress these brave but humble men Victor Groom lent me his tunic. So for a brief hour I masqueraded as a Group Captain with two splendid rows of decorations.

Apart from this episode all measures to implement our plan had been taken out of our hands by ISSB. Each morning Lumby spent an hour doing *The Times* crossword puzzle. Then there was to be seen, stumping across Horse Guards Parade, a tall, thin, dark Lieutenant-Colonel with a wooden leg, accompanied by a shortish Pilot Officer, made bulkier by his long, heavy greatcoat, on their way to the ISSB meeting. A long, long lunch hour followed, then we drowsed away the afternoon skimming through endless papers.

It soon emerged that many of our ideas for implementing our plan could not be carried out because of opposition in various departments. Had we been allowed to interview their Chiefs ourselves we might have got some action, but we

First Faltering Footsteps 41

were strictly forbidden to make ourselves known to anybody.

Mention of uniform reminds me that by this time I had defied convention and had had my greatcoat lined with scarlet satin. As it was grey-blue and cut very long it gave me the appearance of a cross between an officer in the Brigade of Guards, who also had scarlet linings to their greatcoats, and an officer on the German General Staff, owing to its length. It was also against regulations for an officer of the RAF to carry any form of stick or cane; but I felt quite lost without one, so I had Wilkinson's make me a couple of swagger sticks, about eighteen inches long, such as many Army officers carry; but instead of brown leather mine was covered in blue and, as a precaution against trouble in the blackout, they were sword sticks containing a fifteen-inch blade.

Early in February it occurred to me that, although our Forces were so thin on the ground that a decent-sized army could not be allocated to implement a really telling deception threat to the enemy, the Russians had plenty of men; so why should we not propose such an operation to them?

At that time the Russians still held the Crimea, and they had considerable shipping on the Volga which could have been brought down via the Volga–Don Canal to the Black Sea. The gist of my plan was that the Russians should use this shipping and their divisions in the Caucasus to menace the mouth of the Danube with a seaborne assault across the Black Sea, in which the Soviet fleet was still dominant. This, I suggested, might have the effect of causing the Rumanians to withdraw their best divisions from the Odessa region, where they were then operating, for the defence of their homeland, discourage the Bulgarians from giving any further help to our enemies and render it less likely that the Germans might attempt the invasion of Turkey with the object of driving through to the oil wells in Iraq, from fear of having a Russian army arrive in their rear.

The FOPS vetted my plan and Stanley liked it but, to my amazement, he then told me that we had no military link whatever with the Russians; so there were no easy means by which we could propose my plan to their General Staff. The best that Stanley could do was to speak to Anthony Eden about it and suggest that he should put the idea into the head of the Soviet Ambassador, Mr Maisky, when next they met.

February 1942 was marked by a new milestone in Organized Deception. General Sir Archibald Wavell, who was then Commander-in-Chief India, decided to form a deception section at his HQ, and it was Peter Fleming who was sent out to him. The choice was excellent, for Peter was a highly intelligent and adventurous man. Moreover, he had been an officer in the Grenadier Guards and had been employed on numerous secret activities connected with resistance to a possible invasion.

After the débâcle in Malaya he pulled off a splendid *coup* in Burma. During the retreat he put a number of 'most secret' documents containing false information into a suitcase with a spare uniform belonging to Wavell, put the suitcase into the boot of a car and overturned the car down a steep embankment where the advancing Japs were certain to come upon it an hour or so later.

After the retreat he operated from General Wavell's HQ at Delhi, and on one occasion when a high-powered Anglo-American-Chinese staff conference was held there he succeeded in selling faked minutes of the decisions taken to an enemy agent for 10,000 Chinese dollars.

But, like us in London, he found 'selling' deception to most senior officers extremely uphill work. In a letter he wrote to me in those early days he said, 'This is a one-horse show and I am the horse.'

Although no one entering the RAFVR at that stage of the war could be given a higher rank than Pilot Officer, the appointment specially created for me to fill on the JPS had been that of a Flight Lieutenant, so I was entitled to that rank as soon as Air Ministry regulations permitted my promotion to it. In consequence, on 12 February, having served for two months, I automatically became a Flying Officer and changed the one thin ring on my cuffs for a thick one.

To receive my second step three months' further service was required; so I would not become a Flight Lieutenant until 12 May.

It was on 12 February, too, that the faces of all my Naval colleagues on the JPS became extremely red; and with good

First Faltering Footsteps 43

reason. Under cover of fog and an enormous escort of aircraft the German warships *Scharnhorst*, *Gneisenau* and *Prinz Eugen* broke out of Brest and passed through the Straits of Dover unscathed. This was largely due to brilliant planning by the enemy and their successful jamming of our radar; but there could be no doubt that the Admiralty had been caught napping.

From midday on, desperate attempts were made to retrieve the situation by gallant but belated attacks with destroyers and the reckless sending on a suicide mission of a squadron of torpedo-carrying aircraft, not one of which returned. Their sacrifice was not altogether in vain as they inflicted considerable damage on the enemy, but all three ships got away in the mists of the North Sea.

Three days later, on the 15th, the news came that General Percival, having been given discretion to use his judgement, had surrendered Singapore; which meant that tens of thousands of Empire troops had become prisoners of war, many of them without having fired a shot. It was proving a grim winter.

Chapter 4
I Endeavour to Earn My Pay

March 1942 found Lumby still doing his crosswords and me twiddling my thumbs. Stanley, no doubt recalling the type of papers that I had written before going into uniform, suggested that I should write one on the situation with which Britain might be faced when the war ended. This was right up my street and I produced a paper that ran to over 10,000 words.

Part I – which constituted three-quarters of the paper – dealt with the many different circumstances in which the cessation, or partial cessation, of hostilities might come about. Part II dealt with the probable situation, the divergent interests of the Allies, the resettlement of Europe, the emergence of a new great power in Europe (foretelling a pooling of interests by several nations which has since occurred as the Common Market), and the alteration in the balance of power caused thereby.

My major conclusions about the probable situation were: (i) The United States would endeavour to secure financial control of Europe as a great market for her manufactured goods. (ii) the Soviet Union would endeavour to federate the European states as workers' republics on the Soviet model. (iii) Most of the smaller powers would be striving to regain their independent national status.

That (i) above would, in time, inevitably spell the commercial ruin of Great Britain; and that (ii) above would be detrimental to Great Britain economically and also dangerous to her strategically.

I Endeavour to Earn My Pay 45

My final general conclusions were:

1 That the greatest menace to the continuance and prosperity of the British Empire would come from her two powerful allies, the USSR and the USA, whose interests were divergent from hers and from each other's.

2 That having fought a longer war, the British Empire would be relatively weaker economically and financially than the other two; and must therefore seek outside support to maintain her position and create a new balance of power.

3 That the already proposed federation of the Netherlands, Belgium and Luxembourg with their overseas possessions offered a nucleus of such support to Britain.

4 That possession being nine-tenths of the law, Britain must be ready to implement any Armistice by seizing instantly such key points in Western Europe as would facilitate the establishment of the new federation and thus present her powerful rivals with a *fait accompli*.

Stanley thought sufficiently well of my paper to have it roneoed and circulated to the JPS and its associated bodies. The principal of these was the Joint Intelligence Committee, which consisted of a Foreign Office Chairman with the rank of Ambassador and the Directors of Intelligence of the three services, under whom were several teams of GSO 1s and GSO 2s.

While I was still writing that paper we received a nasty set-back about Hardboiled. We were informed that certain air operations which were to take place over southern Norway would conflict with our deception plan; so the implementation of it must be called off temporarily.

Then, in mid-March, our poor old plan received a body blow. The Japanese were advancing with such rapidity in southeast Asia that the War Cabinet feared they might launch a seaborne invasion of Ceylon. Alternatively they might by-pass Ceylon and establish themselves in Madagascar, which would give them, in Diego-Suarez, a splendid fleet base, rendering Ceylon and India open to attack from both east and west.

Ceylon could be reinforced, but Madagascar could not, because it was held by the Vichy French; and it was quite on the cards that, under pressure from Hitler, Pétain might order his people in Madagascar to allow the Japs to occupy Diego-Suarez.

It had been decided to get in first and send a British Expeditionary Force to seize the port. Of all the troops that could have been sent, which did the Chiefs select? Why, the Royal Marine Division that was implementing Hardboiled – the only Division which, having been trained in mountain warfare, was suitable for use in a deception plan that ostensibly threatened Norway.

Cover plans, quite wrongly since our section had been formed, were still the responsibility of ISSB, but they had the courtesy to call us in and, in their Room 330 at the War Office, we discussed various ways of masking the expedition, which had been given the name of Ironclad. This was tricky, as the Division was to sail from the Clyde assault-loaded and the troops were to be issued with tropical kit. The Eastern Mediterranean was closed to us at that time, with Malta in a state of siege, so all reinforcements for the Middle East had to be sent round the Cape; and the enemy could certainly not have been made to believe that we intended to go into French North Africa with a single division. An attack on Burma seemed equally improbable, but, as the expedition was sailing assault-loaded, it must appear to have been despatched against some enemy-held territory, so Burma was chosen; but with the let-out that the convoy would call first at Ceylon for re-grouping.

Two further headaches were that it had to pick up supplies in ports on the West African coast, where the French interpreters sent with the force might give away its real destination; and that the South African government was contemplating breaking off relations with Vichy France. If they did so when the expedition reached the neighbourhood of the Cape, that would be as good as notifying the French that the capture of Madagascar was our immediate intention. The last straw was that, before undertaking the assault, the convoy would have to put into Durban for re-assembly. This was contrary to practice for convoys going to Ceylon, and by

I Endeavour to Earn My Pay

then, too, the cases of maps would have been opened for study; so everyone aboard would know that Diego-Suarez was their objective, which meant a big risk that careless tattle in the port would give the show away.

On the 17th a DDSD meeting was called and it happened to be Lumby's day off, so it fell to Flying Officer Wheatley to attend this conference.

In one of the larger rooms of the War Office there had gathered a formidable array – five Generals, two Admirals, an Air Vice-Marshal, ten Brigadiers, a covey of full Colonels and a spattering of Captains RN and Group Captains RAF. I had, of course, been admitted on showing my special pass, but as I took my seat at the long table, I was aware of numerous curious or surprised glances being cast at the single ring on my two sleeves.

For the best part of an hour, the senior officers present discussed with the Force Commander-designate, Major-General Sturges, Royal Marines, the composition of the expedition. It was to consist of the Royal Marine Commandos, the 25th Infantry Brigade and two Brigades of the 5th Division. They talked of the transport required, naval escort, air reconnaissance, communications, stores, interpreters, medical supplies and a score of other matters.

At length they came to the question of a cover plan. General Sturges, evidently of too lowly a rank to have been let into the secret that a special section of the Joint Planning Staff had recently been formed to deal with such matters, had, very properly, told a member of his staff to think one up, and he proceeded to outline it.

During all this time I had remained silent but, seeing that the General's plan had no relation to that devised by Lumby and myself, I thought it time to pipe up.

'Sir,' I addressed the Director of Staff Duties. 'With due respect, I fear I cannot agree to this.'

There followed a moment of stunned silence. All eyes were turned on me with amazement, except for those of my good friend Eddie Combe, whom I saw grinning in the background. Then I went on to say: 'I am here to represent the Joint Planning Staff of the War Cabinet, by whom a cover plan has already been formulated which has received the approval of the Chiefs of Staff.' One could have heard a pin drop as I went on to tell them what they were required to do.

After showing some reluctance, General Sturges accepted the plan I put forward. The others, I think, thought it rather amusing that an officer who held the lowest of all commissioned ranks, the RAF being the junior service, should have been sent to give them their orders.

To implement our cover plan, Peter Fleming gave invaluable help by flying to Ceylon and commandeering scores of buildings to accommodate the Division during the fortnight it was supposed to be going to spend there; and General Smuts rowed in most handsomely by drafting the whole of his security police to Durban and temporarily interning everybody who could even remotely be suspected of being an enemy agent.

Owing to these measures and a very great deal of luck the cover plan succeeded and the expedition achieved complete surprise. When the convoy arrived early one morning off the west coast of the northern tip of Madagascar, within a day's march of Diego-Suarez, the only people to be seen for miles were a man and his girl bathing.

General Sturges then threw away the splendid advantage he had been given. On finding that the man was a French officer, instead of making him a prisoner, then marching through the jungle to take the great port in the rear and by surprise, he sent him off ahead to announce that the British were on their way and request the French C-in-C to surrender.

The French General sounded the alarm, had every gun in the place manned and for several days fought like a tiger, with the result that we suffered quite unnecessarily a considerable number of casualties before our warships shelled the port into submission.

Meanwhile, the job of deceiving a body of troops into believing they were to be sent to Norway, in the hope that careless talk would reach the ears of enemy agents, had to be started all over again. For this purpose the 52nd Highland Division was allocated to Hardboiled, took over the Arctic equipment left by the Marines and was made to run up and down rocky Scottish hillsides.

Lumby and I remained in semi-somnolent seclusion, but

I Endeavour to Earn My Pay

the Prime Minister did not. In spite of Britain's continued inability to strike a worthwhile blow against the Germans, and the fact that by conquering many million square miles of territory the Japanese had rendered our hopes of final victory even more remote, Mr Churchill still found odd moments in which to demand that his planners wrote papers on how we ought to set the world to rights when that happy day arrived.

The FOPS were fully occupied on a plan for our return to the Continent. The original conception was that we should land on the Normandy beaches, then cut off the Cotentin (Brittany) peninsula. By such an operation pressure could have been taken off Russia in any case and, if we were successful in holding the peninsula, it would make an excellent base in which to build up a big Anglo-American army for an advance to the Rhine. In consequence Stanley decided to relieve the enforced idleness of Lumby/Wheatley by turning over these near-end war problems to them.

One proposition we were required to examine was a proposal from the Norwegian government in exile. Like Mr Churchill they feared that Germany might launch another world war in twenty years' time, so as an insurance against their country's again being overrun they asked that Britain and the USA should, after the war, occupy permanent bases in Norway. Another came from the Dutch and Belgian governments in exile and was the original conception which later led to the commercial union of those countries, together with Luxembourg, as Benelux. They, too, offered to receive Anglo-American garrisons with the object of making their federation a spring-board for immediate resistance in the event of a future attack by Germany. It was also suggested that Britain should establish permanent military airfields along the French coast from the Pas de Calais to Brittany.

On 28 March Lumby went on leave and, as I had been off duty on the previous day, he left a memo in my tray, which read:

'The day has brought forth absolutely nothing – not even a lemon.'

This conveys how frustrated and useless he felt himself to be. As we were getting nowhere with military deception, I turned my thoughts to political warfare. By 10 April I had completed a paper which I called *Deception on the Highest Plane*.

The gist of it was that we should try to take advantage of the fact that, as Hitler had failed to achieve victory in the West by 1942, and had added the United States and Russia to Germany's enemies, great numbers of Germans must by now have lost faith in him and, recalling the miseries they had suffered after their defeat in the First World War, be dreading the terrible experience that lay ahead. The time was ripe to play upon their fears and persuade them that their one hope of escaping the worst was to make a complete reassessment of spiritual values. This, I suggested, could be done by causing them to believe that a new leader would prove their salvation.

This leader, who of course would have no real existence, was to be a Christ figure on lines acceptable to modern thought; no virgin birth but born of poor parents, period of retirement from the world, demonstration of supernatural powers and, finally, revelation of his mission. He was to have been seen in places all over Germany, preaching his doctrine of peace, universal brotherhood and passive resistance to all further war activities.

Every possible means was to be used by our political warfare people to spread rumours about him; so that in due course the Nazis would be forced to run a counter-campaign denying his existence, thus making the belief more widespread that he did exist. In such circumstances there are always queer characters who, to gain notoriety, will swear that they have actually seen such a mystic figure; so there was a good hope that within a few months he would become the talk of Germany.

When Lumby returned from leave he was enthusiastic about my plan. Having a German mother, he had considerable knowledge of the German people, and he said they had a streak of sentimental mysticism in their nature which made them particularly susceptible to such ideas. He added the excellent suggestion that my mystic should be called the '*Bote*' – messenger – and be a descendant of the Emperor Barbarossa.

Stanley liked the paper and when I took it at his order to

I Endeavour to Earn My Pay

General Brooks at PWE he also agreed that it had possibilities and said he would have it examined by his German experts.

My next job was rather a farcical one. Oliver Stanley, having read some of my books with occult backgrounds, asked me to write a paper on the unorthodox assumption that I had killed a black cock and white hen, and, having performed certain curious rites, was granted a supernatural preview of a map of the world showing the situation on all battle fronts, as published in a copy of *The Times* on the day the war ended.

Naturally, this *Cessation of Hostilities* paper could only be a wild extravaganza.

Seen in retrospect the biggest joke in the paper was the date chosen by me for the German collapse. I put it as 8 November 1942.

In view of what we know now, that must seem fantastically silly, but it was based on two major assumptions, both of which seemed valid at the time. Firstly, the Joint Intelligence Committee believed Germany to be already in great difficulty over oil and that within another six months she might find herself desperate for that commodity. Moreover, the JIC were of the opinion that the German war effort was by then being hampered by many shortages and that a considerable proportion of the people were turning against Hitler.

Later, I learned the reason for these ill-founded beliefs. While MI5, which was responsible for home security, did an excellent job and succeeded in catching nearly every spy sent over within forty-eight hours of his arrival, MI6, which was responsible for our spies in enemy and neutral countries, was pathetic.

In the First World War that organization had been the finest in the world; in the Second it was hopelessly incompetent. We had no secret agents worthy of the name. Hence the JIC were not even aware that Hitler had started to build huge factories for the production of synthetic oil, so there was not the least likelihood of German supplies drying up; and that, far from being half-starved and out-at-elbows, the Germans were living on the fat of the land by forced buying, with almost worthless currency, of food, clothes and all sorts of things from the countries they had over-run.

Secondly, I could not believe that the German General Staff would allow Germany to fight on until she was utterly exhausted and would suffer again the terrible times of the early 1920s. It seemed to me certain that, when they realized there was no longer any hope of victory, they would eliminate Hitler and seek a compromise peace while their army was still strong and German industry intact; so that a swift recovery would be possible. Therefore, with another Russian winter in mind, and the reported shortage of oil, I felt there was a reasonable hope that a further six months would see the Germans asking for an Armistice.

That, on the information I had, such a hope was not altogether unreasonable was borne out by Stanley's comment when he had read my paper. He said: 'I think you put the German collapse a little too early. I should have given them another three months and put it at February 1943.'

Towards the end of April another blow was struck against the young deception section. The FOPS had become conscious that their work suffered from their being up on the third floor, so far removed from their colleagues, the STRATS, who worked in the basement. In consequence, accommodation was found for Stanley and his two teams of planners there. When they moved down, Lumby and I were deprived of the opportunity to learn what was going on during the FOPS daily tea parties and were left up on the third floor in even more splendid isolation.

Early in May we were asked to do a paper on *Deception and Attrition in the Pacific*; its object was to draw the maximum number of Japanese forces away from the Indian Ocean. On the face of it that was the sort of work we had been brought in to do, and we proposed a number of measures which might have had some small effect. But in fact it was no more than an academic exercise to give us something to do, since the Pacific was an American sphere, and it was they who would have had to implement the plan. At that date they had never even heard of strategic deception, and it was to be a long time before we initiated them into its mysteries.

Poor Lumby realized the futility of what we were doing,

I Endeavour to Earn My Pay

and had become more and more depressed. It was a sad waste that an officer who had been Chief Instructor at our Military Intelligence College should spend much of his time doing crosswords.

My case was very different. I could only have done some routine 'I' job in a junior rank, but had had the incredible luck to get into the very brain of our war machine, where every idea I had that might possibly inflict grief and despondency on the enemy would at once receive serious consideration on a very high level. Moreover, I had been greatly widening my acquaintance among the officers who were running the war. Later this proved absolutely invaluable in forwarding the interests of my section.

It was still the first week in May when one afternoon Lumby positively danced into our palatial room, hopping on his sound leg, waving his ancient cap in one hand and his heavy stick in the other.

'I've done it!' he grinned, 'I've done it! At last I've managed to get out of this deadly deception racket. I've been appointed GSO 1 to SOE in West Africa.'

As he was to leave England at the end of the month, he at once set about making his arrangements and claimed the fortnight's embarkation leave to which he was entitled. A Lieutenant-Colonel Bevan was appointed to succeed him, and Stanley was anxious that Bevan should join us at once; so as to have as much time as possible to take over from Lumby. But GHQ Western Command, where Bevan was GSO 1 Intelligence, said they could not spare him until 1 June. Then SOE said it was absolutely essential that Lumby should do a fortnight's special course before sailing for West Africa; so, apart from one brief visit, we never saw him again. A year or two later, this wise, witty and kindly old chap was killed in an aircraft crash.

Meanwhile, Stanley's wife Maureen, the daughter of Lord Londonderry, had become seriously ill; so he spent much of his time sitting at her bedside. During the month Lady Maureen grew worse. It became obvious that she was dying, and Oliver took a fortnight's leave so that they could spend her last days together.

The result of all this was that for the last three weeks of

May I had no master or even a colleague, and, alone in my glory with the surroundings of a forgotten Cabinet Minister, became solely responsible for such deception work as there was to do.

Before Stanley left he asked me to write a paper that might help matters in the Far East. For this I created an imaginary task force consisting of two infantry and one armoured division and chose for its objective the Kra isthmus. Had we actually had such a force available, by seizing a belt of territory about a hundred miles long, along the narrow neck of the isthmus we could have cut Japanese communications between Malaya and Burma. But we could only implement the deception by putting out rumours; so I don't think it had much effect. It is, however, of some interest to record that several months later Mr Amery, who was a Cabinet Minister but not a member of the War Cabinet, put in a paper with exactly the same idea but proposing that it should be carried out as a real operation.

On 21 May a telegram came in from General Wavell. In it he again stressed the splendid work Dudley Clarke had done for him in Egypt, and the amateur but successful contribution now being made by Peter Fleming in the Far East. He reproached the Chiefs of Staff for neglecting to use the invaluable asset of stragetic deception in Europe, or to support him in the Far East.

It was obvious that he knew nothing of our efforts to help him by our paper *Deception in the Pacific*, and had not even been informed about Hardboiled. This made it clearer than ever that we, or rather now I, was the 'lost section' of the Chiefs of Staff organization, and that no one even bothered to pass on to GOCs overseas what we were doing. In consequence, having sent him a long telegram to put him in our picture, I made a recommendation that I had already urged on Stanley, namely that there should be a meeting each week of the Controlling Officer and his staff with representatives of ISBB, PWE, SOE, MI5, SIS, MEW and the directors of plans, to co-ordinate strategic deception in all theatres. Stanley had already turned it down on the grounds that we must keep our work super-secret; and, presumably for this same silly reason of putting an unjustified degree of security

I Endeavour to Earn My Pay 55

before efficiency, my recommendation was not adopted.

On the day General Wavell's telegram came in, the Prime Minister had the bright idea that we should deceive the Japanese into believing that we were converting Madagascar into a bastion similar to that which Singapore should have proved.

To meet this suggestion I wrote another long paper in which I pointed out that, although we had captured the great port of Diego-Suarez, this gave us command only of the northern tip of the huge island; that the rest of it, with its 2500 miles of coast-line, remained in the hands of the Vichy French and hostile to us; moreover, to implement such a plan properly, we should need considerable forces which were not available.

Frankly I considered the idea quite impracticable, but, not wishing to appear wanting, I proposed that the imaginary Dumbo force should be used for this, and thought up a long list of rumours to support the plan.

Since 1 May, our target date for Hardboiled, I had been gradually compiling a report on the operation, and, when it was completed, sent it in to the Chief of Staff. In spite of the setbacks and the distressing lack of co-operation we had met in many quarters, it had proved by no means unsuccessful.

On information from the JIC, I was able to report that, to meet our deception threat, German forces in Norway had been nearly doubled, bringing them up to a strength of 200,000 men; that Bergen Harbour had been closed to all shipping from 11 p.m. every night; that owing to shortage of food on account of the greatly increased occupying force, the Germans had called up a further 30,000 Norwegians for agricultural labour; that the Gestapo in Oslo had been greatly increased; and that three German Generals known for their ruthless methods, Daluege, Gelis and Rodeise had been sent to take over the command of the SS troops and police.

So, all things considered, by tying up an extra 100,000 Germans who might have been sent to Russia and causing the German authorities quite a lot of unnecessary trouble, we had done very much better than we had had any reason to hope.

Towards the end of May, I received from General Dallas

Brooks's senior staff officer, Colonel Chambers, the comments of their German Section on my *Deception on the Highest Plane*.

Chambers started off by saying that, while they were entirely in agreement with the basic principle of the plan, it would be difficult to implement because, to start with, rumours of a new anti-Hitler leader could be plausibly put out only inside Germany and our means of doing this were very limited. He went on to say that the German section of PWE did not think that a Christ-like mystic was the sort of thing the Germans would fall for, but they had adopted some of the ideas in my paper and from 10 April had been putting out such rumours as they could in Germany about a mysterious personality who was a creation of their own. He was to be known as Z, looked a little like Bismarck when he was young, and had already established an underground organization. Pastor Niemoller was said to be backing him, and Falkenhausen, Willi Messerschmitt and Sacht were in with him. They were buying up corner houses to be used as machine-gun posts that would dominate the main squares of cities when the time came to rise against Hitler; but one could join Z's organization only if one spoke perfect English.

Obviously PWE's German section had missed the whole point of my paper. How they thought they could spread pacifism among the German people, or do Hitler any harm, by spreading rumours about a young Iron Chancellor who had no real existence, Heaven only knows! As for the idea that no German should be allowed to join a subversive organization unless he could speak his enemy's language perfectly, I have rarely heard of anything more crazy.

On 29 May I wrote another paper pointing this out as politely as I could, but it got us nowhere, and neither, of course, did their absurd adaptation of my plan.

That was the last of the ten independent papers that I wrote under the aegis of Oliver Stanley. The one upon which our deception bible was based was undoubtedly my *chef d'oeuvre*, and in the others there were several quite useful suggestions which were adopted. It may well be that during the following two and a half years I should have been of more value to the JPS had I continued to be used as Stanley used me, to write on any aspect of the war as required, in-

I Endeavour to Earn My Pay

stead of becoming one of a team confined solely to drafting deception plans. But it was decreed that henceforth I should do only the work for which I had been brought in.

On 1 June, Lieutenant-Colonel John H. Bevan, MC, arrived in my office. Shortly afterwards Stanley left the FOPS to become Secretary of State for the Colonies, our section ceased to be part of the FOPS and Bevan was appointed London Controlling Officer, which post he held till the end of the war.

It was upon his taking over that the section gradually began to move from a position of near impotence to one of such influence and power that, had Johnny Bevan asked the Chiefs of Staff for a couple of divisions to play with, they would have given them to him without argument. To his utter absorption in the section's problems, courage and tact in handling senior officers, fine intellect and wide knowledge of world affairs, we owed it mainly that, when our work was done, the Chiefs sent us a minute recording 'our unbroken series of successes' and stating that we had made 'an outstanding contribution to victory'.

Chapter 5
Colonel Bevan Takes Over

'Johnny', as he was always affectionately called by his staff, was 46 years of age when he took over. He was a rather frail-looking man of medium build with sleepy, pale-blue eyes and thin fair hair which turned grey from the strain of the remarkable work he accomplished in the three years following his appointment.

By profession he was a stockbroker, the son of a Chairman of the Stock Exchange and head of the great firm of David A. Bevan, Simpson and Company, in which, after the war, he had nearly a score of partners under him. But his pleasure lay in fishing, gardening and other country pursuits. After we had been cooped up together for a few weeks he said to me one morning, 'Dennis, wouldn't you love to have mud on your boots again?' There was nothing I would have liked less, but I tactfully refrained from saying so.

He was a much tougher person than he looked and, despite lack of exercise, managed to keep very fit; except that he suffered badly from bouts of insomnia. He walked with a slight slouch and a glimpse of his character was given to me by a friend of his who was his contemporary at Eton. When things were looking pretty bad for his side at cricket, he would shuffle in, about sixth wicket down, knock up 100 and shuffle out again looking rather ashamed of himself.

He was the most modest of men and whenever we pulled off a great deception coup, he would always give the credit to Lieutenant-Colonel 'Tar' Robertson of MI5, a really charming man who ran our double agents for us, or Major

Colonel Bevan Takes Over

Roger Hesketh, who later did so with equal efficiency for the deception organization at SHAEF; although, in due course, it became fully realized by our masters that Johnny was the unsleeping mind that watched over, co-ordinated and, to a very large extent, made possible nearly all our great successes.

His most notable feature was a very fine forehead, both broad and deep; and one of his greatest assets an extraordinarily attractive smile. During periods of great strain, when he was sleeping particularly badly, he was often irritable and curt. That he was aware of this and unhappy about it is to his credit; for his wife, Barbara, daughter of the Earl of Lucan, once told me that often when he returned to her in the evening he would say, 'I've been horrid today. How my staff put up with my bad temper I can't imagine.' But, even on those bad days, if one of us made a joke or suggested that he should knock off for a few hours and come out to dinner, that smile which lit up his whole face would immediately flash out. Off duty he made a charming companion and was himself a delightful host.

It was partly on that account that all of us who worked under him ignored his occasional downright rudeness; but even more because we were so fully aware of the terrible responsibility he carried. If the cover plan for one of our major operations had gone wrong and failed to deceive the enemy, not only would the Commander-in-Chief be deprived of the invaluable asset of surprise but many thousands of lives would be lost and a whole campaigning season on that front be wasted. He was, after all, only an amateur soldier and had no precedent to go upon for planning strategic deception; yet the Chiefs of Staff put their faith in him and never failed to accept his recommendations. It is hardly surprising that at times he appeared hag-ridden; but he was a man of remarkable resilience and, just when it seemed that he must crack under the strain, he would be calm, brisk and smiling when he joined us the next morning.

He had received his first commission in 1911 as a Territorial officer in the Huntingdonshire Regiment. In due course he went to France and served for the greater part of the First World War as an infantry subaltern on the Western Front. Then the sort of queer thing happened which does sometimes give reason to believe that certain people are marked out by destiny to play a more important part than their fellows.

One day early in 1918, without any reason being given, he was summoned to join Field Marshal Sir Henry Wilson at the Supreme Allied Headquarters at Versailles and told by the Field Marshal that he had been selected to fill a special appointment.

The Bolshevik revolution in the previous November had brought about the final collapse of the Russian Army and it was known that the bulk of the German forces on the Eastern Front was being transferred to the West. Johnny, then aged 25, was to be given any clerical staff he required and all the secret information available. His task was to assess the probable German Order of Battle for the Spring offensive and appreciate where the enemy would strike his final blow in the hope of achieving a peace of compromise. After many weeks of labour, one afternoon early in March, he gave an exposition of the great wall map he had flagged to Clemenceau, Lloyd George, Churchill, Foch, Haig, Pershing and all the French and British Army Commanders. In the event it proved that he had divined the front on which the enemy would attack to within ten miles and assessed his Order of Battle correctly to within three divisions.

It was at this time that Winston Churchill, then staying at the Ritz in Paris, sent for him to elaborate further his views about enemy intentions. So intrigued was Churchill that he had Johnny stay to dine with him in private. Then, next evening, he sent for him again and, walking round the Place Vendôme, they talked till three o'clock in the morning. It was this extraordinary ability to charm and interest men of great intellect and power which won for him the complete confidence of the Chiefs of Staff and the personal friendship of the CIGS, General Sir Alan Brooke, a fellow bird-watcher, with whom, after his appointment as Controlling Officer, he dined regularly two or three times every month.

Had he had his choice I am sure that he would have made the Army his career, but his father had insisted on his going into the family business and in 1919 he returned to it. But in 1939, when he saw the Second World War looming up, he secured for himself an interesting post. It became his responsi-

Colonel Bevan Takes Over

bility to ensure that far-reaching censorship arrangements could be put into operation at any moment. When the war came he went into uniform and, as an officer of MI5, occupied an office at their war-time headquarters, the one-time prison at Wormwood Scrubs.

He was not long content to accept such static employment. Early in 1940, he succeeded in getting himself transferred to the active Intelligence list and, as a Major, went with his Division to Norway. After the evacuation and his return to the UK, he was posted to Western Command as GSO1 Intelligence.

While at Western Command, Johnny's principal employment was lecturing on security to some forty battalions of Home Guards; so, for all practical purposes, he vegetated until the unpredictable call to great affairs came once again.

He knew no one who was concerned with the high direction of the war except Sir Charles Hambro, who was then the head of the Special Operations Executive. But Johnny had three valuable assets: firstly, his own personality; secondly, that his brother-in-law was Field Marshal Sir Harold Alexander; and, thirdly, myself.

For nineteen months my twenty war papers, written as a civilian, had brought me into intimate contact with a number of officers on the Joint Planning Staff and for a further five months, as a commissioned member of it, I had made the acquaintance of many others. Moreover, my circle of wartime friends extended far outside it, to officers and others whose co-operation could assist our work.

With very few exceptions the senior officers to whom I'd been sent to make requests for assistance in our plans had received me in a most friendly fashion. Partly, perhaps, that was because I adhered rigidly to the behaviour expected of junior officers during the First World War. On being shown into the room of an Admiral, General or Air Marshal, I stood rigidly to attention until addressed. This usually resulted in a smile, or invitation to sit down and the offer of a cigarette.

I then relaxed, said my piece cheerfully and, if I had to argue a point, spoke as though to an equal; so the interview often ended by our laughing together. Then, as I got up to go, I said, 'I wonder, sir, if you happen to have a day free to lunch with me?'

Such invitations from very junior officers were unusual; but many of them had read my books, they had to lunch somewhere and doing so at their clubs became monotonous; so, after only a very slight hesitation, they nearly always accepted. Once the ice had been broken in this way I asked them to dinner. The majority had sent their wives to the country, so it made a pleasant change for them to enjoy a meal with Joan and Diana.

In consequence, not a week passed but Admirals, Generals and Air Marshals dined or lunched with me, or I with them; so I was able to introduce Johnny on the 'old boy' level to all these people.

And he took swift advantage of it. Poor, dear old Lumby was both too shy and lacked the means to entertain. But not so Johnny. In no time at all he followed up the series of lunches and dinners I gave for him by inviting many of my other guests to a meal, turned on the Bevan charm and had them eating out of his hand.

For the first fortnight or so that Johnny and I were together, he remained very quiet, reading his way into the war as I had done five months earlier, attending ISSB meetings with me every morning and generally getting his bearings.

Johnny also read a number of my papers written before and after I joined the Joint Planning Staff and displayed considerable interest in the former; although I don't think he at all approved of the latter, as in his view it was unseemly that a very junior officer should presume to advise and criticize departments outside his own. Then one day he remarked, rather acidly and apparently apropos of nothing in particular, 'Our staff duties are pretty poor, aren't they, Dennis?'

I had always laboured under the illusion that the term 'staff duties' applied to the obligation of a junior officer to act as nurse, ghillie, guide and general factotum to his superior; and I was considerably hurt by his implying that I had failed him in this, as I had always secretly prided myself on being the perfect staff officer

It transpired that he was making no aspersions on my personal conduct; but, still mystified as to the meaning of the expression, I replied cautiously, 'No, sir, I'm afraid our staff duties aren't quite all they might be.'

Actually, he was referring to my paper on military deception, which he was then studying. From the beginning I had, of course, split my papers into sections and numbered the paragraphs but, as I was ignorant of it, not according to the procedure laid down by Staff College. They were, too, in the form of long essays instead of beginning 'Object of the operation', going on to 'Factors in favour', 'factors against', 'Conclusions' and ending with 'Recommendation'. It was this, and the regulation of references such as A(c)(IV), etc., that went by the singularly inappropriate name of 'staff duties'.

Having digested my paper, Johnny rewrote it in accordance with these canons. Henceforth, it became the *deception bible*, upon which the implementation of the deception plans in all British and, later, American commands were based.

Another matter which I then learned came under the heading of staff duties was the proper keeping of files and numbering their contents correctly. Lumby had had his own distinctly personal system in dealing with the few files that we then possessed. He would never let our pleasant and competent secretary, Joan Eden, handle our papers but filed them himself, without any cross-indexing or enumeration. He was allergic to files and he had confided to me in a gleeful whisper that once, when one of his files had become too bulky to fit on a shelf, he had taken it out and burned it. So it was not to be wondered at that Johnny, with his tidy mind, was far from happy at the state in which he found our filing cabinet.

Joan Eden was called in and instructed how, by bending a folder backwards, a proper file could be made. She had had no previous experience of this delicate art but, being a clever girl, took to it like a duck to water and, henceforth, our few files assumed an admirable degree of order.

Soon afterwards Johnny decided to keep a file of his own and labelled it 'Lt Colonel J. H. Bevan – Personal'. Casually he remarked to me, 'The papers in this are just intelligence material with which you need not bother yourself, Dennis.'

It was a tactful way of telling me that I was not to look in it, and that rather amused me, as I could get all the secret information that I wanted from my friends in the Air Ministry. But Johnny was obsessed by security.

As a young man he had lived for a considerable time in Scandinavia; so it was not surprising that his thoughts should turn to making use of that territory for the work with which we had been charged. For several days he worked hard writing a paper which he headed *Strategic Deception – Sweden* and gave it the reference JB and DW/SD No. 1; which was a kindly compliment to me as I had contributed very little to it.

The object was to bring Sweden into the war on the side of Britain or, failing that, to make Germany believe that Sweden was about to enter the war against her and:

(a) forestall such a possibility by invading Sweden or,

(b) tie up further reinforcements in Norway and withdraw numerous squadrons of the German Air Force from other fronts to base them on the north German coast as a threat to Sweden.

I thought it an excellent paper but, having already had some dealings with the Foreign Office, greatly doubted if they would agree to its being put into operation.

Sad to say, I proved right. In the pre-war years the Foregin Office had been very conscious of Britain's military weakness, with the result that they had had to soft-pedal any policy which savoured, however remotely, of aggression. Even when the point was reached that we were making 1000-bomber raids on Germany, and the Americans had enormous forces in Europe fighting with us, the FO continued to be desperately anxious that we should not give offence to neutrals.

Two-thirds of the way through June, Johnny had become as depressed about our uselessness as Lumby had been, but he was made of different mettle and he said to me:

'Dennis, we are never going to get anywhere like this. We might just as well both be on leave for all the good we are doing. No one tells us anything or gives us any orders. We have got to have a directive. And as no one else seems

Colonel Bevan Takes Over

prepared to give us one, we must write one for ourselves.'

'Yes, sir,' I replied dutifully. I had, of course, already read many directives, which were in fact terms of reference to force commanders and others, setting forth in black and white what the Chiefs of Staff wished them to do, the powers with which they were invested and their limitations. But I did not know that they were termed directives, so I had no idea what Johnny meant.

However, he got down to the job and the Chiefs of Staff, having only the vaguest idea of what deception might entail, passed it without argument. It gave us the power to require the aid of anyone who could assist us to mystify and mislead the enemy. And, from that point, Johnny Bevan and I went to work.

Chapter 6
We Move to the Basement

Johnny Bevan's next move was a physical one. He had reached the conclusion that, as long as we remained in our palatial offices on the third floor, we would never secure the full cooperation of the STRATS and the FOPS or be regarded by them as an integral part of the Joint Planning Staff. He therefore agitated for us to be moved down to the basement.

To accomplish this was by no means easy. Such rooms in it as were not already occupied by the planners, or as sleeping quarters for Generals Ismay and Hollis, Sir Ernest Bridges (the Secretary of the War Cabinet), Sir Desmond Morton and others were earmarked as emergency quarters for Churchill, Attlee, Eden, Beaverbrook, Bevin and their staffs in the event of German paratroops being dropped on London. However, Johnny was a persistent person and eventually succeeded in getting two rooms loaned to us, the larger of which was, in an emergency, to have accommodated the War Cabinet typing pool, the smaller just large enough to accommodate Joan Eden and our files.

Well aware as I was of the soundness of our move, I could not help regretting having to leave our luxurious quarters for our new 'utility' ones. Our room could not have measured more than fourteen by twelve feet. At one end it had two doors which virtually made it a passage, at the other end there was a single desk and flanking that, on either side, two others. Instead of the vast mahogany ministerial desks to which we had become accustomed, all five were small, oak affairs and there was not even room to move between them. Instead of

We Move to the Basement

the acres of thick pile carpet upstairs, the floor was bare linoleum.

I had the job of supervising the move and did what I could to give the room a more cheerful look by pinning maps up on the walls and importing a long Persian rug to carpet the space between the two doors. I also persuaded Mr Rance to let me take down one of our huge leather armchairs for any visitors we might have, although there was only just enough room for it between the five desks.

'Mr Rance's room' was the cover name given to the Joint Planning Staff's quarters. He was in fact a civil servant from the Office of Works and responsible for all the furniture in the War Cabinet offices. This charming old gentleman had at one time been a Warrant Officer in the army unit garrisoning the Indian penal settlement on the Andaman Islands. He was no stickler for red tape, became a very good friend of mine and on numerous occasions enabled me to secure extra amenities for our section.

Every morning he went the round of the offices carrying a large chronometer and by it adjusted the clocks to exact Greenwich time. He did this, so he told me with a smile, on a direct order from the Prime Minister. It had been the practice of the Joint Planning Staff to keep their clocks five or ten minutes fast in order to be certain of being on time for their meetings. One day Mr Churchill had suddenly decided to attend a Directors of Plans' conference. On arriving he looked at the clock, thought himself late and politely apologized. Then, glancing at his watch, he discovered that he had arrived dead on time. Most annoyed, he ordered steps to be taken so that this 'should never occur again'.

When we had moved down to our dungeon, Johnny set about tackling two other major problems. Firstly, it was obvious that while the ISSB was in many ways helpful to us, it was in other respects a barrier to securing the implementation of deception plans with the maximum efficiency and rapidity. He felt that direct contact with numerous departments in the service ministries was essential; yet if we took on the implementation of our own plans we should require a considerable increase in staff. He thereupon drafted tentative proposals for a new establishment which would give him posts for six GSO 2s working under him that could be filled as required; one Naval, four Army and one Air.

It was at about this time that I met a man named Umberto Delgado who was later to create quite a stir as a revolutionary. He was then a Major-General, chief of the Portuguese Air Force Mission and a professor at the Portuguese Military Academy. Passionately pro-Ally, he had come to England with proposals for Britain to be given facilities to establish an air base in the Azores.

In view of the heavy sinkings still being inflicted on our shipping by the U-boat packs in the Atlantic, a base in the Azores could prove invaluable; but to secure it was going to be a tricky business. The Governor of the Azores was believed to be strongly pro-German and it was thought that, unless he was threatened with a considerable display of force, he would not allow us to land. The Americans could supply such a force but we, at that time, could not and, while the Portuguese government was willing to allow us to establish a base there, they flatly refused to allow the Americans to do so.

My good friend Roland Vintras had been put in charge of these negotiations and, as host to Delgado, wished to give him while in London as good a time as possible. In restaurants rationing to two courses had by then become very strict and these generally consisted of indifferent food; so Roly asked if he might bring Delgado to dine one night at Chatsworth Court.

I readily agreed and it proved a most entertaining evening. Delgado was a shortish, plump man, a gifted raconteur with enormous vitality. I put only one foot wrong by opening in his honour, as a Portuguese, a bottle of ninety-year-old madeira. Courteously, he waved it aside and said he would much prefer whisky!

In the event a compromise was reached by which, if I remember, the Americans went into the Azores accompanied by a token force of British, the whole being under the British flag.

Many years later I heard the inside story of this decidedly unorthodox operation. I was staying with Bill Elliot, who had by then become an Air Chief Marshal and head of the

We Move to the Basement

British Chiefs of Staff Mission to Washington. Our Ambassador to the United States at that time had a wife who refused to do any but absolutely essential entertaining; so Bill's wife nobly filled the gap by giving dinners two or three times a week. At one of these I again met Delgado, who had been appointed Portuguese Ambassador to Canada in order, I suspect, to get him out of the way.

Over the port he gave a vivid description of the affair. The Governor of the Azores had, as anticipated, refused to permit the Allied expedition to come ashore, upon which Delgado had drawn his pistol and threatened to blow his brains out unless he rescinded his orders to resist the landing.

Years later Delgado became prominent in the news as the leader of a movement to overthrow President Salazar. Based on Brazil, his principal adherents seized a liner in mid-Atlantic. He then went to Spain and one night ill-advisedly crossed the frontier into Portugal to confer with his fellow conspirators. He was betrayed. He and the girl friend who accompanied him were set upon and brutally beaten to death.

The second problem with which Johnny was concerning himself after our move to the basement was liaison with the Americans. The reception of their first contingent in Northern Ireland had given the ISSB a nasty headache, for the Prime Minister had minuted the appropriate authority to the following effect, 'Our gallant allies are about to arrive on our shores. Pray see to it that they have everything to which they are accustomed – plenty of showers, breakfast cereals, marmalade to eat with their bacon and so on.'

To have provided any large quantity of such items in the barracks the American troops were to occupy, when our own were kept on tight rations, would at once have given away to the local population that a convoy of Americans was expected. Southern Ireland had remained neutral and the news would soon have got through to the German Embassy in Dublin, with the result that a pack of U-boats would promptly have been despatched to intercept and play havoc with the convoy. On these grounds, the Prime Minister was persuaded to forgo his hospitable intentions and the Americans landed safely.

It was obvious that the United States forces would play an ever-increasing part in the war in Europe; yet, as far as deception was concerned, we had no contact with them at all.

Johnny asked the DMI that an officer should go to Washington, explain the possibilities of strategic deception to the American Chiefs of Staff and, when possible, assist in the implementation of our plans through United States channels.

As at that time deception was still regarded, except by a very limited number of imaginative people, as of most dubious value, the DMI proved loath to nominate a fully trained Intelligence officer solely to this work. But he did agree that one who was going out to join the Intelligence Branch of the Joint Staff Mission should act for us on a part-time basis. This officer, Major Michael Bratby, was then posted to us on a ten-day attachment, so that he could be indoctrinated into our mysteries.

Michael was in his early thirties, by far the youngest officer ever to be attached to our London Controlling Section. He had learned his first lessons in Intelligence at Matlock under old Lumby and had a great admiration for him. Lumby had never been distinguished for the smartness of his appearance. On his recall to the Army in July 1939 he had bought a Service cap which by the spring of 1942 was a shapeless bag that he wore slightly on the back of his head, and he told me that he had every intention of making it last until the war was over. Michael had been much influenced by his original preceptor!

Johnny, who habitually wore the best-polished shoes in the British Army, subscribed to the doctrine that a tidy appearance indicated a tidy mind. Since I also believed that staff officers had a duty to be smartly turned out, Michael did not immediately strike a happy note with either of us. Privately we deplored the fact that such a fellow should have been selected as one of the representatives of the Imperial General Staff in Washington.

In this we proved wrong, since Michael had got on exceptionally well with the Americans in his previous job as a Divisional Intelligence officer in Iceland, and he did even better with them in their own country. In peacetime his

We Move to the Basement

hobby was bird-watching and, in collaboration with Peter Scott, he wrote books which gained him a wide public among nature lovers. He was a stockily built fellow with a rather plump face, weak eyes for which he always wore spectacles, and a gentle smiling manner.

His first reaction to Johnny and me was no more enthusiastic than ours to him. He showed great interest in our work but loathed the atmosphere of our map-lined but still cell-like room. After spending two days in it he confided to me that he would not be prepared to stay there permanently if offered a fortune.

Later, we all got to know and appreciate one another's personalities. But Johnny was heavily involved in his campaign to by-pass ISSB, and I had too much routine work on my hands to give a great deal of time to our visitor. Michael's ten days of incarceration were soon over and he left us to do a similar period in the more congenial atmosphere of the ISSB, whose interests he was also to watch as a part of his duties in Washington.

The last general 'appreciation of the situation' got out by the STRATS had been a most depressing document. It laid down that we were not yet strong enough to invade and hold a bridgehead on the Continent anywhere along the stretch of coast over which we could give our troops fighter cover, because it was in that area (naturally) that the enemy had his greatest concentration grouped to resist any such attempt; and that for us to invade any part of enemy-held territory outside the range of fighter cover would prove suicidal. In other words, we must sit on our bottoms until many thousands more Americans had arrived and our air strength had become superior to that of the Luftwaffe – which could not be hoped for until the following summer.

Enraged by this, the Prime Minister wrote a paper in reply. He never wavered from the basic principle that it was folly to attack the enemy at his strongest point. Therefore, from the beginning, he had been firmly of the opinion that we should not attempt to re-enter the Continent by way of northern France or Belgium, and it was only under pressure from the Americans that he eventually agreed to the direct assault against Hitler's 'Atlantic wall'. But in his paper he pointed out that the Luftwaffe could not be in great strength everywhere at once along the 2000 miles of enemy-held coast-line. He then proposed that six separate expeditions, each composed of 100,000 men, should be prepared and all of them launched simultaneously at different places, hundreds of miles apart, between northern Norway and the Pyrenees; those that failed to get a foothold would at once be withdrawn and despatched to support those that succeeded.

I do not believe for one moment that he expected his plan to be accepted, since he knew perfectly well that we had not got the shipping. He was simply twisting the tails of the Chiefs of Staff. After the evacuations from Dunkirk and Greece they had become over-cautious and were unwilling to mount any major offensive until we should have the over-whelming strength to make its success 100 per cent certain. On the face of it, such caution is proper. But there is another side to it. No country has ever won a war by standing in-definitely on the defensive, and long periods of inaction in-evitably lead to despondency and a lowering of morale among the troops. In this case, if by sitting tight for another year we allowed Russia to be forced out of the war, the whole of Hitler's mighty Army there could be withdrawn. Such a re-inforcement in the West could make it impossible for even a great army of Americans in addition to our own ever to re-turn to the Continent, while a part of the German forces might well be used to over-run Turkey, deprive us of our oil in the Middle East and, eventually, join up with the Japanese in India.

It was, I feel certain, these considerations which made Churchill regard it as imperative that we launch a major offensive somewhere during 1942. He was asking the Chiefs for the sun and the moon. He knew he would not get them, but he hoped to ginger them into giving him at least an important planet.

Johnny's swift mind seized upon the Prime Minister's paper as an excellent opportunity to show our flag. His thesis was that, while the risk of actually attempting a landing on the Continent outside fighter cover might be considered too great, we might deceive the enemy into believing that we intended to do so. If this succeeded, the enemy would have

We Move to the Basement

to withdraw considerable forces from Russia, to form a powerful reserve in central France and to strengthen his garrisons along the now lightly held coasts northward from the Pas de Calais and southward from Cherbourg.

This excellent paper, which included the means by which we proposed to deceive the enemy, went in as JB and DW2, *Deception – Return to the Continent*.

Personally I had much more forceful views on how the situation should be handled; but as they had nothing to do with deception, they were outside our terms of reference. Therefore, as soon as I had given Johnny such assistance as I could with his paper, I started one of my own. I called it *The Art of War*. Having examined the possibilities everywhere, I concluded that in 1942 we could not without great risk launch an offensive against any enemy-held territory; but that the time had now come when, with the United States behind us, we were quite strong enough to stand no more nonsense from the neutrals.

Spain was allowing Hitler to use her ports to shelter U-boats and helping the enemy in other ways, but was reported to be in a desperate way for food and raw materials; so I suggested that General Franco should be offered a choice. Either he should throw the Germans out, accept the Allies' protection and allow them to establish bases in Spain; in which case the United States would feed his people and send him the essentials to keep his industries going or, when it suited us, we would invade Spain and take the country over.

Franco might possibly have agreed. If he did not, my plan was that we should go into northern Spain, both from the Atlantic and the Mediterranean simultaneously, so as to seize swiftly the great barrier of the Pyrenees before the Germans had time to bring south sufficient forces to launch a counter stroke.

The occupation of Spain would have been invaluable to us. By dominating the Mediterranean coast we could have much more easily reinforced Malta and, in due course, have mounted an operation against French North Africa, or the south of France, or have seized Sardinia as a stepping-stone to Italy.

Even a threat to Franco could have produced most valuable

repercussions. If Franco decided not to play with us, he would have to call on Hitler to help him make the long coastline of Spain secure from invasion, and that would have meant withdrawing anything up to twenty divisions from the Russian Front or a dangerous thinning out of those that were holding down France, Belgium and Holland.

The next problem was to whom to send my paper. To submit it to the STRATS and the FOPS was useless as this confrontation of a neutral was a Foreign Office matter, and it was certain that the Foreign Office would have a fit at the mere suggestion. Somehow, I had to get my paper right to the Prime Minister.

I consulted my old friend Maxwell Knight of MI5, and he solved it for me. The Prime Minister's personal assistant was Major Sir Desmond Morton, and Maxwell Knight and he were old friends. Max, having read my paper, gave me an introduction to Sir Desmond.

As a result, towards the end of July, I penetrated Mr Churchill's quarters where, however frequently he worked in No. 10 during the day, he always slept when he was not at Chequers for the weekend or abroad for conferences. The ground floor, immediately above our basement, had been converted into private apartments for him and Mrs Churchill, a map room and work-rooms for his secretaries. On the mezzanine floor above it were the offices of Desmond Morton, Professor Lindemann, Commander Tommy Thompson (the Prime Minister's ADC) and a small mess for the 'Prime's' entourage.

Desmond Morton was a great character; deep-voiced, forceful, decisive, the sort of buccaneering personality that Churchill loved. He was constantly in attendance on the Prime Minister, and fully informed about every plan pending and every aspect of the war.

I realized afterwards that by taking my paper 'upstairs' I was asking to be thrown out of the Cabinet Offices. While I was a civilian I was perfectly entitled to express my views about the conduct of the war to anyone who would listen. But as a very junior staff officer all I was entitled to do was put my idea informally up to the STRATS, whose function it was, not only to make plans for such operations as their

We Move to the Basement

masters were contemplating, but to write papers on others they considered feasible and put them forward with the opening sentence, 'In anticipation of the wishes of the Chiefs of Staff....' They could, therefore, had they liked my suggestion, have written an official paper on it which would have gone in turn to the Directors of Plans, then the Chief of Staff and, if not thrown out by either, been submitted to the Foreign Office. But I had had the impertinence to by-pass the lot.

Fortunately, Sir Desmond Morton received me kindly and gave the best part of an hour to discussing my paper with me. He shot it down on the grounds that: (1) the Foreign Office would never agree; (2) Spain would prove a much tougher nut to crack than I imagined (he instanced the desperate resistance put up by the Spanish people against the French in the Napoleonic wars); (3) the Germans' swiftness of reaction was well known and they would have troops across the central Pyrenees before we could close in from both sides; (4) we should have tied up a great part of our forces in Spain indefinitely.

Desmond Morton and I became great friends. He lunched with me the following week, returned the lunch soon afterwards at the 'Senior' and later came several times to dinner with us at Chatsworth Court. So my unorthodox effort was far from wasted; henceforth, I had the ear of a man next to the Prime Minister and was able to use it on numerous occasions to the advantage of my section.

It was late one afternoon in July when Johnny was sent for by the Chiefs of Staff. He returned with tremendous news. A firm decision had been taken to mount an expedition against French North Africa that autumn.

The Chiefs had instructed Johnny that he was at once to set about the preparation of a cover plan, and that in no circumstances whatever was he to mention the work on which he was engaged to anyone else. Not even the ISSB or the other members of the JPS were to be told. The latter had, of course, written the plan for the operation, but they had also written numerous others for possible use and it was not until nearly a week later that they were informed that Torch had been adopted.

During these few days we worked with intense concentration and far into the nights; for we were very conscious of the great responsibility we had been given, the lack of prestige that our section had so far laboured under, and the handicap of being amateurs with only a rudimentary knowledge of campaigns conducted at the highest level.

It was little more than two months since Johnny had taken over. Now he was faced not only with the task of preparing a detailed deception plan to cover the greatest amphibious operation since the Spanish Armada, but also with the immense labour of thinking out scores of minor pieces of information which, suitably conveyed to the enemy, would give him the false picture we wished him to accept.

Moreover, by his own directive, Johnny had freed himself from the ISSB, who had previously been responsible for implementing all cover plans. This meant that we should have to undertake the innumerable tasks connected with implementation ourselves. In consequence, when he sent up our proposals for deception, he also submitted his request for an increase in our Establishment. The result could not have been more heart-warming. Early in August, the Chiefs took our proposed cover plan for Torch and gave their approval to the general conception. They also agreed that arrangements should be made as a matter of urgency to provide Colonel Bevan with the necessary staff.

Johnny Bevan had won his spurs. And he deserved them.

Chapter 7
Preparations for Torch

Johnny and I spent many hours discussing ways by which we could conceal from the enemy the British intention of landing an army in North Africa. Eventually, towards the end of August, I wrote a paper outlining our recommendation for circulation to the JPS and ISSB.

The expedition was to sail from the Clyde, and the forces composing it would be concentrated in that area. The assembling of these masses of ships and men could not be concealed from German air reconnaissance, so the enemy was bound to become aware that we were preparing a large-scale overseas operation. Our task, therefore, boiled down to misleading them about its destination.

Aerial reconnaissance would also have informed the enemy that we had a large concentration of troops in southeastern England, and they probably knew that the backbone of this force was the Canadian Division.

The Clyde would certainly have been the base chosen by us had we meant to make a landing in force in Norway; so, for deception purposes, we put out that this was our intention. Had we in fact meant to return to Norway we should obviously have endeavoured to prevent the Germans from reinforcing that country; so it was plausible to lead them to believe that, simultaneously with the despatch of the expedition to Norway, we should use the Canadian Division and other troops in the south for a cross-Channel operation against the Pas de Calais, in order to force the Germans to keep a maximum number of troops in that area.

To the deception plan for the landing in Norway we gave the code name Solo One, and for that against the Pas de Calais Passover. These were chosen in the hope that a bright German Intelligence officer might associate the anagram Solo with Oslo, and Passover with the crossing of the Channel.

In addition there were many minor plans to mask the innumerable activities in preparation for the operation. I drew up a large chart which showed every step to be taken from day to day until the actual sailing of the expedition.

Although posted to the Cabinet Offices, for pay, rations, etc., as an Air Staff Officer, I now came under Air Commodore (Bill) Elliot, who had succeeded Dickie Dickson as Director of Plans (Air). Owing to his good offices I had put up my second ring as a Flight Lieutenant early in the summer. Now that Johnny's application for an increased staff, which included a GSO 2 Air, had been passed, I was automatically promoted to Squadron Leader. But this did not make me one whit more competent at 'staff duties', and some ten days after the passing of our plan poor Johnny was at his wits' end owing to the innumerable problems he had to tackle, in which I could give him little assistance. Running his hand distractedly through his thin hair one morning, he said to me: 'Dennis, we can't go on like this. We must have help, and at once.'

He then went upstairs to see General Ismay. The following morning Major Harold Peteval reported for duty.

Peteval had been Johnny's GSO 2 at Western Command, where they had worked together for the best part of two years. He had been just too young to participate actively in the First World War and in peace-time had managed a soap factory. However, he had been in the Second World War from the beginning, had spent several months in France and had been evacuated from Dunkirk. People who had known him in France spoke of his remarkable imperturbability under shell fire, and later we learned that 'our Harold' frequently went out at night to get the best possible view of an air-raid, in order to see if either the attack or defence had developed new techniques.

Very reserved by nature, he was a large, solemn man with a mass of thick, smooth, black hair, a heavy moustache (later reduced to more elegant proportions on his marriage to the Bishop of Chichester's daughter), and heavy-lensed spectacles. Whenever he spoke of our work, it was with the low-voiced intensity which seems to become habitual to many officers long associated with Intelligence and jealously guarding its secrets; but if one got him on his own, it soon became apparent that his serious mien hid a delightfully subtle sense of humour and that, having thought deeply upon many problems, he always had an interesting and often original point of view on them.

In any case, now that Johnny was irritably demanding of me innumerable trivial services that any ordinary Intelligence officer would have regarded as part of his normal work, the arrival of the tried and proven Harold was for me sweeter than the answer to any maiden's prayer.

On the first occasion that Johnny sent him off to represent us at a high-level conference, he waylaid me outside our room. Being so shy, he implored me to go with him. I said that it was pointless for two of us to go and I would willingly relieve him of the job. We then made a pact that he should take on all work connected with the office, while I attended all conferences and, as required, bearded Generals in their dens.

Early in September the London Controlling Section acquired a fourth member, Major Ronald Wingate. Several candidates for the post had been interviewed by Johnny, but from the time Wingate's name was first mentioned it was clear that he meant to get it if keenness could secure it for him. He not only rang Johnny up repeatedly, but also lobbied Pug Ismay, who was an old friend of his. Pug made it quite clear that the decision lay with the Controlling Officer, but he sent down a note strongly recommending this old companion of happy days in India, and Ronald was taken on.

It is a curious concidence that Ronald had earlier held the post of G S O 1, S O E West Africa, which Lumby had left the Cabinet Offices to take over, and that both were Companions of the Most Distinguished Order of the Indian Empire; but their careers and personalities had little in common.

Lumby had spent all his Indian years in Simla or Delhi

and, on the rare occasions when he did take long leave, had returned to England; whereas Wingate had, for lengthy periods, represented the King Emperor in the remotest parts of the sub-continent living, as he liked to describe it, in 'lice-ridden hovels'; but on each trip home he spent the accumulated earnings of two years motoring across Europe from one luxury resort to another. Lumby was a modest efficient servant of the Crown, but had never basked in its reflected splendours; Wingate had ended his Indian political career as Governor of Baluchistan, ranking as a Lieutenant General, and had ridden in state with an escort of Lancers. Poor Lumby's wooden leg restricted his recreations; whereas Wingate had been a very active man – a fine shot, fisherman, polo player and golfer. He was also a great *bon vivant* and knew all the best restaurants in most of the European capitals. He was the son of a great man, Sir Reginald 'Wingate of the Sudan', had taken a double First at Balliol and, as a very young Political Officer in the First World War, had been sent to the burning hell of Aden in the days when there were no refrigerators or wireless communications. There he had negotiated the treaty which gave Britain a protectorate over all the oil sheikdoms of the Gulf. He counted kings among his friends, had a great self-assurance and a delightful sense of humour, assets that opened all doors to him; so we could not have had a more valuable addition to our section.

Ronald was a slender man of medium height with grey hair and a neat grey moustache. He had small, twinkling, triangular-shaped eyes and, when he joined us, was 54, several years older than Johnny. He had left the Indian Political before normal retiring age, because of some difference of opinion with the Viceroy.

On the opening of the Second World War he had got himself a job with the Ministry of Economic Warfare. Later he sailed as Political Agent with the ill-fated expedition to Dakar where, had he been allowed to go ashore, things might have turned out very differently, since he spoke French as fluently as a Frenchman, was on excellent terms with General de Gaulle, yet appreciated the Vichy point of view, and was as cunning as seven serpents. After his return to England he had gone to West Africa as GSO 1. SOE. It had

Dennis Wheatley as Squadron Leader

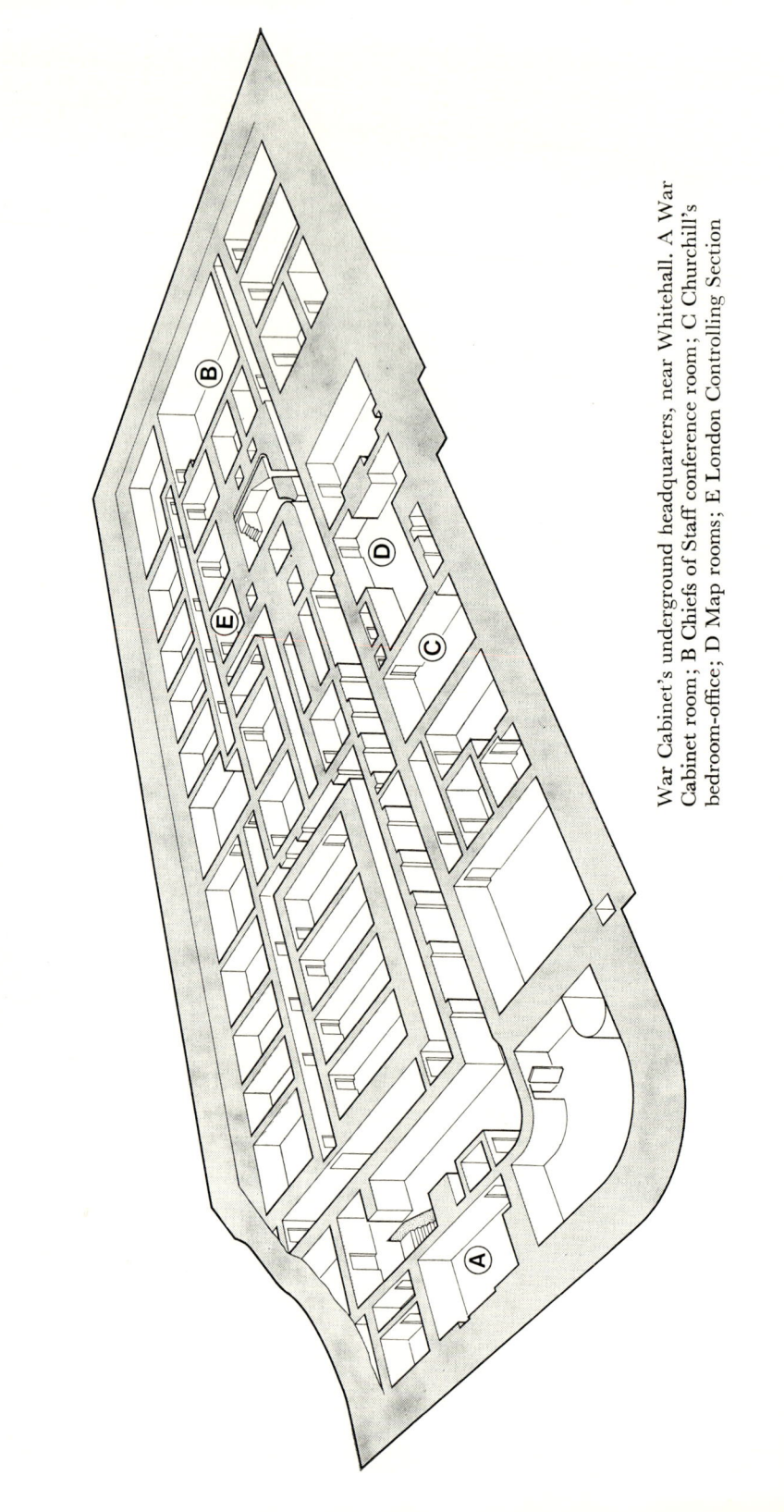

War Cabinet's underground headquarters, near Whitehall. A War Cabinet room; B Chiefs of Staff conference room; C Churchill's bedroom-office; D Map rooms; E London Controlling Section

Colonel John Bevan

The London Controlling Section. (*l to r*) Maj Derrick Morley, Maj Neil Gordon Clark, Maj Harold Peteval, Jnr Cdr Lady Jane Pleydall-Bouverie, Col John Bevan, Wg Cdr Dennis Wheatley, Lt-Col Ronald Wingate, Cdr James Arbuthnott, with Cdr Alec Finter from Cairo

General Lord Ismay

Above: Joan Bright welcoming Field Marshal Sir John Dill to the Quebec Conference

Opposite above: Air Chief Marshal Sir William Elliot

Opposite below: Major-General Sir Leslie Hollis, RM

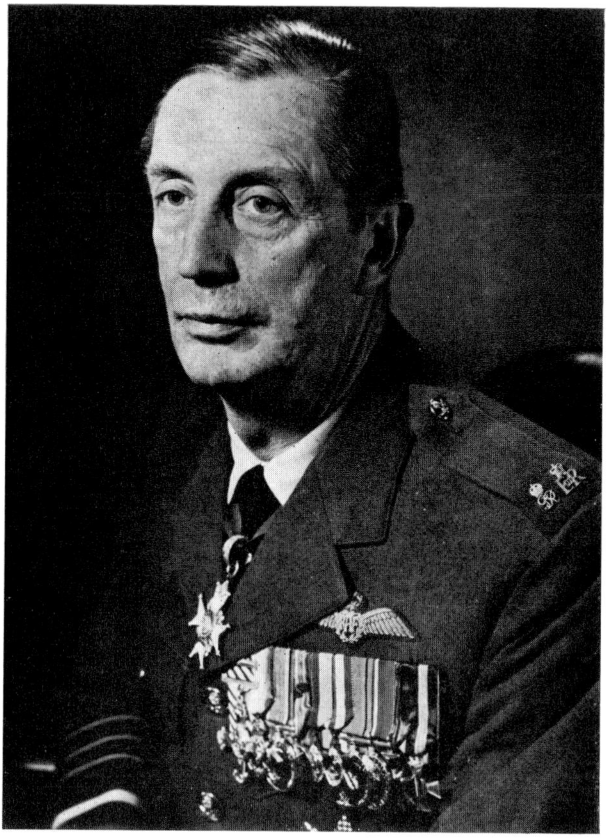

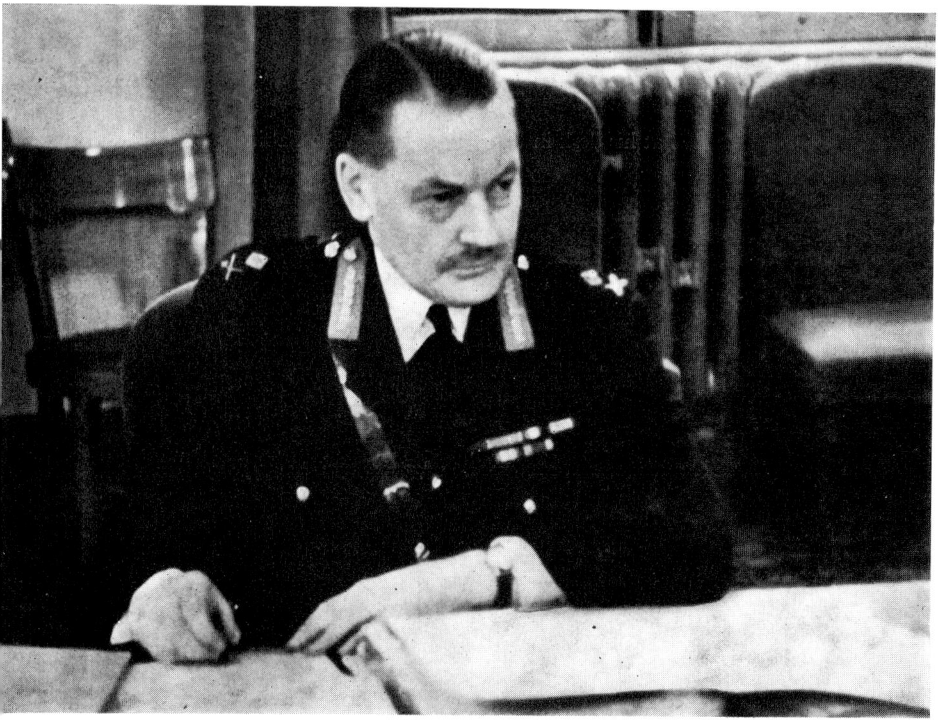

DW at his desk in the offices of the War Cabinet

Preparations for Torch

turned out to be an extraordinarily tricky post to fill, as the Governor was constantly at loggerheads with the Commander-in-Chief and, by a most unfortunate arrangement, SOE owed a partial allegiance to both.

Lumby found it an equally difficult post and, after a year there, was recalled owing to a reorganization of the Inter-Service Security Board. This also affected us, as we still worked closely with it and I continued to attend its meetings every morning. Old Colonel Graham, who had filled the dual role of the Military Member and the head of MI1 (M) (appointment of and contact with all Military Attachés posted to Embassies abroad), was retired. Major Eddie Combe, promoted to Lieutenant-Colonel, replaced him as Chairman and Military Member ISSB. Captain Eric Goudie, promoted to Major, replaced Combe as Secretary to the Board and a new post was created for a 'Cardinal' Colonel (so-called because entitled to a scarlet hat and gorgets) to concern himself exclusively with the work of MI1 (M). Lumby was appointed to this new post and in it would have proved a most valuable friend to us, but, alas, the aircraft that was carrying him back from West Africa crashed on the coast of Ireland and he was killed.

As the oldest inhabitant of our village, it had fallen to me from the beginning to indoctrinate all newcomers. For this purpose I drew up a large chart like a family tree, showing the chain of authority from the Prime Minister, in his capacity as Minister of Defence, through the War Cabinet, the Chiefs of Staff or the Defence Committee, the Vice-Chiefs or the Directors of Plans, to the various sections of the Joint Planning or Joint Intelligence Staffs, the ISSB, and other bodies outside the Cabinet Offices who would implement decisions.

Many months later I found that a big chart similar to mine had been printed off, giving the names of all the people concerned, for the information of officers newly appointed to the JPS to fill the places of others who had been posted elsewhere. I was interested to note that the only omission was any mention of the London Controlling Section; so we were evidently still considered to be super-secret.

Ronald Wingate proved a swift learner. He knew no more

about the organization of the modern army than I did about the Royal Air Force, but all his life he had dealt with government hierarchies and his knowledge of politics – domestic, imperial and international – was encyclopaedic. He displayed an amusing cynicism about his ex-fellow civil servants and had a vast experience of 'the working of the protocol', as he termed it; thus, by using exactly the right approach, he was often able to achieve results which would have been beyond the scope of anyone lacking such highly specialized knowledge coupled with his particular form of guile. He used at times to declare that his one aim in life was to 'give everyone pleasure', and his unruffled calm, polished wit and unfailing good humour were in times of stress a blessing to us all.

The basic plan which Johnny and I had drawn up was never departed from in principle, but it developed many ramifications. Solo had become two separate plans: the first concerned with the shipping concentration in the Clyde, the second with the 52nd Highland Division's notional invasion of Norway. There were also Passover, Cavendish, Overthrow and Kennicott, and to merge these plans successfully was like wrestling with a hydra-headed monster.

To implement them became an ever-greater headache as, although we still had the valuable co-operation of ISSB and permission to go direct to certain departments outside it, we were in no position to issue instructions to C-in-C Home Forces or the C-in-C of the Expedition now forming.

In consequence, at Johnny's instance, the STRATS had sent a paper up to the Chiefs, outlining our situation and difficulties, as a result of which it was agreed that the controlling officer should henceforth be responsible to the Directors of Plans, who would be charged with assisting him with the implementation of deception. The way was now open for us to make use of the Executive Planning Sections, each of which carried out detailed planning in their respective ministries on plans that had been approved. But this was only one fence crossed; we soon found ourselves up against all sorts of dead ends and, at times, wilful obstruction.

The three ways of conveying false information were: through double agents controlled by MI5; by initiating certain activities in neutral countries; by leading the forces

Preparations for Torch

concerned to believe that they were being sent overseas when this was not actually the case, or, alternatively, to believe that they were being despatched to a country which was not, in fact, their destination. The object of the third method was that careless talk by the forces concerned would be picked up by enemy agents or neutrals in this country, and be passed either deliberately in the first case, or as interesting gossip in the second, to the enemy.

When the Torch convoys sailed it was to be anticipated that they would be sighted by enemy U-boats or long-range aircraft, steaming west and out into the Atlantic, instead of north; so their cover destination was then to be changed to the Azores. On arriving outside the Straits of Gibraltar, this cover would also be blown and the enemy was to be told that the convoys were on their way to invade Sardinia. This final cover destination was later changed to the east coast of Sicily, then Greece.

Meanwhile the United States forces, which were actually to land at Casablanca, were to be told that they were being sent via the Cape as reinforcements for the Middle East and, to account for the fact that the ships were assault loaded, that they were to undertake operations against the Azores on the way.

We had to overcome many obstacles to make our stories plausible.

If the Torch forces had really been going to the Middle East, they would have been issued with tropical kit, but for North Africa in winter tropical kit was not required; for service in the Middle East the engines of all aircraft would have been dust-proofed, while for North Africa this was not necessary; for the Middle East all tanks and vehicles would have been painted with desert camouflage, whereas in North Africa the terrain was greenish-brown; the medical supplies required for the two places differed greatly; Army nurses were to be taken in the second wave of the assault and they would have been redundant if the force had been proceeding to the Middle East; if the 52nd Highland Division and other forces in Scottish Command earmarked for Solo had really been going to Norway they would have needed pack transport, but the War Office refused to find us any mules.

Passover presented even greater difficulties. To make a threat to the Pas de Calais ring true, however much we might add by ruses to the notional size of the force, we needed a real one of considerable size as a basis for our deception, and one that believed itself fully fitted to go into battle.

For this we had counted on the Canadian Divisions and other units which had been concentrated in southeast England to carry out operation Roundup when required. Then at a meeting held at the War Office to nominate a force for us, we learned to our utter amazement that, even after three years of war, there was not a single division in the UK that was in a state of readiness to proceed overseas. Even the forces to be used in Torch could not be brought up to active warfare establishment and fully equipped without robbing every other division that was to be left behind of some of its men, guns, vehicles or radio sets. This meant that the depleted divisions would automatically become aware that they were not to be employed in active operations for many months to come; so what hope had we of leading their personnel to believe that they were shortly to be the spearhead for the liberation of Europe?

In addition to this, nearly everyone we approached scarcely bothered to conceal the fact that he thought this new-fangled deception racket a lot of nonsense. They had their own jobs to do and regarded it as a shocking waste of time and material to train troops for operations in the sort of territory where they were not to be sent, to study maps which would never be used and amass medical stores which would never be required. No wonder Johnny Bevan's temper became frayed and his hair began to turn grey.

The worst of all our headaches was Gibraltar. It emerged that tank landing craft have a comparatively limited life, after which they must be reconditioned. The voyage out to Gibraltar proved to be about their limit, and the Admiralty informed us that from a month to six weeks would be required to recondition them there. This meant that the TLCs – unmistakable vessels which could have no possible use except for an assault landing – would be arriving in Gibraltar roadsteads as early as the last week in September, and D-Day had now been postponed until 8 November.

Preparations for Torch

In addition, from the end of September onwards, the fortress would show unusual activity in a dozen different ways. The size of the airfield was to be increased; boxed fighter aircraft were to be sent out in a very considerable number, together with great quantities of spares and stores of every kind. This meant many more ships than usual calling to unload at the port, and scores of specialist personnel had to be sent out well ahead of D-Day.

These matters would have been of less concern had the port possessed a considerable hinterland of Allied-controlled territory, but the colony's area was only a few square miles. Everything that went on in it could be observed by telescope from Algeciras, and many thousands of Spanish entered it each day to work, leaving again in the evening. However stringent the security measures, it seemed that the enemy must gain knowledge of the war-like activities in progress and infer that a major operation against some Axis-dominated territory in the Mediterranean was pending.

Dudley Clarke was giving us all possible assistance by implementing our cover plans, as far as he could, through his channels in the eastern Mediterranean, but, as far as we knew, neither General Mason MacFarlane nor General Lord Gort, the Governors of Gibraltar and Malta respectively, knew anything about organized deception. They were probably working in the dark on such instructions as the Chiefs of Staff were sending them at our instigation. Johnny decided that, to achieve the best results, it was essential that both military Governors must be put fully in the picture. He asked the DMI for an officer he could send out on a mission to them.

Major David Strangeways of the Duke of Wellington's Regiment was the officer selected. We found him to be the complete antithesis of Michael Bratby. He was a regular officer and so beautifully turned out that, even in battledress, he looked as if he had stepped straight out of a bandbox. When I asked him to dinner, regardless of the absurd regulation that forbade it, he appeared in immaculate 'blues'.

He was a small, good-looking man, with a brisk, efficient manner and a very quick mind. While displaying the most punctilious military manners when addressing Johnny, he had not the least fear of expressing his own opinions with the utmost frankness.

After a few days with us he had mastered our current plans and left England by air with 'most secret' despatches for Generals Mason MacFarlane, Lord Gort and Sir Harold Alexander in Cairo.

We used his journey to endeavour to pull a fast one over the enemy. My old friend Henry Hopkinson had been posted to Cairo as Foreign Office advisor to Mr Casey, our Minister of State, and there could be nothing suspicious about my sending Henry an autographed copy of my last-published book by hand of Strangeways. Placed loosely in the book was a letter on Cabinet Office paper from me introducing Strangeways to Henry and telling him of my good fortune in having been taken on to the Joint Planning Staff. I then went on to gossip a trifle indiscreetly, but in guarded language, about forthcoming events. While containing a certain amount of harmless truth, the facts about our build-up at Gibraltar were so distorted as to lead the enemy to false conclusions; yet the letter had nothing in it that Henry and I might not plausibly have written to each other; and, of course, no mention of my being employed in deception.

We had already been informed that the hotels in Gibraltar were insecure and that the luggage of officers passing through was searched by enemy agents as a matter of routine. So we felt reasonably confident that if Strangeways left the book and letter in his suitcase, the letter would be read and its contents passed on to the *Abwehr*.

Having completed his mission with characteristic efficiency, Strangeways returned to England. Thereafter Generals MacFarlane and Gort gave us most valuable help, which included a broadcast by the former to the garrison at Gibraltar calling on the forces under his command to do their utmost in the preparations which were now going forward for 'the permanent relief of beleaguered Malta'.

As a result of having been drawn into our deception racket Strangeways was sent out, a few months later, to Dudley Clarke, who put him in charge of 'A' Force sub-headquarters in PAIFORCE. In due course, he was transferred to the

Preparations for Torch

Eighth Army and played a leading part in 'A' Force activities in the great advance from El Alamein to Tunisia.

During the final phase of the campaign he was in command of Dudley's brigade of dummy tanks and visual deception devices. On the first sign of the German collapse he abandoned deception to take an active part in rounding up the enemy. Dashing ahead in an armoured car, he was the first man into Tunis, shot his way into the German HQ, blew open the safe and seized all the secret documents before they could be destroyed; for which he received the DSO.

General Montgomery thought so highly of him that, on the General's return to England, he asked for him as his adviser on deception. As a result, this brilliant young officer became a Colonel on the Staff of Twenty-first Army Group and responsible for tactical deception after our landing in Normandy.

Chapter 8
Torch

While David Strangeways's mission was a considerable help in our attempts to provide the enemy with plausible reasons for the increased activity at Gibraltar, this was in the main a Naval problem, so the question arose as to whether we ought not to have a sailor as a permanent member of the LCS.

About the advisability of this I had no doubts whatever, but Johnny, with his strange antipathy to officers of any but the 'Brown Job' service, appeared loath to do so and expressed doubt whether enough work could be found for a Naval officer to do.

He consulted Lt. Commander the Hon. Ewen Montagu, RNVR, the distinguished barrister who, earlier on, had been the deputy representative of the Admiralty on ISSB. On leaving the ISSB, Montagu had been put in charge of Naval ruses; so he was now our principal contact at the Admiralty. He proved strongly in favour of Johnny's asking for a naval member for his staff and added that, should it be found that LCS could not provide him with full employment, he, Montagu, would ensure that the newcomer's spare time was profitably filled by 'devilling' for him.

So far, LCS consisted of a stockbroker, a thriller-writer, a soap manufacturer and a retired civil servant, all disguised as officers only for the purpose of the war. As regular Naval officers of any rank were at a premium by 1942, we naturally expected that at best the Admiralty would send us an intelligent peace-time yachtsman now ranking as a Lieutenant

RNVR. Instead of which, towards the end of September, Captain Cuthbert of the FOPS brought to our office as our new member James Arbuthnott, a full Commander RN.

Arbuthnott had served in the first World War, retired from the Royal Navy in 1926 and became a tea planter in Ceylon. There he had risen to Chief Executive of Scottish Lands, the biggest tea-planting corporation in the island, and ruled as their representative over scores of square miles of plantations, many white subordinates and thousands of native labourers. On the outbreak of the Second World War he had been recalled to the colours and posted to Admiral Sir James Somerville's Indian Ocean Command. He had become very friendly with his Admiral, which stood us in good stead, as Somerville was now based on Gibraltar as Commander, Force 'H'. Mention of Somerville reminds me of an oft-told but amusing story. When he was given the further honour of a KCB to add to his KBE, Admiral Sir Andrew Cunningham sent him the following signal: 'From C-in-C Mediterranean to Flag Officer Force "H" – Fancy, twice a knight at your age. Congratulations.'

From Ceylon James had been transferred to the Middle East, and had worked in Cairo for over a year. After Johnny had given his usual lucid dissertation which always preceded my more prolonged indoctrination of new members, James remarked quietly, 'Of course, we had nothing of this kind in Cairo.'

As he had worked at GHQ Middle East for over a year, knew Dudley Clarke slightly and must have rubbed shoulders often with 'A' Force officers, this was an extraordinary tribute to the high degree of security maintained by Dudley and his organization. When questioned, James said he had heard of 'A' Force but had no idea what it did; yet it was over two years since Dudley had started practising deception and he now had under him over 100 officers.

James Arbuthnott was a tallish man with slim hips, a thin face and greyish, slightly wavy hair. He had the quiet manner so often associated with the 'silent' service and one of those bronzed, attractive features that go so well with Naval uniform. The corners of his eyes and mouth were wrinkled with much smiling. His unassuming, rather shy demeanour would not have led one to suspect that in civilian life, on behalf of his company's directors in Scotland, he had wielded such power in Ceylon, but once one got to know him the reason for his having been selected soon became apparent. He was not particularly inventive or imaginative, but his judgement was extraordinarily sound and he possessed in a very high degree those qualities that go to make a great Pro-Consul – an inbred sense of justice, toleration and sympathy for the under-dog.

With the punctilio that I had made a rule, on his arrival in our office as my senior, I addressed him as 'Sir'. Then, on his first day with us when I took him out to lunch, he said, 'My name is James and I'd like you to call me by it. With a number of officers working together on a staff, I don't think it a good thing for them always to be saying "Sir" and be standing up saluting their seniors.'

This seems an appropriate place to record the type of relationship which developed between Johnny Bevan and his officers. He made it clear to each of them on joining that, since we were all much of an age and had all held responsible positions in civilian life, he did not favour a strictly military set-up. We were not children to be checked in and out, and he felt sure we could be relied upon to do our jobs to the best of our abilities as a little group of friends rather than a group of officers of varying seniority.

His occasional bouts of irritability occurred only in periods when he was under great strain, and during our long association I doubt if a happier office existed in any service ministry. The wisdom of his attitude was proved beyond all question, for a very real friendship grew up between us all. Never a week passed in the many months we worked together without several of us lunching or dining with one another, and over many a good bottle of wine we discussed informally with Johnny the progress, improvement and possible extension of our deception activities.

I remained the only airman in the party and James, for over a year, the only sailor; whereas in due course the soldiers increased to five. It was only natural that, as the sole representative of our services, coupled with the great liking we felt for each other, James and I to some extent shared our work. When I took my day a week off or went on leave, James took over all Air matters and when he was away I kept an eye on Naval affairs. This worked admirably, as neither of us was involved in Intelligence or order of battle deception, which, as our spider's web extended, took up a great deal of the time of the military members.

James's greatest contribution to our efforts was perhaps his capacity for 'keeping his eye on the ball'. When the section had got itself fully organized it was frequently the lot of three or four of us to hold round my table long planning sessions. The rest of us were all too apt to go round in circles and get carried away into arguments about some side issue. It was James who would bring us back to the crux of the matter.

He had a far more difficult row to hoe in establishing satisfactory relations with his Service Ministry than did the rest of us. As Controlling Officer, Johnny had ready access to 'Pug' Ismay, Joe Hollis, CIGS, VCIGS, the DMO, and DMI; and Ronald's personal charm soon gained him his own circle of highly placed friends and the friendship of many Generals. Peteval rarely left the office. My long association with the JPS had enabled me to become on excellent terms with more people concerned in the high direction of the war than any of the others, and in the Air Ministry I had a chain of friends running up through Roland Vintras, my charming Director of Plans, to the VCAS, Sir Charles Medhurst.

James was unfortunate in that all the senior officers with whom he had become friends while serving in the Royal Navy were now overseas and the only contact with whom we could provide him, Commander Hutchinson, the Naval member of ISSB, proved anything but helpful. He was already sickening with the disease that, after an operation on the brain, brought about his death in the spring of 1944. It was this, no doubt, which caused him to fret about his work. He was often querulous in his manner and perpetually badgering James to give him unnecessarily detailed information about our plans for his master, the DNI, while showing marked reluctance to give James much information in return.

James supported his difficult position with commendable patience and, in due course, side-stepped the DNI's unhelpful bodies by establishing good relations with Captain Buzzard, RN, the Naval 'GSO1' of the STRATS, and Captain Charles Hughes-Hallett, RN, the Chief of the Naval Executive Planning Section, who, after the war, as Admiral Sir Charles, a director of Hutchinson and a City tycoon, became a good friend of mine.

The coming of James Arbuthnott filled the fifth desk in our cell-like office. Johnny sat in the centre below the clock; Ronald and James sat on his right and, facing them, Harold and myself on his left. This crowded room was so lacking in comfort that James and I christened it 'the schoolroom'.

We could no longer complain of isolation. The telephone rang from dawn to dusk, often two or three of us were talking on it at the same time, and our stream of visitors was almost constant. No sooner was one problem in connection with Torch cover plans settled than others presented themselves. Johnny's hair was always an indication of the state of his mind. Every morning he appeared with it brushed smoothly back from his fine forehead, but when worried about anything he had a habit of running his fingers through it; from about noon on it was always in a state of disorder for the rest of the day.

The atmosphere became so tense that it led to a minor revolt. Old Lumby and I had always shut up shop promptly at six o'clock. When Johnny replaced Lumby, I continued to leave at that hour, but Johnny nearly always stayed on and often returned after dinner, although there was nothing for him to do except read past plans and papers. Immediately we received the order to prepare cover plans for Torch, I willingly stayed working until the small hours, but once we had matters in hand and nothing urgent had to be done, I saw no reason to do so. I therefore took a middle course, staying on some evenings and excusing myself on nights when I had a dinner party. Harold, of course, would never have gone to bed at all if Johnny had decided to remain up. Ronald adopted my attitude, as did James for a short period after his arrival. For five of us to sit on there until seven or eight o'clock several evenings a week when we had finished our day's work was manifestly absurd; so James and I got together and decided to do something about it. That evening, at six o'clock, we both stood up, put on our greatcoats and caps, saluted politely and said, 'Good night.'

Johnny looked up in surprise, murmured a not very cordial 'Good night', and returned to his reading. On the days that followed James and I went through the same procedure. Ronald, always a cautious man, waited for a few nights, then joined us in our unannounced strike. Henceforth, except on occasions when there was really urgent work to do, Johnny and Harold were left to their own devices for as long as they cared to remain at their desks.

We had done what we could to explain away the activities at Gibraltar but, as the weeks went on, it became apparent that our story that we meant to relieve Malta permanently was not good enough. As the only base from which Allied forces operating in North Africa could be readily supplied, Gibraltar was being crammed to bursting with every type of store and ammunition. Hundreds of boxed fighter aircraft were shipped there and vast quantities of fuel. Details of scores of branches of the services not normally stationed there were being sent out, and an advance party of American officers was due to arrive to prepare an HQ for General Eisenhower when the landings took place.

Obviously we had to think again and, while maintaining our deceptive threats to Norway and the Pas de Calais, we felt that we had to provide yet another notional objective to cover the build-up of our forces at Gib.

Johnny gave me the job of having first crack at the problem and I wrote a paper for him on the following lines:

A second attempt to land at Dakar was ruled out because it would have alerted the French throughout the whole of North Africa. Sardinia was undesirable because it, or possibly Sicily (which was settled on later), was to be the cover objective for our final phase, and pointing to either prematurely might result in the Axis strengthening their forces there and thus render our landings in Algeria more hazardous. A breakthrough in the Med. to reinforce the Middle East was not plausible, because that could have been done without casualties by following our then normal practice of sending troop convoys round the Cape.

But the threat of a landing in Southern France, then only

occupied by Vichy forces, could suit our purpose for the following reasons. If Vichy reinforced her south coast with units from North Africa, this would be all to the good. If the threat resulted in the Axis taking over Vichy France and sending German forces south, these were unlikely to be drawn from the Channel coast, owing to Passover (our threat to the Pas de Calais), so they would have to withdraw troops from Russia for this purpose; which again would be all to the good. And a stronger garrison in the South of France would not be near enough to North Africa to prejudice our landings there.

Johnny accepted my arguments and put them in proper shape for submission to the Chiefs of Staff, who approved them. We then began passing new information through our secret channels to the Germans to build up my picture

We also wrote a long paper on *Information to the Press.* It would not have been politic to put an embargo on British newspapers and periodicals being sent to neutral countries; so our dailies were flown out regularly to Lisbon, where copies were bought by the German Embassy and sent on to Berlin. Their contents, including the advertisements, were minutely scrutinized by German Intelligence. Obviously our deception plans would be greatly assisted if we could bring about the appearance in the press of articles slanted in the direction required.

The top men in Fleet Street were, within certain limits, trusted, but not with particulars of forthcoming operations (until so near the date when the operation was to take place that they had usually found out about it for themselves) and never anything to do with deception; but we could put ideas into their minds through the Directors of Public Relations in the service ministries, whose rank was on Brigadier level.

For this purpose we produced several lines of thought which would support a belief that we meant to invade Norway, others which would support a belief that, simultaneously, we intended to attack the Pas de Calais, and a greater number which indicated various reasons why it would be ill-advised to attempt to go into North Africa. From then on, hints were dropped by the DPRs to the military correspondents, which led them in their speculative articles on future strategy to give the enemy the picture we desired.

It was during those weeks that we first came into direct contact with the Americans. General Eisenhower, until quite recently only a Divisional Commander, had arrived in England as President Roosevelt's nominee to be C-in-C Torch. He had been given Norfolk House as his headquarters and a combined staff of American and British officers to carry out the detailed planning.

Our main contact with him was through Brigadier Mockler-Ferryman. He was a great friend of Charles Balfour Davey's, who by then had been made Commandant of our Staff College. With Charles I had met him before the war, which was all to the good. He was known to his friends as 'the Moke'; but, far from there being anything mulish about him, he was a most receptive, highly intelligent and very charming man.

'The Moke' had several American officers under him and he charged a Lieutenant-Colonel Goldbranson with keeping in touch with us and doing everything possible to aid our deception plans. In civilian life a shrewd Middle West railway executive, he was both competent and cordial. In due course he sailed for North Africa with 'the Moke' and for some months was in charge of the first Deception Section in Algiers.

Among our other American visitors was a regular Colonel who had been the American Military Attaché in Rome. He was a most intelligent man and did all he could to help us sell our new-fangled toy by bringing several American Generals down to see Johnny, so that he could explain it to them personally.

Most people, if responsible for implementing Torch cover plans, would have felt that they had quite enough on their plate; but not Johnny Bevan. He was also concerning himself with many other problems, the chief of which were how to get Washington fully into the game, the new measures which would be necessary to coordinate deception between Dudley Clarke and Goldbranson once the Torch forces were established in North Africa, and the spheres of influence over which the various Commands and ourselves should exercise direct control; for nothing had ever been laid down about this, which was constantly leading to muddles.

Early in October, he decided that the best way to straighten things out was to call a conference in London. To it he invited Dudley Clarke, Peter Fleming and Lieutenant-Colonel Peter Cooke, the Washington representative of the DMI, under whom our liaison officer, Michael Bratby, was working.

The preparations for the conference were immense. For days all of us sweated blood getting out a vast agenda, writing long papers on the innumerable ways we might hope to deceive the enemy, upon grades of operators and spheres of influence, and arranging accommodation for our visitors.

One by one, having flown thousands of miles from their respective continents, the mystery men came in. For the conference we had secured the loan of the room in which the Chiefs of Staff held their meetings on nights when there was a blitz – the second largest in the basement, the biggest being that in which the War Cabinet held theirs. When the great morning came, everything and everyone was ready for the meeting round the spotless mahogany table at ten o'clock – everyone, that is, except me.

The initial cause of my non-appearance is still a mystery to me. Joan was on leave and with Joan and Charles Beatty up at Welshpool; so I was alone in the flat. I cannot recall whether I dined out or had a friend to dinner with me the preceding night. One thing is quite certain, with such an important occasion before me on the following morning, I did not go out on the tiles or get gloriously tight. And normally I was accustomed to wake up without being called at about seven o'clock. Yet, when I woke and looked at my clock, it said five past eleven.

I naturally assumed that, for some reason, the clock had stopped the previous night. Getting out of bed I walked into the sitting-room to get the right time from the electric clock there. To my horror that, too, gave the time as five past eleven.

I hurriedly shaved, scrambled into my clothes and took a taxi to the Cabinet Offices. When I walked into the Conference room it was just on a quarter to twelve. The only thing to do was to tell the truth and shame the Devil. Coming to attention I said to Johnny, 'I'm terribly sorry, sir. I overslept.'

He stared at me for a moment, then burst out laughing. The others followed suit and an absolute roar went up. I could not have made a more striking entrance had I planned it.

For the next three days, seated in well-sprung elbow-chairs, we debated this and that, reaching agreement on all essentials, and a great deal of good resulted from our deliberations.

We had all heard so much about Dudley Clarke that we were most intrigued to see the 'great deceiver' in the flesh. He proved to be a small, neat, fair-haired man, with merry blue eyes and a quiet chuckle which used to make his shoulders shake slightly. He was a 'Gunner', but had served very little of his time with the Royal Regiment, having been selected again and again for unorthodox assignments.

He had been among the first officers to land in Norway, carrying £10,000 in notes, which had been thrust upon him at the last moment. He had surveyed the route from Mombasa to Cairo as a possible means of reinforcing our forces in the Middle East. He had originated the Commandos and, after Dunkirk, been the first officer to land again with a raiding party on the coast of France. It was whispered that in Spain he had slipped up and been arrested while disguised as a woman. In fact, he was a truly legendary figure. He got a great deal of fun out of intrigue of every kind. He even had the crowns on his shoulders, red Staff gorgets and medal ribbons fitted with press studs so that, by removing them, he could appear at will to be an inconspicuous subaltern; although the pilot's wings of the Royal Flying Corps on his tunic gave it away that he had served in the 1914–18 war.

By his kindness, humour and the truly courteous way in which he deferred to our own, non-Regular Lieutenant-Colonel, he won all our hearts, and we were tremendously impressed by his grasp of all deception problems. He and I soon became the best of friends and have long continued so. In 1965, he generously brought me back from Paris a china figure of Marshal Marmont to add to my collection of Napoleonic soldiers.

Major Peter Fleming, another unusual personality, I had

already met. Unlike many authors of travel books, who turn out to be pale, bespectacled little men, his bronzed, tight-skinned face always gave the impression that he had only just returned from an arduous journey across the Mongolian desert or up some little-known tributary of the Amazon. His lithe, sinewy figure, dark eyes and black hair reminded one of a jaguar, until his quiet smile rendered the simile inappropriate. Physically, he was as fit as any troop-leader of Commandos and, in fact, he had been Chief Instructor at the London District Unarmed Combat School before being sent out to initiate deception in the Far East. He was always immaculate in the gold-peaked cap and freshly-pressed tunic of his regiment, the Grenadier Guards. There was only one thing I disliked about Peter. He smoked the foulest pipe I ever came within a yard of, and when he used to sit on the edge of my desk puffing at it, I heartily wished him back in the jungle. But we were most fortunate in having such a courageous, intelligent and imaginative man as our colleague for the war against Japan.

Welcome as our visitors were, during the week following our conference they added further to the congestion and turmoil of the 'schoolroom'. They had numerous contacts to make while in London, and our cell was the only base they had in which to make their arrangements and where telephone messages would be certain to reach them. Whenever any of us went out to our ministry or elsewhere, on our return we would always find one of them temporarily occupying our desk. But, in spite of the bear-garden in which he was compelled to work, somehow Johnny managed to complete the last phases of the Torch cover plans.

Our conference had been held in mid-October. The first Torch convoys were due to sail and troops were now moving to concentration areas preparatory to embarkation. The mass of shipping in the Clyde was constantly increasing. With growing anxiety we listened every morning to the Home Security reports furnished by ISSB on enemy air reconnaissance over the UK. So far we had been lucky. For weeks past no German 'recce' aircraft had flown over the Clyde. But we felt our luck was too good to last. One glimpse of the tremendous activities now taking place up there, and the

Torch

Luftwaffe might be sent in force to create havoc among the closely packed shipping. But our good fortune continued. Right up to D minus 12 the enemy apparently remained ignorant of the fact that a great expeditionary force was about to be despatched against him.

At last the Armada sailed. It was routed far out into the Atlantic but, even so, there was the risk that it might be sighted by a long-range Focke-Wulf and that the large packs of U-boats then scouring the Atlantic might be concentrated against it. Every morning at nine o'clock James went to the Admiralty War Room, took note of the latest U-boat dispositions, brought them across to us, then plotted them on a chart which we had installed for that purpose.

At that time the U-boats were mostly in the neighbourhood of the Canaries. As the convoys passed out of the range of enemy reconnaissance aircraft they came ever closer to the main hunting ground of the U-boats. It needed only one of these to sight the Torch Armada and, whatever the risk, she would break wireless silence to call up the whole U-boat fleet and send the news to Berlin. Yet our luck still held. Stray U-boats roving north caused great anxiety, but on D minus 6 the convoys arrived off the Straits of Gibraltar, still unreported.

For some reason, the Admiralty had insisted that, before entering the Mediterranean, the convoys must have a whole two days in which to regroup for the assault. In consequence, for two days while we held our breath, the ships milled round one another 100 miles outside the Pillars of Hercules Then, at night, with all lights out, they passed the Straits. The die was now cast.

In that vast array of ships was a large number of the Regular officers, non-commissioned officers and men who had been brought off from Dunkirk. As experienced leaders and instructors to our more recently formed units of civilian soldiers, they were invaluable and irreplaceable. In the ships, too, were our newest tanks, guns and other weapons that for two years our factory people had been toiling day and night to produce. The attitude of the French in North Africa was unpredictable. The best elements of their Regular Army were stationed there, and it was certain that Vichy would order them to resist our landings. If our assault failed, it could prove disastrous. Our forces, driven back to the beaches, would be 2000 miles from home; there could be no rescue operation like Dunkirk.

As the operation had been mounted in the UK, planning the cover for it had been the sole responsibility of the London Controlling Section, but, from the beginning, as far as the Mediterranean theatre was concerned, Dudley Clarke had given us the maximum possible assistance. Now that the convoys were actually moving into his territory he put over to the enemy certain last-minute information which had been agreed between him and Johnny.

On the morning after the convoys passed the Straits, an immediate alert was ordered by the enemy in all Axis-held territories in the Mediterranean as far east as Crete. We held our breath, waiting to see what further reactions there would be.

Would the enemy guess our intentions against North Africa? Had we really succeeded in lulling the suspicions of Vichy? Could the Germans possibly believe the last stories we had put over, first that it was our intention strongly to reinforce Malta, and later that we meant to invade the South of France? Would they fall for our last-minute bogus information that the landings were to be on the heel of Italy or in Greece?

The result is now history. The Torch cover plans succeeded beyond our wildest hopes. In due course 100 per cent proof was forthcoming.

To cite but three examples:

A German U-boat Commander, captured some days later in the Mediterranean, gave it away that all the U-boats in that area had been ordered to concentrate hundreds of miles *east* of our objectives.

The Axis agents in North Africa had not an inkling of our intentions: the majority of them were caught and interned.

On Saturday 7 November Field Marshal Kesselring, who commanded the Axis Air Forces in the Mediterranean based on Southern Italy and Sicily, issued orders that not a single aircraft was to go up; although by that evening our convoys would have been within range and might have sustained

Torch

heavy damage. So confident was he that he could inflict far greater damage on them when they were much nearer his bases that he forbade all action. Instead, every aircraft capable of taking the air was to go up at four o'clock on the Sunday afternoon, when he expected that the convoys would be passing through the narrows of the Straits of Bon, between Sicily and Tunis. Then, at short range, he would smash them utterly. But at midnight on the Saturday, having deliberately passed by their objectives, all unsuspected, the blacked-out convoys turned back, steamed out of range and early on Sunday morning, 8 November, appeared off Oran and Algiers, without the loss of a single ship or man, achieving complete surprise.

We had yet a long way to go and many doors still remained closed to us; but no one who knew of the part we had played in this great operation could any longer doubt the value of carefully planned strategic deception.

Chapter 9
After the Landings

The anxiety we felt when we assembled in our office on the morning of 8 November can well be imagined. None of us could settle to any serious work until we learned whether our cover plan for the Torch forces had enabled them to achieve surprise and land in North Africa almost unopposed or if they were, at that moment, being bombed and shelled to pieces.

At about half past ten a copy of a deciphered signal reached us. The French had been caught napping, the troops were being put ashore faced with only sporadic opposition and we had succeeded in capturing the Maison Blanc airfield, outside Algiers: a key point in the operation.

Immensely relieved, we spent the rest of the morning laughing, chatting and only skimming through the mass of papers that we had to absorb every day; then we celebrated by all going out for a long cheerful lunch at the Berkeley.

Well loaded, we got back to the office at about four o'clock and began to glance through the papers that had accumulated in our absence. After a while James grinned at me and pushed across a memo. It was from the Prime Minister and read:

> General Ismay: for circulation to Chiefs of Staff and JPS.
> The news of our first successes in North Africa is most heartening but it is over a week since I have heard anything of our plans for going into Norway. Pray let me hear more of this as a matter of urgency.
>
> W.C.S.

After the Landings

It was, of course, a joke, for we had not a single battle-trained Division left in the UK, much less a landing craft; and would not have for many months to come, as Churchill perfectly well knew. But it was not intended as a joke by him. It was simply his way of letting his staff know that he would tolerate no letting up.

During the day and those that followed, news came through that General Nogues, the French Resident General in North Africa, was urging his troops to resist us to the utmost of their ability. But, fortunately, the hearts of the majority of them were not in it.

Admiral Darlan also accepted Pétain's order to resist. There is good reason to suppose that, after the fall of France, he continued, secretly, to be pro-Ally. But he could not forgive us for the terrible damage we had done his fine fleet by our bombardment of it at Oran. Nevertheless, realizing the futility of sacrificing further French lives, a few days after our landings he ordered a surrender and would, I think, later have given us his valuable co-operation had he not shortly afterwards been assassinated.

The American landings at Casablanca proved equally successful. That was little short of a miracle, because for nine days out of ten at that season of the year the height of the Atlantic rollers would have made it impossible for landing craft to put troops ashore; and there also they were faced by the opposition ordered by General Nogues.

It was the first time the United States troops had been used in active warfare and giving them assistance in planning this operation caused some appalling headaches. While they were to supply the Naval and Military forces required, owing to distance it was impossible for them to use their own Air Force; so the RAF was charged with the duty of occupying the airfield in the neighbourhood of Casablanca and giving the US troops air cover.

General Patton was the Force Commander for this operation; so measures had to be concerted between him and the Director of Plans (Air), Air Commodore (Bill) Elliot. But Patton proved hopelessly vague and optimistic at their conferences. Elliot had no doubts about our ability to send in sufficient fighter aircraft to do the job, but, as he pointed out again and again, they would remain grounded and useless unless they could be regularly supplied with the requisite quantities of fuel.

One evening, a few weeks before D-Day, I was having a drink with Bill Elliot in our little mess. He had just come down from a conference with Patton and had asked him for the umpteenth time how he proposed to ensure the supply of fuel to our aircraft; which was an American responsibility.

To Bill's frustration and distress, the dashing General's only reply had been to laugh, clap him on the back and say: 'Don't you worry, Air Commodore. Don't you worry. Your boys shall have all the juice they need, even if I have to carry every can in on my own back.'

The tragedy was that the landing at Casablanca was not only a futile waste of effort, but delayed the clearing of the enemy from North Africa for many months.

The original Torch plan made by the JPS envisaged three landings in North Africa – at Oran, Algiers and a third much further along the coast at Philippeville in Tunisia. But the Americans insisted that, instead of Philippeville, the third landing should be made at Casablanca; presumably so that, should our operations in North Africa not lead to the conquest of the country, our forces would have a line of retreat by way of Casablanca.

In the event, the presence of an American army hundreds of miles to the southwest on the Atlantic coast proved completely useless. It could not be used to reinforce our army in Algeria for many weeks, and in the meantime Philippeville remained in the hands of the enemy. The Germans, always swift to react to our offensives, immediately rushed division after division into Tunisia, so that from a comparatively weak force there which might have been taken by surprise and easily overcome, General Von Arnhem soon had under him ample forces to repel our General Anderson's First Army when time enough had elapsed to organize it for a drive along the coast to the east.

The original British conception had been that Montgomery's Eighth Army should launch an offensive into Libya a week or so before D-Day of Torch and for Anderson's

After the Landings

First Army to advance through Tunisia to join up with him, which could have resulted in clearing the whole of North Africa within perhaps six weeks.

As it was, the Americans' refusal to agree to a landing at Philippeville botched one of Churchill's grand designs. It was not until 13 May 1943, six months after our first landings at Algiers and Oran, that General Sir Harold Alexander could send his famous signal: 'It is my duty to report that the Tunisian campaign is over. All enemy resistance has ceased. We are masters of the North African shores.'

As is well known, General Montgomery successfully carried out the part in the great plan assigned to him by defeating General Rommel, early in November, at the famous battle of El Alamein. But thereon hangs a tale.

Following General Ritchie's defeat by Rommel, General Auckinleck, who had succeeded Wavell as Commander-in-Chief Middle East, took personal command at the front and restored the situation. He saved Cairo, but the Eighth Army had been driven back on Mersa Matruh.

The disaster decided Churchill to restore the shattered morale of our troops by making a change in the High Command. General Sir Harold Alexander was nominated to succeed Auchinleck as C-in-C Middle East, and General Gott, a very fine soldier, to replace Ritchie as Commander of the Eighth Army. But while flying back to Cairo to receive his directive, Gott's aircraft crashed and he was killed.

Montgomery was chosen to step into Gott's shoes. Having taken over the Eighth Army, he did a wonderful job. In the next week or two the signals sent back to us embodying his 'general orders' to his troops showed that, reversing many accepted practices, he was putting new fighting spirit into them. But whether he will go down to history as a great General, I regard as extremely doubtful.

As far as El Alamein is concerned (and it was Johnny Bevan, Alexander's own brother-in-law, who gave me the following account), Monty was responsible for the battle, Alexander, as his superior, only for ensuring him adequate supplies and reinforcements. But before the battle opened Alexander joined Monty at his forward headquarters. He remained there with him during the desperate fighting that took place in the first four days. What advice and help Alex gave Monty during this critical period will never be known. But on the fifth day, after the decisive breakthrough had been achieved, he said to Monty: 'Carry on, Monty. The battle is now all yours.' And Alexander returned to Cairo.

There is an interesting sequel. Many years later, when Monty retired from the post of Deputy Supreme Commander of the NATO forces in Europe, a dinner was given in his honour at the Royal Hospital, Chelsea, by the Army Council. Every available Field Marshal was present and a few very senior Generals, including Freddy de Guingand, Monty's extraordinarily able Chief of Staff, who had come from retirement in South Africa to attend. The only non-Army officer invited was my old friend, Marshal of the Royal Air Force Sir William Dickson, because by then he had become Chairman of the Chiefs of Staff Committee.

In his speech of thanks, Monty said: '... my success I owe to three things: the courage and initiative of the British soldier, the unfailing support and wise advice of my old friend, Sir Alan Brooke, and the untiring work of my Chief of Staff, Freddy de Guingand.'

The dinner over, the party retired to another room for more drinks and cheerful talk. Addressing them again, Monty said, 'Gentlemen, as you know, I am a teetotaller and I like to go early to bed; so you will forgive me if I leave you.'

As he was about to leave the room, Alexander and Dickie Dickson were standing talking near the door. Alex caught Monty's attention by saying quietly: 'Monty, when you made your speech acknowledging the help you had received in achieving your victories, didn't you forget something?'

'No,' replied Monty, pulling up abruptly. 'I don't think so.'

'Yes, you did,' said Alex quietly. 'You forgot me.'

It was a mild but deserved rebuke from a great gentleman and, as will be recognized in due course, by far the finest soldier that Britain produced in the Second World War.

This episode was related to me by Dickson, who was an eye-witness of it.

Had not General Gott's aircraft crashed, it is doubtful if many people outside the Army would ever have heard of

After the Landings

Monty. It is by no means rare for Fate to take a hand by ordaining that certain people should be so placed at a certain time that an unforeseen happening will alter their whole lives and bring them to the top. Of this I can give another striking example.

When the war opened Richard Gale was a Major in the Warwickshire Regiment. Previously, during the troubles in Palestine, he had been the Military representative in the first ever Joint Planning Staff – a little committee of three GSO 2s, one from each service, formed to co-ordinate the plans of the Army, Navy and Air Force. In due course, as a competent Staff Officer, he was selected to become Personal Assistant to Field Marshal Sir John Dill, the CIGS during the early years of the war.

As the Army expanded, the Warwickshire Regiment increased from one to three or four battalions. Having done his two years at the War Office, Richard was promoted to Lieutenant-Colonel and given command of one of these new battalions. Every soldier's ambition is to get his battalion so Richard was delighted, and it far outweighed what to many might have been a depressing thought – that it was earmarked to form part of the garrison of Iceland.

Early in his embarkation leave, Richard ran into my old friend, Charles Balfour Davey. By then Charles had become a Brigadier and the Commandant of the Staff College at Camberley.

Happily Richard told Charles of his good luck. Having congratulated him, Charles said: 'Do you think that before you go you could spare an evening to come down and give my chaps a talk on Joint Planning?' Richard agreed and, a few nights later, dined and gave his talk at Minley Manor.

These occasions are most pleasant as I well know, having myself several times given such talks at Minley after the war. The atmosphere is informal. After a good dinner the officers assemble in a large ante-room with a blazing fire, round which there is a settee fender. The visitor sits on that and, with a brandy and soda close at hand, talks to his friendly and highly intelligent audience.

Dark as were those days of the war when Richard gave his

talk, our ever-resolute Prime Minister had no doubt at all that the time would come when we would liberate Europe. He had already gone so far as to nominate the Force Commander who was to do the job, and his choice was General Sir Harold Alexander.

This, of course, was before Alex was given an overseas command, and when we were still suffering from our set-back at Dunkirk; so he could be given no troops or even a Staff. He was simply sitting at home doing nothing, and so he decided to spend a few weeks taking a refresher course at Staff College.

Thus it chanced that, when Richard Gale gave his talk, Alex was among his audience. After the talk Charles took Alex and Richard to his sitting-room for a nightcap. There Alex asked Richard what he was doing. With pardonable pride Richard replied that he had got his battalion and, in a week or so, was taking it to Iceland.

Alex remained thoughtful for a moment, then asked, 'I suppose you will be seeing General Dill to say good-bye before you go?' On Richard's replying that he would, Alex sat down at the desk, wrote a brief note, handed it to Richard and said, 'When you see General Dill, please give him this from me.'

Next day Richard went up to the War Office and gave General Dill the note. Dill read it and made no comment, but an hour or so later, one of his Staff Officers rang up Richard and simply said: 'General Dill has asked me to tell you not to buy any more Arctic clothing.'

A few days later Richard was summoned to the War Office. Dill then showed him Alex's note. It said: 'Are you crazy to send one of the few officers who has had experience of Joint Planning to Iceland? Keep him here and when the time comes I'll give him any job for which he likes to ask on my Staff for the return to Europe.'

So, greatly disappointed, Richard never got his battalion. Instead, he was put into another Staff job, with the curious title of 'C C Air'. This entailed organizing and training our first parachute troops and glider-borne formations.

When, at length, a British Army did return to the Continent, to the great harm of Anglo-American relations and the

After the Landings

conduct of the campaign it was not under the command of Alexander, but of the much inferior Montgomery. Richard, however, instead of going as a simple Staff Officer, went as Major-General commanding the 6th Airborne Division. It was the spearhead of the army of liberation and he was the first British General to land in France.

Had he gone to Iceland with a battalion of the Warwickshires, all the odds are that he would have remained there on dreary garrison duty for two years, and been lucky if he ever reached the rank of Brigadier. But Fate had ordained that he should give a talk at Minley and that Alex should be among the audience. Owing solely to that, he ended his career as General Sir Richard Gale, GCB, KBE, DSO, MC, having succeeded Monty as Deputy Supreme Commander of the NATO Forces in Europe.

In my own case, had not lack of capital in my business forced me to sell it at the time of the 1930 slump, I should still be a wine merchant instead of having become a successful author. Still more remote was the possibility that I should have been the only civilian ever to be commissioned direct to a post on the Joint Planning Staff of the War Cabinet. That would never have happened had I not 'chanced' to meet and talk with 'Uncle' Max of MI5 at Charlie Birkin's cocktail party where the other guests were uncongenial.

I do not suggest that Fate entirely dominates our lives and that every phase of them is preordained. Nearly all our reactions to any situation are automatically dictated by our upbringing and past experience; but at times of crisis we still have free will and, whether we take it or not, our consciences tell us beyond all question which course is the right one. Nevertheless, I regard it as beyond doubt that, at times, Fate does create for us entirely unforeseen circumstances which give us the chance to make the best use of our abilities.

On New Year's Eve 1943, Joan and I gave a party at Chatsworth Court. People dined early in the war, so the big restaurant in the basement there was usually clear by soon after eight o'clock. I arranged with the management that, when the last diners had gone, it should be handed over to me, and invited our guests for nine.

We had over 100 people. Pug Ismay, Jack Slessor and a

dozen other Generals, Admirals and Air Marshals, Desmond Morton, Tommy Thompson and other members of the PM's entourage; all my own colleagues, except Johnny Bevan, who was on leave, several members of ISSB and MI5, and most of the officers of the STRATS and FOPS; also, of course, such wives as had remained in London, although the majority had been sent by their husbands, with their children, to live more safely in the country.

Thanks to the mass of stores I had laid in we were able to give them not only lashings of champagne, but a splendid spread, including such things as foie gras, which by that time was almost impossible to obtain; so the party went with a swing.

It was not until after three in the morning that our last guest left, and by then I had something else to think about. Johnny Bevan being on leave, Ronald Wingate, who had been made Deputy Controlling Officer, was temporarily my chief.

Before leaving he drew me aside and said, 'Dennis, I've a special job for you. It's just up your street. This month there is to be a high-powered conference at Casablanca. The President is coming over to meet the PM there. For the first time he will be crossing to our side of the Atlantic; so it is super-super secret. This afternoon I was charged to prepare a cover plan to prevent anyone from getting wind of the fact that the President is coming over, and that the PM, the Chiefs of Staff and all the rest of them have left England. Don't come to the office tomorrow. Spend the day quietly here, thinking it out. I'm sure you will produce the answer.'

What a charming and clever old fox Ronald was. By his flattery he could get the best out of anybody; and how wise he was to give the job first to one person and tell him to take the day off. Johnny Bevan would never have done that. He would have had all of us arguing for hours round our conference table, while telephone calls and urgent signals being brought in constantly disturbed us.

The two men got on excellently together, but their methods were as different as chalk from cheese. Except for his rare periods of leave Johnny worked tirelessly and far into the night for months on end. Ronald always went home at six

After the Landings

o'clock and was almost professionally lazy – except when Johnny was abroad on a conference. Then he rarely left the office. Whenever a crisis arose, Johnny became harassed and displayed ill-temper. If one of us happened to be going on leave he would have thought very badly of us had we not volunteered to remain and give such help as we could. Whatever the trouble, Ronald was completely unperturbed. I recall one such occasion when I was due for leave and offered to postpone taking it. Smiling at me with his little triangular eyes half-closed, he said:

'My dear Dennis, if any one of us is not competent to run this section on his own, he has no right to be here at all. Of course you must start your leave tomorrow. Have a good time.'

Ronald was therefore much the more pleasant master to work under. But let it not be thought that Ronald was the better man for the job of Controlling Officer. Shrewd, charming and able as he was, I do not believe that he could ever have won the confidence of the Chiefs of Staff to the extent that Johnny did. During the latter years of the war they positively ate out of Johnny's hand, accepting every plan that he put up to them. Had he asked for a battleship and escort of destroyers to implement one of our deception plans, I believe they would have let him have them.

Chapter 10
The Casablanca Conference

Next day I spent putting such wits as I have to devising satisfactory measures to cover Symbol – the code name given to the Casablanca Conference – and the following day I handed my plan to Ronald. Having read it, he said that it was exactly what he wanted. Then he rewrote it himself, retaining parts of it but altering and improving it immensely.

Our worst headache in this job was that Casablanca was within bombing range of southern Spain. Throughout the war General Franco played his cards with the utmost skill. Both Hitler and Pétain, who was an old friend of the Caudillo, did their utmost to persuade him to bring Spain in on the side of the Axis; but, by the exercise of extraordinary tact and by giving concessions, such as that U-boats might use Spanish ports, he succeeded in keeping his country neutral, so that it might have a chance to recover from the ravages caused by the Civil War. But those ravages had made Spain extremely vulnerable, and she was in no state to resist should German troops be sent in to occupy the peninsula.

We feared, therefore, that if the enemy learned about the Conference, Hitler might threaten Franco with invasion unless he allowed several squadrons of Luftwaffe bombers to take over the airfields in southern Spain.

As the conference was being attended not only by the President and Prime Minister, with their personal advisers, but also by the Chiefs of Staff and Directors of Plans of both Britain and the United States, together with a score or so of

The Casablanca Conference 113

the most gifted officers on both planning staffs, no imagination is needed to realize what a devastating blow it would have been to the Allied cause had even a sizable percentage of these fine brains been eliminated by a series of concentrated heavy bomber raids.

We felt reasonably confident that security measures would keep the enemy in ignorance for several days that a conference was being held, but it was to last for ten; and it was too much to hope that the enemy would not learn, well before the conference ended, that the President and Prime Minister had left their countries to meet.

It was decided, therefore, that about half-way through the conference we should leak it that one was being held, but put out misleading information as to where.

For this I had chosen Madeira as a plausible half-way house between the USA and the UK, but the objection was that, if the island had really been the place where they were to meet, arrangements would have had to be made with the Portuguese government. As they would not be, German agents in Lisbon would almost certainly have satisfied themselves that the rumour was false.

Finally we decided on Khartoum and a good story to leak which would account for the capital of the Sudan having been chosen. Churchill was always asking his intimates for advice, but rarely took it unless it coincided with his own views. To this General Smuts was an exception. They were great friends; he would always listen to Slim Jani's wise counsel and nearly always acted on it.

Smuts was then an elderly man and had recently been ill. So it was to be put out that he was not sufficiently recovered to undertake a very long journey, and the PM valued his views so greatly that he had decided the conference should be held in Khartoum, which was not too distant from South Africa.

Our first job was to conceal the fact that the PM had left England at all. This was far from easy, as he would be taking with him Generals Ismay, Hollis and Jacob, the Chiefs of Staff and the Directors of Plans – not to mention a score or more of joint planners, secretaries and others. The sudden disappearance of this galaxy would be a clear indication to scores of people who worked in their offices that the PM had gone overseas.

A little research led me to the rather alarming discovery that in the Chiefs of Staff organization and their offices in their own Ministries no fewer than 700 people – officers, secretaries, filing clerks, etc. – had access to the minutes of their daily meetings.

I suggested to Johnny Bevan, who had by then returned from leave, that we should try, during the Chiefs' absence, to – for lack of a better word – have their minutes forged. He approved the idea and asked me to do what I could about it.

During my year in the Cabinet Offices, the only man of importance who worked in them that I had not so far met was the Secretary of the War Cabinet, Sir Edward Bridges. Johnny had not met him either; but he was obviously the only person who had the authority to do what I wanted, so I went upstairs and bearded him in his den.

Like all the top civil servants I have ever met – or top men in any service for that matter – he proved affable, brisk and willing to hear what I had to say. He signed me to come and sit with him on a big horsehair sofa in front of a roaring fire, and I said my piece.

He agreed at once, and adopted my suggestion that, as the Vice-Chiefs deputized for the Chiefs when they were away, on this occasion instead of their names' appearing in the daily minutes, these should read: 'Sir Alan Brooke said' – when actually it had been the VCIGS General Nye, who had spoken, and similarly with the representatives of the other two services. Thus the number of people who would become aware that the Chiefs had left London would be enormously reduced and virtually restricted to a very small circle normally in personal contact with them. Bridges then said he would follow the same line with the minutes of the War Cabinet, and have the PM's name substituted for Attlee's.

Secrecy about Symbol also brought me into contact with the PM's doctor Sir Charles Wilson, who afterwards became Lord Moran. Tommy Thompson tipped me off that the doctor had ordered two tropical suits. As he accompanied Churchill everywhere, nothing could have been a clearer indication to the people who were to make them than that the PM was going not only abroad, but to a hot country. I saw the doctor and courteously read him the riot act; insisting that he must cancel his order on the excuse that he had thought it a good idea to have the suits made while material was still available, for use immediately after the war, and that he had now changed his mind. He was very huffy and sulky about it, but agreed to do as I required.

Owing to his exceptionally close association with the PM that was a case which might have led to a serious leak, but I have often wondered if many of our security precautions were really necessary, because rumours – except those deliberately put out by us through diverse channels – had little chance of reaching the enemy. MI5 was extraordinarily efficient. It had tabs on every enemy agent in Britain before the war and had them all behind bars within twenty-four hours of its outbreak. And those who were landed from submarines or parachuted in afterwards were always picked up within a few days.

Obviously it was up to me to ensure that the RAF security people fully understood the rôle they were to play during the departure from the airfield. I therefore went down to Horseferry Road where Air Intelligence had its Headquarters, and asked for the Chief of Air Security. He proved to be a Group Captain, an enormously fat man. When I stood before him and saluted, instead of asking me to sit down, he enquired what I wanted.

For security reasons, I had not mentioned the object of my visit before asking to see him, and when I gave it he at once became voluble. 'Oh yes, Wing Commander, of course we've got all that in hand.' He then proceeded to reel off an entirely different cover plan for the departure of the party. Still standing, I shook my head and said, 'I'm afraid, sir, that your proposals are quite unacceptable.'

'What the hell d'you mean?' he exclaimed angrily.

With devilish delight I replied, 'The section of the Joint Planning Staff to which I belong has already devised a cover plan and it has received the approval of the Chiefs of Staff. So I am here only to give you your orders with regard to its implementation.'

Collapse of Group Captain.

In the event, had the party deliberately decided to bitch the cover plan, they could not have done better. At about eight o'clock on the evening of 12 January, Addison Road (now Kensington Olympia) Station was closed, a police cordon kept pedestrians well out of sight of the station, the fleet of blacked-out cars duly arrived there and their occupants boarded the waiting special train.

Somewhere in Berkshire the train decanted them, and they boarded another fleet of cars which was waiting to drive them to the airfield. (The PM was driven the whole way by car.) On entering a village a mile or so from the airfield, some bright boy in the leading car of the convoy discovered that there was still three-quarters of an hour before the time set for take-off. So he said to his companions, 'Let's pull up and have a drink at the village pub.'

Everyone being in holiday mood, his suggestion was immediately accepted. The entire convoy halted. Brooke, Portal, Mountbatten and a score of others, smothered with gold braid and their chests a sunset of medal ribbons, crowded into the little bar parlour. The publican, his eyes bulging at such a sight, hastily produced his very limited stock of hard liquor and they proceeded to drink the place dry. What a story he would have to tell his friends on the morrow, of the mighty warriors who had patronized his pub on their way to the airfield.

As soon as MI5 learned of this occurrence, they acted with great promptitude. They did not actually cast the unfortunate landlord into prison, but they placed him, his family and his staff under house arrest, put his pub out of bounds to the public for a month and set a guard on it to prevent any of its occupants telling others about the night when a gilded throng had made merry on the premises.

The Symbol conference was not to be held actually in Casablanca, but at Anfa, some miles up in the hills. The village consisted of a large hotel and a number of commodious villas. As the airfield was a considerable distance from Anfa, to reach it the distinguished visitors would have to be driven through several Arab hamlets. Codrington, the head of Cabinet Offices Security, had been sent on ahead to make suitable arrangements for the reception of the PM. From

The Casablanca Conference

the aircraft he was taken straight to a small plain van, shut inside and driven to his destination. So none of the locals caught even a glimpse of that rotund and famous figure.

Not so the President. His compatriots received him with a guard of honour. He and his entourage were ushered to a long cavalcade of cars and, preceded by a score of motor cyclists armed with sub-machine guns, took the road for Anfa.

Let no one say, though, that the Americans did not realize the necessity for security. They had enclosed the whole area of Anfa in a great barbed-wire fence and stationed half a dozen batteries of field artillery all round it. Who they thought was likely to attack the place, God alone knows, but they were ready and willing to sacrifice their lives in defence of their President.

Still, let us give praise where praise is due. They were the hosts and nowhere in the world could you find better ones. That evening the half-starved British were invited to the hotel, fed to bulging point on delicacies they had not seen for years and filled to the brim with good liquor.

It was after dinner that we have yet another example of the lack of appreciation of security in the great. Churchill was at the bar, thoroughly enjoying himself. Dickie Mountbatten came up to him and said:

'While you're here, sir, you must go down to the harbour and see the wreck of the *Jean Bart*. She is piled up on the rocks outside it.'

The *Jean Bart* was the great French battleship that was to have been the pride of the French Navy. When the war opened, she was still unfinished, but her barbettes had been installed so she could act as a stationary fort and fire her great guns. On 8 November, when the United States invading force was sighted, she was ordered to do so. The American warships had far less gunpower, but they were not sitting targets. While taking evasive action they succeeded in shelling her into submission.

'Yes, Dickie,' replied the Prime Minister. 'That's a splendid idea. We must all go to see this great ship of war that has been destroyed by the guns of our allies. We'll go tomorrow morning.'

Codrington, who was standing nearby, overheard this conversation and immediately took alarm. To view the *Jean Bart* meant driving down right through the narrow streets of Casablanca, which would be swarming with Arabs. He knew that his master would certainly be recognized, and could not be prevented from acknowledging the cheers of the crowd and giving the V-sign.

He knew, too, that Churchill had a complete disregard for danger, so it was useless to suggest that he would be exposing himself to possible assassination. But the real menace of such an excursion lay in the fact that, once Churchill was seen in Casablanca, it would become evident that a high-powered conference was being held there. Berlin would be informed of it within a matter of hours. And the next day was only the first day of the conference. There would be nine days left in which Hitler could blackmail Franco into letting him send those bombers down to southern Spain. Long before the conference was due to end, Anfa might be blown off the map.

Intensely worried, Codrington wondered what to do. He sought the help of Sir Charles (Peter) Portal. The Chief of Air Staff realized the danger at once. He went up to the PM and said: 'I hear, sir, that tomorrow you are going down to see the wrecked *Jean Bart*.'

'Yes, Peter,' replied the PM happily. 'You must come too, to see this great ship of war that has been destroyed by the guns of our allies.'

'I wonder if that is altogether wise,' Portal said thoughtfully. 'It means going right down through the native quarter, you know, and you are only just recovering from that bout of 'flu you had. In your weakened state, if you happened to pick up some bug, it might easily lay you up again.'

'I'm fully recovered,' declared the PM cheerfully. 'Fit as a fiddle. We'll all go down tomorrow to see this great ship of war which has been destroyed by the guns of our allies.'

Foiled, Portal thought again, then he said, 'That's all very well. I'm happy to know that you are feeling no after-effects of your illness. But you ought to think of the President. He is a permanent invalid and far from strong. You might pick up some bug and pass it on to him.'

At that the penny dropped. The possibility was so far-

The Casablanca Conference

fetched that Churchill realized Portal was really trying to protect the security of the conference without actually asking him to lose face by apparently showing a lack of courage. After a moment he replied:

'Oh, I see. Well, I am a little old to indulge in those pastimes with which native quarters are usually associated; but did I so far forget myself, and have the misfortune to pick up one of those unpleasant diseases which you seem to have in mind, I do assure you that I would not give it to the President.'

So the expedition was put off until the last day of the conference, by which time it would have been too late for Hitler to take any action against Casablanca. Giving the V-sign to the cheering crowds, and with a large cigar sticking out from his chubby face, the great man and his friends went down to look at 'this great ship of war destroyed by the guns of our allies'.

The conference actually opened on 15 January, and day-to-day reports of its deliberations were sent back to us. One of the first subjects discussed was the opening up of the Mediterranean. The key to this was considered to be the occupation of the port of Sfax, round the corner of Tunisia on its coast that faced east. As Anderson's First Army was hopelessly bogged down in western Tunisia, the capture of the port depended upon the Eighth Army, which was then advancing from Libya; and Alexander was instructed to order operations to begin against it on 24 January.

Air Chief Marshal Sir Arthur Tedder said that, once we had established airfields in Tunisia, convoys could be passed through the Med. with only an acceptable degree of risk. The First Sea Lord agreed, stating that convoys of thirty ships every ten days should prove adequate to supply our requirements in the Middle East; and the fact that convoys no longer had to go right round Africa would release no fewer than 225,000 tons of shipping for other purposes.

Figures were produced to show how the strength of the German Air Force had been reduced, and measures for weakening it still further put forward. It was agreed that the Luftwaffe should be provoked into coming up to fight on every opportunity that offered; and that the French in North

Africa (who had now come over to us) should be given the latest types of aircraft to re-equip their squadrons.

It was also agreed to furnish the French Army in North Africa with modern weapons and estimated that they would then be able to put into the field three armoured and ten infantry divisions.

General Charles de Gaulle, having escaped from France at the time of the débâcle, had become the official head of French Resistance outside his own country. This meant that not only was he the Commander of the Free French Forces domiciled in Britain, but he had also been accepted as the leader of Free France in several French colonies in both Africa and the Pacific. He was, therefore, already a power to be reckoned with.

While in England he had proved incredibly haughty, rude and difficult to deal with; so he was by no means Churchill's favourite man. Nevertheless, the PM admired his defiance of the enemy and felt it to be only just that he should continue as the head of all French forces which came over to the Allies.

President Roosevelt held a different view. His nominee for the command of any French Army of Liberation was a General Giraud. Giraud had been captured by the Germans in 1940, but later escaped and, as he was rabidly anti-Pétain, had been helped by the Americans to make his way in secret to the South of France, from where he was taken off in a submarine and conveyed to Gibraltar shortly before the D-Day of Torch.

Giraud was violently anti-British and refused to be taken off in a British submarine. But the American submariners knew so little about the Mediterranean that they would not risk the loss of one of their submarines by taking her sufficiently close inshore. The result was a compromise. A British submarine did the job but flew the American flag, and had on board an American officer who was nominally in command.

But when they got the old boy to Gibraltar, they found that they had picked up a real hot potato. The idea had been that early on D-Day Giraud should give a rousing broadcast to the people of North Africa, telling them that the gallant

The Casablanca Conference

Americans were coming to free them from the tyranny of the Nazis, enforced through poor General Pétain who was now too old and weak to resist them.

Giraud flatly refused. He had come with his own broadcast in his pocket. In it he declared that *he* was about to liberate North Africa and was to be the Supreme Commander of all the Allied Forces occupying those French territories.

Eisenhower was justifiably annoyed. Whether he actually had a gun held against the Frenchman's back, history does not relate; but Giraud made his speech – larded, of course, with plenty of the old nonsense about 'the honour of France' – more or less on the lines the American desired.

Like him or not, the Americans had saddled themselves with Giraud and, as he was greatly senior in rank to de Gaulle, they agreed that he should become C-in-C all French Forces. Like him or not, Churchill was saddled with de Gaulle and argued that, having raised the banner of Free France in the desperate days when Britain stood alone against the might of Germany, he had a better claim to that position.

A compromise was reached, if I remember rightly, to the effect that Giraud should command the French Army in North Africa, while de Gaulle returned to England and continued to command the Free French Forces there and in the French colonies which had repudiated Vichy. The two Generals reluctantly were made to shake hands in front of the cameras, then parted: Giraud soon to fade from the public eye; the troublesome but resolute de Gaulle to become the greatest man his nation has produced for several generations.

However, the main object of the conference was to decide on Allied strategy for 1943. From the beginning, the Americans had convinced themselves that the quickest way to end the war was to launch an invasion from England against the Continent. A plan for this distant possibility had been drawn up by the FOPS in the spring of 1942 and given the codeword Roundup. To implement it, for many months past the Americans had been carrying out operation Bolero – the despatch of large US forces to Britain. In the summer of '42, Churchill had persuaded them that the German resistance would be too strong for Roundup to have any chance of success for some time to come, and to undertake the occupation of North Africa instead. Then, in the autumn of '42, the Americans urged that after Torch our next major operation should be Roundup, to be undertaken in the early summer of '43.

Churchill's conception of Roundup was not a mighty invasion such as eventually took place on the Normandy coast in 1944; but, as the codeword implies, a landing to 'round up' any German units that might still be resisting after the defeat and disintegration of the German Army had been achieved by some other means. Almost to the end he endeavoured to dissuade the Americans from attacking the enemy in his strongest place, which could result in our butting our heads against a stone wall and sustaining enormous casualties without achieving victory.

At the Washington Conference he had again induced them to forgo Roundup in 1943 and, North Africa taken, exploit our success in the Mediterranean. The British wished to do this by invading Italy and putting her out of the war. To that the Americans would not agree because to tie up large forces there would have prejudiced the possibility of Roundup, upon which their hearts were set. The furthest they would go was that we should carry out operations which would render the Mediterranean safe for Allied shipping. With Tunisia in our hands, this could have been achieved by the capture of Sicily. And, with the tacit understanding that Sicily should be our next objective, the conference broke up.

Churchill never wavered in his opinion that the speediest road to victory lay in striking at what he termed, 'the soft underbelly of the Axis'. The Italian troops did not show anything like the fighting spirit of the Germans. By a determined effort Italy could be put out of the war; and what splendid dividends that would bring us – we could at once open up a second front against Germany and so take pressure off the Russians, as they had been pleading with us to do. From Italy we could cross the Adriatic and, supported by Tito's partisans, strike across the Danube at Germany's reluctant allies, Hungary and Rumania, with a good chance of putting them, too, out of the war, or we could strike through the passes of the eastern Alps, towards Munich and Vienna.

The Casablanca Conference

These cogent arguments caused the Americans to think again and concede that, after our capture of Sicily, the project of extending the campaign to the Italian mainland should be given serious consideration.

It was then that General Eisenhower expressed the opinion which I quote from his book, *Crusade in Europe*:

My own opinion, given to the conference in January [Casablanca], was that Sicily was the proper objective if our primary purpose remained clearing the Mediterranean by us for Allied shipping. . . . On the other hand, if the real purpose of the Allies was to invade Italy for major operations to defeat that country completely, then I thought our proper initial objectives were Sardinia and Corsica. Estimates of hostile strength indicated that these two islands could be taken by smaller forces than would be needed in the case of Sicily, and therefore the operation could be mounted at an earlier date. Moreover, since Sardinia and Corsica lie on the flank of the long Italian boot, the seizure of those islands would force a very much greater dispersion of enemy strength in Italy than would the mere occupation of Sicily

From Major-General Sir John Kennedy's book, *The Business of War*, we learn that Admiral Sir Andrew Cunningham also favoured Sardinia and, as C-in-C Mediterranean Fleet, it would have been his responsibility to put the invading force ashore. Churchill (who had shown such interest in my paper, written in the dark days of 1940, suggesting that we should seize Sardinia) gave it as his view that we should 'not crawl up the leg of Italy like a harvest bug'.

But Alan Brooke, as is plainly stated in his *War Diaries*, edited by Sir Arthur Bryant, favoured Sicily; and, in London, before the conference, had succeeded in overriding the opinion of the JPS and arguing his colleagues round because the Americans had already agreed to an invasion of Sicily.

Nevertheless, at Casablanca there occurred a revolt against him. To quote from his own diary:

And now suddenly the Joint Planning Staff reappeared on the scene with a strong preference for Sardinia. . . . They had carried with them Mountbatten (the Chief of Combined Operations) . . . Peter Portal (the Chief of Air Staff), Admiral Cunningham (C-in-C Mediterranean Fleet) while Pug (General Sir Hastings Ismay) was beginning to waver. . . . I had a three-hours' hammer and tongs battle to keep the team together, and to stop it from wavering I told them that I flatly refused to go back to the American Chiefs of Staff and tell them that we did not know our own minds and that, instead of Sicily, we now wanted to invade Sardinia.

The CIGS possessed extraordinarily persuasive powers coupled with a will of iron and usually got his way.

There are good grounds for suggesting that this decision was one of the most important taken in the whole war. It was the Allies' opening move in carrying the war into the enemy's country as a prelude to his final defeat. The choice of the place at which we should re-enter Hitler-held Europe lay with us, and while many places, such as France and Holland, were unsuitable because the enemy could have brought stronger forces against ours too swiftly, there remained a choice of several where the resistance he could put up to begin with was strictly limited – Sicily, Sardinia, the Adriatic coast of southern Italy, and Yugoslavia. These varied in their geographical conditions, and some presented many more natural obstacles than others. The time-factor was of immense importance; if we could have got into Austria, Hungary and Germany while the Russians were still at death grips with the main German forces deep in Russia, it would have enabled the United States and Britain to dictate the future of Central Europe.

Had they been in a position to do that, how utterly different, and more happy, might the world situation be today.

On 10 July General Montgomery launched his successful invasion of Sicily, but, within a week, he was brought to a standstill in the mountains in the north-east of the island, which surround the great volcano, Mount Etna. He was bogged down there for *seven weeks* – ample time for the enemy to reinforce the toe of Italy – and it was not until early September that our first landings in Italy took place.

There then began the long, hard climb up the leg of Italy, which included the terrible slaughter at Cassino, and the bitterly contested landing at Anzio. It was not until *nine months* later that General Sir Harold Alexander, having forced his way half-way up the peninsula, succeeded, on the day before the Normandy landings, in capturing Rome.

The Casablanca Conference

Eleven months later this brilliant general, having fought his way over many more mountains and rivers, reached the valley of the Po. Had not many of his best divisions been taken from him for the American landings in the South of France, there is good reason to suppose that by that time he would have been in Vienna. As it was, he accepted the surrender of over a million German troops while still on Italian soil.

It is always invidious to speculate on 'might have-beens' but, on a question which is of such immense historical interest, I think we are justified in taking a look at the possibilities had we, instead of going into Sicily, gone into Sardinia.

Instead of being held up by the mountains in north-east Sicily for nearly two months, from Sardinia the Allies might have landed on the Italian coast between La Spezia and Genoa in August 1943. That would have saved us the many thousands of casualties and *twenty months* of bitter fighting that it took us to reach that area. It would have placed us at one step within a hundred miles of the valley of the Po, thus, with the asset of air bases in Sardinia, giving us an excellent chance of cutting off from Germany the Axis forces to the south, and so catching in the bag another enemy army as great as that which had surrendered to us a few months earlier in Tunis.

Had that then become, as it almost certainly would have, our main theatre of operations, either General Montgomery or General Alexander might well have penetrated through the eastern Alps by the Ljubljana Pass that summer. The final battles would have taken place in Austria and Bavaria, with the odds on the war being shortened by many months and the Allies reaching Vienna and Berlin while the Russians were still hundreds of miles distant.

In my opinion, the decision to invade Sicily rather than Sardinia lost the Allies the chance to save Central Europe from the Russians and led to the war's continuing for six months longer than it need have done.

But at Casablanca the die was cast. After Tunisia had been cleared of the enemy, the Allies were to invade Sicily; and the code name chosen for this operation was Husky.

Chapter 11
The Completion of the Deception Section

When the conference had ended, the PM sent a message that he intended to go on to Cairo to see General (Jumbo) Wilson (who had succeeded Alexander as C-in-C Middle East) because 'we shall be requiring such a large part of his army for Husky'.

Since no part of the forces for Husky was being sent from Britain, it was not our responsibility to prepare a cover plan for the operation, but that of Dudley Clarke, who now had a headquarters in Algiers. It was, however, up to us to give him our utmost assistance by threatening enemy-held areas from which, otherwise, reinforcements might have been sent to Sicily.

Of the other matters which kept us busy in the spring of 1943, the most important to us personally was our move from the crowded 'schoolroom' to more pleasant and more spacious quarters. As long as there was a risk of invasion, nothing would have persuaded Churchill to forgo having Headquarters Home Forces immediately under his hand. One of his first acts on becoming Prime Minister had been to have a large basement adjacent to that of the JPS cleared of the Home Office civil servants who worked there, and C-in-C Home Forces, General Sir Bernard Paget, with his staff installed there instead. But by the end of 1942 it was decided that the second fortress-basement might be put to better use by relieving the congestion in the JPS basement and also bringing into it the Joint Intelligence Staff, which would save much time previously spent in visiting and telephoning.

The Completion of the Deception Section

The Joint Intelligence Staff worked under the Joint Intelligence Committee and consisted of several teams of officers of each service together with a few odd bodies from the Foreign Office and the Ministry of Economic Warfare. The task of allocating accommodation in the basement was given to Lieutenant-Colonel Denis Capel-Dunn, a key figure in the Chiefs of Staff organization.

At the time these arrangements were being put in train, Johnny Bevan was about to leave the country to attend a conference abroad; so, before his departure, he charged Harold Peteval with the job of seeing that we were given suitable quarters. In due course, Peteval discussed matters with Capel-Dunn. Peteval then came to me and said unhappily: 'Dennis, I'm terribly worried. Capel-Dunn insists that as we have only two rooms in the old basement, all we need is two in the new one. The Colonel will be furious. But I don't see what I can do about it.'

Ever greatly concerned for my own comfort and that of my friends, I told Harold that I would take over the matter.

When I went to see Capel-Dunn his reception of me was far from genial. In vain I pointed out that, under the establishment granted to Johnny by the Chiefs the previous summer, the London Controlling Section could be expanded to seven officers, five of whom were already functioning in it, and that, as Colonel Bevan frequently received visits from very senior officers who talked with him about super-secret matters, he must be given a room to himself.

Grudgingly, Capel-Dunn conceded one extra room. But I declared that not to be good enough. The rooms were only about ten foot square and to expect six officers, Johnny's personal assistant, a filing clerk and two typists to work in two such confined spaces was absurd. Moreover, now that the section had expanded, I considered that we were entitled to a conference room.

To my insistence the Colonel took great exception. He told me sharply that his decision about the allocation of accommodation was final; and that for an officer like myself, who was his junior, to tell him his business was an impertinence.

Distinctly riled by this treatment, an hour or two later I

went upstairs and put the situation to Lawrence Burges, the Deputy Secretary of the War Cabinet. This Pickwickian little man was already a friend of mine, who had lunched several times with me and dined with Joan and me at Chatsworth Court. He was a jolly chap, modest and easy to talk to, and his powers far exceeded those of Capel-Dunn. I told him our maximum requirements, to allow for expansion, and he told me to leave matters to him.

The result was that we were given no fewer than nine small rooms, situated at the far end of the basement. By having several partition walls removed, I reduced the number to five; one each for Johnny and Ronald, two more for Harold and Johnny's ATS assistant, a double one for our typists and filing clerk, and a triple one for James and myself which was L-shaped, one-third of it to be occupied by our conference table.

As time went on, it proved none too much. Harold was given another officer to assist him with his Intelligence work, we had one male and two female civil servants to devil for us and do our typing; and, in my big room, two other desks were later occupied by Major Neil Gordon Clark and a Foreign Office representative: Sir Reginald Hoare who, until the Nazis went in, was HM's Minister in Rumania.

Honour satisfied, I invited Capel-Dunn to lunch. Not only did he accept, but he happened to be a lover of fine Hock. From then on we became firm friends.

I decided to furnish the big room suitably and, at the same time, protect some of my better belongings, then in store, from possible destruction in an air-raid. I brought in my big, oval dining table and a set of Chippendale chairs, and covered the linoleum on the floor with some £800 worth of silk Persian rugs. I then covered the walls with maps; big ones, consisting of many sections pasted together, of Europe, Italy and North Africa, and smaller ones of the Eastern Mediterranean, the Atlantic, the Pacific and the Far East.

On Johnny's return, he was delighted; and soon after we were fully installed in our new quarters, General Ismay came down to inspect them. As he entered our big room he gave a swift glance round this, for any ministry, uniquely luxuriour accommodation, looked at me, standing at attention

The Completion of the Deception Section 129

behind my desk, and asked: 'Dennis, where are the girls?'

Johnny, ever obsessed with 'security', had decided, perhaps rightly, to divide us into two groups, 'Intelligence' and 'Plans', in order that the knowledge of secret intelligence should be confined to fewer of his people. Harold was now segregated in his separate room where he daily flagged enormous charts marked with cryptic signs, indicating the many agents and double agents through whom the enemy was being fed with false information; while James and I, in our room, made the first drafts of all plans.

Ronald having been elevated to Deputy Controlling Officer, it was decided that James and I ought to have another soldier to assist us. A very able lawyer named Buckley, who represented the Home Office on ISSB, recommended for the job his brother-in-law, Major Neil Gordon Clark, who duly joined us.

In the latter part of the First World War Neil had served in the Royal Tank Corps. Rejoining in 1939, he had been given command of a formation of the Home Guard; so on being pitch-forked into our outfit he was, to begin with, somewhat overawed and hopelessly at sea. But he swiftly absorbed the indoctrination that it was my job to give him and later proved of great value to us.

There emerged, too, a special bond between Neil and me, because he and his brother were the heads of Messrs Matthew Clark and Sons – the agents in the UK and numerous other territories for Martell brandies. We talked wine, became excellent friends, and have enjoyed many a good bottle together.

He was rather diffident, but could be very firm on occasions, and we could not have had anyone better for the job he was given to do. In addition to helping James and me to formulate plans, he became responsible, in association with Harold, for maintaining our Fake Order of Battle. This was rather like inventing a new crossword puzzle every day, but Neil handled it most efficiently.

The other officer who joined us permanently was Major Derrick Morley. Derrick was a strange cross between a playboy and a very able financier. An Irishman with no great capital behind him, he had travelled extensively in Europe

E

during the late 1920s and early 1930s, always with introductions to princes and millionaires. While in Paris he had formed a liking for the Impressionists and expended some £2000 of his limited capital in buying works which later became worth tens of thousands of pounds.

In the thirties he had gone into the great merchant banking house of Messrs Helbert, Wagg & Co. Ltd. On the outbreak of war, although the Army was anathema to him, he endeavoured to join up but was rejected on medical grounds because he had flat feet. Undeterred, he pulled such strings as he could and, one morning, a friend of his – I think the chairman of Fortnum and Mason – telephoned him to go for an interview at the War Office.

The Army was then recruiting knowledgeable civilians who could do the rather small-time job of becoming Intelligence Officers at our innumerable training centres. On being questioned, Derrick said that he was a banker, then admitted to speaking several languages and having a considerable knowledge of international affairs.

The Major who was interviewing him said, 'Right. You are just the man I have been looking for. You can judge the sort of chaps who are capable of doing low-grade Intelligence work just as well as I can. I am a Regular and I want to get into the war. I'll have you gazetted as a Captain. Report here tomorrow and take over from me.'

The Major later became General Sir Gerald Templer.

Having asked to go on active service, Derrick was sent to the Middle East, but his feet let him down and on his return home he was posted to our section to act as Harold's number two. But Harold was so secretive that, intelligent as Derrick was, he remained completely mystified about what Harold was trying to do.

However, in due course, Johnny found another use for him. He became our roving Ambassador and was flown out to Sweden, Portugal and Spain to instruct our Ambassadors in those neutral countries how best they could help in furthering our deception plans. That was much more his cup of tea, and in such work he proved invaluable.

When detailed planning began for the Normandy landings, Derrick became our liaison officer with General Freddy

Morgan, COSSAC, whose staff were making all the preparations for the invasion until General Eisenhower took over. Their headquarters was Norfolk House in St James's Square and, after one of Derrick's daily visits there, I asked him how he was getting on.

Sadly he admitted, 'I'm getting nowhere. Johnny regards his stuff as so secret that he has forbidden me to mention it to anyone except General Morgan, and I hardly ever see the General; so my going to Norfolk House is a sheer waste of time.'

'Now listen, Derrick,' I said. 'You are still looking on yourself as just one of the thousands of Majors who are everywhere like pebbles on the beach. But you are not really that any longer. You are a member of the Joint Planning Staff of the War Cabinet; so outside it you are vested with immense prestige. The lowest of us should think of ourselves as having the rank of at least a Brigadier. You must do that and tomorrow ask General Morgan out to lunch.'

Derrick was not only a member of the JPS. In civil life he was a merchant banker, he owned a fine estate in Ireland, was a member of the Turf, Buck's and the St James's, and was on Christian-name terms with half the nobility in the kingdom. He took my advice and invited Freddy Morgan to lunch; no man could have been a more charming host. Over the meal he and the General became firm friends, and after that Derrick met with no more difficulties.

During the war Derrick lived at the Ritz, but the food had become so indifferent there that he always appreciated being asked to dinner with us at Chatsworth Court.

Curiously enough, Derrick and I did not really become intimates until some time after the war. Derrick put me up for the St James's Club, and later for both Pratt's and White's, for which, as I made many other friends in these clubs, I can never be sufficiently grateful. As the years passed we became ever closer, so that I now look upon him as my best friend. Never have I met a man with more exquisite manners, shrewd intelligence and enchanting wit.

A later comer to our basement was Sir Reginald Hoare, a member of the great banking family, known, for some reason, to his intimates as 'Ralph'.

When Johnny asked for a representative of the Foreign Office to become a permanent member of our section, Sir Reginald, who was then unemployed, came to us on the recommendation of the Chairman of the Joint Intelligence Committee.

This distinguished diplomat had been HM Minister in Rumania until Hitler absorbed that country into the Axis. He was an elderly, grey-haired man with a pronounced stoop. He contributed positively nothing to our activities and told me once that he had taken the job only because, like Kipling's elephant's child, he suffered from 'a satiable curtiosity', and could not bear to be kept out of the secrets of the high direction of the war.

Johnny, who had an ingrained distrust of everyone not wearing uniform, told him as little as possible, showed impatience at his slow, deliberate manner of speaking and at times was downright rude to him. This engendered in him an intense dislike of Johnny who, he once said resentfully, 'treated me like a footman'. Being a law unto himself, he put in only a few hours a day at the office just to learn what was going on. But he had a subtle wit, a lovely sense of humour, and James, Neil and I, whose office he shared, delighted in his companionship. We christened him 'Ambassador', and always addressed him in that way.

The last to join us, and then only as an attachment who came in to sit with us for a few hours two or three times a week, was Professor H. A. de C. Andrade – known to us, at his request, as 'Percy'. Johnny had asked for a scientific adviser and the powers that be had done him proud, as Percy was the President of the Royal Society.

But here again, in an even more marked manner, Johnny displayed his illogical distrust of civilians. He ordained that none of us was to give the Prof. any information whatever about future operations.

This was a minor tragedy because, unlike the 'Ambassador', Percy was willing and eager to give his fine brain to helping us further our designs. I soon found that his knowledge of Germany and the psychology of the Germans was encyclopaedic. He knew more about the mentality of the enemy and what they were likely to do than all the rest of

The Completion of the Deception Section 133

us put together. Moreover, although he was only consulted on such matters as gas and bacteriological warfare and, later, about the prospects of producing a nuclear bomb, he was constantly suggesting ideas as to how we could mislead and mystify the enemy in ordinary military matters.

His moods were unpredictable and he would frequently discourse on subjects that were far above our heads; assuming that even semi-educated people such as us would understand what he was talking about. But it was a great pity that we did not make more use of him.

Work in our office continued at high pressure; endless reading of minutes and papers of all kinds, long hours spent round our conference table and occasional crises.

I managed at least to reduce the hours which we formerly had to devote to reading by putting it to Johnny that for all of us to read every paper circulated to the JPS was an absolute waste of time and that we ought to divide this work.

He agreed, and it was decided that I should read the minutes of the War Cabinet, of the Defence Committee, of the Chiefs of Staff meetings and Foreign Office telegrams, in and out; that Ronald should read all JPS papers on future plans; that Harold should read all JIC appreciation of future enemy intentions, and the Intelligence summaries; that James should read all directives to Force Commanders and reports regarding operations then in progress; and that Neil should read all papers concerning the movement of forces, resources, report on the previous day's decisions at ISSB and attend their meetings, which he took over from me.

Then, at the nine-thirty meeting that we all attended every morning, each of us should tell the others the salient points in the papers he had read the previous day. When the 'Ambassador' and Derrick Morley joined us, the former took over Foreign Office matters from me and the latter kept us informed of all that was going forward among General Eisenhower's people at Norfolk House in preparation for the Normandy landings.

On one day of the week, Wednesday, I was always late

for these meetings as another of my jobs was that of liaison officer with the Political Warfare Executive. This had its headquarters at Bush House, in the Strand, and was under the direction of my, by then, old friend, Major-General Dallas Brooks.

Every Tuesday night Dallas agreed with his Foreign Office associates the items of propaganda that were to be put out during the ensuing week on the 'white' (true) and 'black' (false) radio broadcasts for neutral and enemy consumption. On Wednesday mornings I went to his office to go through it with him and ensure that nothing should be said on either white or black that would conflict with our deception plans.

Dallas never arrived at his office until ten o'clock. This, if I left Chatsworth Court at my usual time and took a taxi instead of going by underground, gave me the best part of three-quarters of an hour's leeway; and I employed the time to good purpose. First stop Harrods, second stop Jacksons of Piccadilly, third stop Fortnum and Mason. These excellent establishments having only just opened, I had first choice of the very limited stocks of off-ration luxury edibles that came in each morning and were snapped up within the hour. Then on I went to Bush House.

Dallas would have just arrived and be sitting in his shirt-sleeves while one of the pretty girls he employed as secretaries cleaned his tunic buttons. He was a most friendly man and his invariable greeting to me was, 'Come in, big boy. Sit down and tell me the news.'

For five or ten minutes we swapped tidbits of highly secret information, then co-ordinated the propaganda that was to be put out during the week. Another taxi took me back to the Cabinet Offices, and I usually got there just in time to make my report before our meeting closed.

I have mentioned Dallas's pretty girl secretaries, but the man who excelled in surrounding himself with lovelies was the head of the Special Operations Executive, Major-General (later Sir) Colin Gubbins, known to his intimates as 'Gubby'.

Gubby was a bachelor and a dapper little man. Instead of the slacks or battle-dress worn by the majority of Army officers employed in War Departments, he always wore beautifully cut Bedford cord breeches, highly polished field

The Completion of the Deception Section

boots and spurs. His office was in Baker Street, but he lived in a large flat in Bayswater overlooking the park.

Joan and I went to several parties he gave there. The majority of the guests were officers of the Free Forces – Poles, Frenchmen, Norwegians, Belgians, Dutchmen and Czechs – daring fellows who from time to time were dropped by parachute into enemy-occupied territory either to carry out sabotage missions or take instructions to Resistance groups. But the hostesses were a score or more of beauties, mostly ex-débutantes, hand-picked by Gubby from the hundred or more girls that he employed in his office. SOE had 'resources', so there was always a splendid buffet and a never-failing supply of good liquor.

Another party to which Joan and I went had most unpleasant results for her. It was given by one Tom Green and his wife. Tom was one of the many 'cloak-and-dagger' characters whose acquaintance I made while lunching at Rules with Eddie Combe – and 'character' is certainly the word to use when referring to Tom.

He was an enormous Irishman who positively exuded blarney and spoke with a heavy brogue. Even that famous author of spy stories, E. Phillips Oppenheim, could not have dreamed up such a fantastic personality for the man from whom all our secret agents in France took their riding instructions.

Tom was a great gourmet – on one occasion, God alone knows how in the London of 1943, he actually produced a sucking pig for lunch. We got on famously together; so Joan and I were asked to this party in a huge flat that was situated on the top floor of a big block somewhere in the neighbourhood of Sloane Avenue.

The place was crammed with foreigners, now temporarily in London, so wearing uniform, but spending most of their time in their own countries as spies; and dozens of pretty women. The latter were handing round trays of champagne and a variety of cocktails. Champagne had never agreed with Joan, so she took what she believed to be a White Lady. Soon afterwards she went green in the face and began to feel extremely ill.

I got hold of Tom's step-daughter, a large but ravishing

blonde, who took Joan off to a bedroom. Poor Joan passed out for a while and was then terribly sick, while Mrs Green did her best for her and I hovered unhappily in the background. It was well over an hour before we could even get her on her feet and into a taxi. When we did get home, she was still incapable of undressing herself so I had to get her to bed.

In due course, I learned the explanation for this most distressing occurrence. There had been a Polish officer at the party who was suspected of double-crossing us. Tom Green and his subordinates had planned to knock out the Pole and, while he was still so ill as to be incapable of coherent thought, shoot questions at him which would lead to his giving himself away. Owing to mismanagement in arranging the glasses on the tray of drinks offered to Joan, she had had the ill luck to pick up the Mickey Finn that had been intended for the Pole.

Our move from the 'schoolroom' to the ex-Home Office basement had one result that caused me considerable annoyance. The little JPS mess had originally been started for the benefit of map-room officers who, if I remember, did two days on and thirty-six hours off. As only six of them were on duty at one time, there was room enough for Pug Ismay, Joe Hollis, Ian Jacob, the STRATS and the FOPS also to use it when they were not lunching or dining out. Having been a FOP during my first months in the Cabinet Office, I automatically became a member and, in due course, as part of the JPS, so did Johnny and the other officers of our section. But it had gradually increased from three of us to seven, and now the staff of the Joint Intelligence Committee – consisting of a score of officers – had moved into our fortress basement. Even if each person had a meal there only two or three times a week, it would obviously now be impossible to accommodate them without long delays, as our two bridge tables put together seated only six at a time.

A meeting of the mess committee, which consisted of General Jacob, Wing Commander Kershaw (from the map room), Lieutenant-Colonel Weber Brown and myself, was called and the situation discussed. It was then decided that only the original members of the little mess should in future be allowed to use it and the ex-Home Forces HQ mess up

The Completion of the Deception Section

on the ground floor was to be taken over for use by the Joint Intelligence Staff and Johnny's London Controlling Section.

This was a sad blow and, as I pointed out, the work of my section would suffer since, by personal contact with the JPS and others in the little mess, we were often able to save much time in forwarding our plans. However, the best I could secure was the concession that I and my colleagues should still be allowed to buy drinks there.

I was very lucky in having so many friends who returned the hospitality they received at my Hungaria lunches and little dinners at Chatsworth Court by taking me to lunch at their clubs. Most of them, being Regular officers, belonged to the Senior, the Rag, the In and Out, the Cavalry or the RAF. But Johnny and Ronald belonged to Brooks's, Neil to the Royal Thames, Derrick to Buck's, Eric Goudie to the Travellers and others with whom I lunched less frequently to White's, Boodle's and the Garrick; so at least twice a week I was able to enjoy a good meal in pleasant surroundings.

When writing of our mess committee, I mentioned Lieutenant-Colonel Weber-Brown. Buster, as he was known to his friends, was an interesting little man. At the time I joined the FOPS, he was one of the dozen, mostly elderly, officers of the three services who staffed the map room. In addition to sticking pins in maps to show the movements of troops on all battle fronts, the position of every ship in the Royal Navy and every squadron of the RAF, it was part of their duty to get out a daily report based on the signals received from all C-in-Cs, particulars of shipping that had been sunk, enemy aircraft shot down, and it was one of Buster's jobs to take a copy of this 'twenty-four-hour summary' every morning to the King at Buckingham Palace.

But a time came when Buster left the map room and was given a large room to himself upstairs on the second floor, near that in which the Chiefs of Staff met. In due course he confided to me what he did in this room and took me up to see it.

If one went into the map room after dinner one could be pretty certain of seeing a Cabinet Minister and one or two other 'high-ups' having the latest situation on the battle fronts explained to them by the watch-keepers; so in the evenings they were kept busy. But at times during the day, and still more so at night, there were no visitors and often long periods elapsed between signals coming in, so the watch-keepers had nothing to do. Bored by this, and every sort of information being readily available, Buster had amused himself by making graphs based on statistics in connection with the war.

I think it was General Hollis who realized how valuable such graphs could be, and suggested that Buster should devote his whole time to making them. From then on he worked entirely on his own, except for a girl artist who came in three mornings a week to colour the graphs. When I visited his room there were dozens of graphs pinned up on the walls and on screens. Among other things, they showed over a period of months the stocks of petrol and certain key foods such as wheat, sugar and meal available in the UK; the sinkings of our shipping and enemy U-boats; the weight of bombs dropped on our cities and those of the enemy; the losses in aircraft by the RAF and the Luftwaffe; the tonnage of the Royal Navy and available landing craft; the numbers of men in each service and the munition factories; the strength of every division in the UK, and the degree to which it had been equipped with the latest weapons; and even what the Beveridge plan would cost the British tax-payer up to 1960, provided the ratio of births and deaths remained constant.

As Buster remarked to me cynically, 'It is generally accepted that the higher the rank, the more infantile the mind becomes; so the Chiefs of Staff are no longer capable of reading. But once a week they come here, I take them by the hand and show them my pretty pictures, which gives them an idea how the war is going on.'

Behind the joke there lay a grain of truth. The Chiefs had so much on their minds that they could not possibly give sufficient time to reading more than a small proportion of the papers sent up to them, but half an hour spent in Buster's room enabled them to absorb a mass of valuable information.

There was another thought which gave me cold shivers down the spine. Had an enemy agent penetrated Buster's room he, too, could in half an hour have absorbed every

The Completion of the Deception Section

principal fact about Britain's war potential. No wonder that Buster's work and his room were looked on as super-secret. Very few officers in the JPS had even heard of it. Johnny had not, until I asked Buster if I might bring him up there. No one else I knew had ever entered it; so I regarded it as a great compliment to have been shown Buster's 'pretty pictures'.

Chapter 12
'Nothing to Hide'

Sicily being in the Mediterranean theatre, the cover plan for Husky was Dudley Clarke's responsibility; but it was up to us to aid him in any way we could, and we got out a paper which we sent up to the Chiefs of Staff.

Its main objective was to conceal from the British forces to be used their true destination, in order to minimize the chance of careless talk being overheard by an enemy agent.

This was not easy as three forces were to be despatched: an Eastern group from Egypt, a Central group from Malta and Tunisia, and a Western group from Algiers and Britain. And all were to sail assault-loaded, so the troops they were carrying would know that they were not just being sent somewhere as reinforcements but were to take part in a landing on enemy-held territory.

We decided that it should be put about among the Eastern group that they were to seize some of the islands in the Dodecanese; among the Central group that they were to take the little island of Pantellaria, which lies near Malta and was still in the hands of the Italians; and the groups from Britain and Algeria were both told that they were part of larger forces which were to attack a French port in the Bay of Biscay and the South of France respectively.

With regard to the force from Britain, we recommended certain measures which could have been taken, such as: brief Force Commanders and secure their co-operation; have models made of the Biscay coast to be put in rooms where a certain number of people would have access to them;

'Nothing to Hide'

issue English–French phrase books and, to Force paymasters, suitable currency for an occupation; attach French interpreters, carry out mine-sweeping off the Biscay coast, bomb communications with the ports there and indicate an increase in sabotage by dropping dummy parachutists.

However, we were debarred from putting in hand any of these ideas owing to a directive by the Chiefs of Staff, who instructed Johnny that he was not to request the service ministries or the Combined Commanders to take any steps in the UK until a Supreme Commander had been appointed, and that all implementation would then be his responsibility.

In the event, Lieutenant-General 'Freddy' Morgan was appointed COSSAC (Chief of Staff to the Supreme Allied Commander), and given Norfolk House, St James's Square, as his HQ, but not until April. So for two months, as far as Husky was concerned, we had to remain inactive and even then our powers were greatly restricted. This resulted in a stringent complaint by Colonel Sir John Turner about the general lack of deception activities and, such as they were, their co-ordination. Sir John was a quite exceptionally forceful and determined personality – known, owing to his great beak of a nose, as 'Conky Bill'.

When his scathing paper came in, as I knew him and Johnny did not, I was given the job of sending a reply to the Assistant Chief of Air Staff (Ops).

It was a long paper in which I rejected Colonel Turner's assertion that the three services had made no attempt to co-ordinate any large deception plan. I recalled the fact that many months earlier, with members of the ISSB, I had visited him at his HQ and, as we had met several times since, he knew the work upon which I and the other members of the London Controlling Section were engaged. I then gave particulars of our deception plan for Torch and its success, upon which we had received the congratulations of the Chiefs of Staff. Finally, I pointed out that, since we were a highly secret body, even many very senior officers in the service ministries' staff were unaware of our existence and that, with regard to Husky, the Chiefs of Staff had expressly forbidden Johnny to communicate with those ministries.

Despite our success in fooling the Germans, Italians and French in North Africa about the Torch landings, we were still faced with many difficulties in carrying out our jobs. Not only were we largely hamstrung by the very high degree of secrecy we were ordered to maintain about our very existence but, due to the failure of the Chiefs to issue proper instructions, we could still only 'beg' instead of 'require' the assistance of the heads of such departments as we had been allowed to get in touch with; and many of them continued to regard our requests as a time-wasting nuisance.

However, as it turned out, no forces were to be sent from the UK to participate in Husky, so it was unnecessary for us to lay on measures calculated to persuade such forces that they were to make a landing in the Bay of Biscay. Our contribution to assisting Dudley Clarke was, therefore, reduced to putting out false rumours regarding our future intentions.

The principal ways in which we did this were: through 'most secret sources', i.e. double agents; through neutrals both abroad and *en poste* as diplomats in London; by apparently careless talk from ourselves and from high-ups 'in the know', who gave us their help; and by asking our own diplomats in neutral countries to make misleading statements at social functions which would be passed on to the enemy.

To tell these groups what lines we wished them to take, we got out several papers. The main ideas we wanted to put into the mind of the enemy were a possibility that we might invade southern France and that, the French army in North Africa having now come over to the Allies, no further British or American troops would be sent there. Instead, we should build up a great Allied army in Britain for the invasion of the Continent by way of Holland or Norway. Timing would depend upon the shipping available as we were still short of the number of ships necessary to put over an invading force of overwhelming strength; but the reopening of the Mediterranean, by which we could reinforce Egypt, instead of going round the Cape, should soon give us the extra shipping required. In due course our forces in Egypt were to be used for an assault on the 'underbelly' of the Axis. We should bypass the Dodecanese and Crete and go straight into Greece. We had many secret scientific

'Nothing to Hide' 143

weapons that had never yet been employed in war. These we were saving for the great day when we went into Western Europe. Our papers ran to many thousands of words, those for the diplomats covering all phases of the war in every theatre, with the exception of our real future intentions.

It was during that April that I had an exceptionally pleasant day off. A month or so earlier it had been decided that an American officer should sit in as an observer at all the deliberations of our Joint Planning Staff. The officer appointed was a Colonel William H. Baumer. He was a delightful fellow and a very able one. Not only did he wear on his chest the large, colourful coat of arms signifying that he had passed through West Point Military Academy, but he had been on Eisenhower's staff when Ike was no more than a Divisional Commander.

From such an officer we had 'nothing to hide' (of which more later), so he was duly indoctrinated into our mysteries and I asked him to one of my Hungaria lunches. Among my guests that day was the Vice-Chief of Air Staff, Air Chief Marshal Sir Charles Medhurst. During the lunch Baumer said how greatly he appreciated the kind way in which he had been received by the British, then added: 'The only thing which disappoints me is that, so far, apart from London I've seen nothing at all of England; and it doesn't look as if I stand much chance of doing so.'

Petrol was then most strictly rationed, so none of Baumer's British colleagues could have offered to take him for a run in the country, but Medhurst turned to me and said: 'We really must rectify that, Dennis. You can have my car and chauffeur tomorrow to take our American friend to see some of our beauty spots outside London.'

On returning to the office I told Johnny about Medhurst's generous gesture and asked him for the day off.

At 9.30 next morning the Vice-Chief's large and comfortable car picked up Bill Baumer at the Cumberland Hotel, then collected me from Chatsworth Court. First we drove to Richmond Park, then on to Hampton Court Palace. We then drove through the lovely Surrey countryside to the Devil's Punchbowl at Hindhead. After lunch we visited Sandhurst and Windsor. And so back to Chatsworth Court, where Joan had an excellent dinner waiting for us. It had been an unforgettable day.

I referred earlier to the phrase 'I have nothing to hide'. It became a standard joke in the Cabinet Offices on account of the following happening.

Pug Ismay's number two, Brigadier (later General) Sir Leslie Hollis, had a civilian personal assistant named Jones. He was a very efficient but nevertheless an ordinary little man, with the appearance and manner of the actor Robertson Hare in a Tom Walls' farce. In most of these plays Hare's rôle had been that of a highly nervous curate who constantly found himself in most embarrassing situations such as, to his horror, being locked by mistake into the bedroom of a ravishing, near-nude blonde. Jones would only have had to learn the lines to go on as Hare's understudy.

As a link with Joe Hollis no one could have served me better. Whenever I rang up, however busy Hollis might be, Jones would say, 'Ha! Wing Commander. You wish to see the Brigadier. Hang on. Hang on for one moment, and I will ascertain at what hour the Brigadier can see you.'

On one occasion when there was to be a conference in Washington, Hollis decided to take Jones with him. On arrival, the Prime Minister and Pug were given rooms in the White House but the Chiefs of Staff and the JPS were quartered in a big hotel about seven miles outside the city. As it was high summer, twice a day they had to make the sweltering drive in, escorted by a swarm of motorcycle police, horns blaring and guns at the ready, to attend the Combined Chiefs' conferences which were held in the White House.

After eight gruelling days the conference was about to end, and on the last morning Hollis said to Jones, 'We are leaving for home tomorrow; so you had better start packing up.' Then he added, 'How have you enjoyed your stay in Washington, Jones?'

Jones, who had never left the isolated hotel, replied with his usual hesitant breathlessness. 'Well, Brigadier, well. Of course, it has been the most interesting experience. But, but, I am a little worried about one thing. When I get home, my family are certain to ask me, "What did you think of the

'Nothing to Hide'

White House?" And, well, I have never had the honour and privilege of going there.'

Hollis, who was the kindest of men, said at once: 'I'm terribly sorry, Jones. I've been so busy that I never thought of it. But, of course, you must see the White House. Come with me now and I'll take you there.'

On arriving at the White House, Hollis took Jones up to the first floor and said to him, 'Wait here a few minutes, Jones. I have to brief General Ismay for this morning's meeting. But I shan't be long and when I come back I'll take you round.' Then he left Jones standing in a long, not very wide, corridor.

Hollis was delayed longer than he had expected but on his return he found Jones exactly where he had left him. With his usual brisk manner, he said, 'Come along, Jones,' and took him on a tour to see Abraham Lincoln's bedroom, the banqueting room and all the other sights of the place. But, after a while, he noticed that Jones, far from showing any interest, remained completely silent and apparently ill-at-ease. So he said, 'What's the matter, Jones? Aren't you feeling well?'

'Oh, er, yes, Brigadier,' Jones replied unhappily. 'I'm perfectly well but I have just been through a rather shattering experience.'

'Why, what happened to you?' Hollis asked.

'Well, Brigadier. You, er, you will recall that you told me to wait for you in that corridor. Not long after you had left me I observed a figure in a wheelchair approaching. Although I have never had the honour of meeting the President of the United States, I have seen many pictures of him and I had no doubt in my mind that it was he who was advancing towards me.

'Naturally, as he was about to draw level with me, I deferentially made way for him to pass. But he did not pass. He abruptly brought his wheelchair to a halt, swung it round facing me and asked: "Is the Prime Minister up?"

'You will appreciate, Brigadier, that not only was I not aware if the Prime Minister was in a state to receive an important visitor, but I did not even know where his apartments were situated. Not wishing to appear entirely at a loss, I replied, "One moment, Mr President. One moment and I will ascertain."

'You will, I am sure, appreciate the unhappy situation in which I found myself. As I stood there completely at a loss how to proceed, the President pointed to the door against which I was standing and said abruptly, "In there! In there!"

'Greatly relieved, I opened the door so that the President might pass through it. To my horror, I saw that it led into a bathroom and the Prime Minister was there, standing up in the bath naked. Imagine my position, Brigadier. There was I in the doorway, caught between the Prime Minister of Great Britain and the President of the United States. For a moment I remained there at my wits end what to do. Then the Prime Minister called out: "Come in, Mr President, come in. I've always told you that I have nothing to hide."'

Among the measures taken during the spring of 1943, to get it put about that a return to the Continent was to take place that summer, Johnny had a number of bank notes printed, carrying the inscription in bold letters, 'British Army of Occupation in France'. All of us carried a few of them about in our pocket books and every time we took a taxi, paid a restaurant bill or bought something in a shop we used one. Then, having allowed the person to whom we gave it time enough to have a quick look at it, we hurriedly snatched it back in apparent confusion and substituted an ordinary pound note.

Towards the end of April, we also got out some further lines for people who were helping us by apparently indiscreet speculation in their correspondence.

As early as mid-February it had become more or less apparent that, providing Husky was successful, Churchill would succeed in persuading the Americans that we should not be strong enough to launch a cross-Channel operation during 1943; so that, instead of Allied forces being withdrawn from the Mediterranean, Sicily should be used as a base for going into Italy. But it was hoped that, instead of our having to fight our way up the leg of Italy, her collapse

'Nothing to Hide'

might be brought about by other means. This was outside my sphere as a deception planner, but Roly Vintras, recalling the papers I had written before I went into uniform, asked me to write a paper upon how this might possibly be achieved. For him and the JPS I produced a very long paper reviewing the many ways by which Italy could benefit, both now and after the war, by renouncing her alliance with Germany, and if she was prepared to treat with us, suggesting means by which our proposals for an armistice could be conveyed secretly to the Italian General Staff.

In this paper I made it clear that unconditional surrender would not be required of Italy. To demand it was the only publicized decision taken at Casablanca. This was one of the most stupid things ever done. Not only had we now to try to tell the Italians that we did not really mean it in the sense of despoiling them of everything; but we had debarred ourselves from any chance of a negotiated peace with Germany. Whereas, had we remained free to offer them terms, it now seems pretty certain that, with the possibility of agreeing an Armistice, the German Generals might have shown much more courage and determination in their attempts to rid themselves of Hitler; so the war could have been brought to an end very much sooner.

By mid-May, our future strategy had become certain. Sicily conquered, we were going into Italy. Now LCS was asked to propose deception measures that might assist in bringing about an Italian surrender.

I happened to know that Dallas Brooks had, as part of his political warfare equipment, a super-powerful radio transmitter, known by the codename of Aspidistra. I had been given to understand that it was capable of blanketing radio transmitters in enemy countries and could be used to put over a broadcast which listeners would believe emanated from their own main broadcasting stations.

It occurred to me that the *coup de grâce* might, at a well chosen time, be administered if Aspidistra put out a broadcast to the Italians purporting to come from their King and ordering them to lay down their arms. I wrote an appropriate speech. To my distress, when I submitted this to General Dallas Brooks, he refused to play. He said that Aspidistra could be used only once, then it would be blown; and he did not consider this the right occasion to use it.

Meanwhile, Johnny wrestled with scores of problems every day and read 'most secret' papers far into the night. Ronald, as his deputy, attended any number of conferences in the various ministries, and kept himself abreast of every development in both our planning and intelligence sections. James was constantly going to and from the Admiralty to co-ordinate our deception plans concerning convoys and landing craft. Harold juggled endlessly in his room with matters about which we were not supposed to know; sticking pins into a chart that looked like a crossword puzzle, but indicated all our secret agents' activities, and also attended the weekly super-secret Twenty Committee meetings, where it was decided what information should be passed to the enemy. Neil had taken over from me in attending the morning meetings of ISSB and, most dreary task, kept track of all the fake units in the 'Order of Battle' created by ourselves, Dudley Clark and Peter Fleming. Derrick kept us informed of all that was going forward at General Morgan's HQ in Norfolk House and, in due course, was to give invaluable assistance to our plans by acting as our secret 'Ambassador' to our diplomats in neutral countries.

We were a team. A good team and, by and large, a happy one.

Chapter 13
Operation Husky

As I said earlier, among the many papers I had to read every day were the minutes of the meetings of the War Cabinet and, when Churchill was overseas attending conferences, the signals he sent back informing the members of the War Cabinet who had remained at home of decisions taken.

One such occasion was during the third Washington conference. The PM reported that he had given a lunch at the British Embassy to five of America's leading statesmen and, at it, told them his views about how the world should be governed after the war. They were, as far as I remember, as follows:

A Supreme World Council should be set up consisting of the United States, Great Britain, the USSR and, if America desired it, China. [At that time China consisted of a so-called Republic dominated by Chiang Kai-shek.]

Regional Councils for Europe; the American hemisphere; and the Pacific.

Europe should be divided into twelve states: France, Spain, Italy, Prussia, the Low Countries, Turkey and Greece, with Central and Southeastern Europe formed into several confederations. In fact, a United States of Europe.

The creation of national and international forces for the maintenance of world peace.

A federal association between the United States and the United Kingdom.

To me, the above had a decidedly familiar ring. It is the essence of my paper, *After the Battle,* written by me three years earlier. Owing to the great length of that paper, I do not suppose for one moment that Churchill ever read it. But the King had; also at least a dozen people who were closely associated with the PM, and it is as good as certain that several of them had talked to him about its contents.

He went on to amplify the ideas he had put to the Americans:

The four major powers on the Supreme World Council should contribute to an international force at the disposal of the Supreme Council.

Bases would be required for the international contingents. Such bases should be mainly on islands, and the USA/GB should take over all islands required for this purpose.

It is fascinating to speculate on the course history might have taken had the USA and the UK virtually become one as he suggested. Would the USA have felt compelled to aid us in the Suez operation, or the UK to send the British Army to fight in Vietnam?

On 10 July the landings in Sicily were duly carried out, and a few days later the Chiefs discussed the operation. Dudley Clarke's cover plan had proved successful and we had achieved surprise, but our casualties had been heavier than expected and unloading by both British and Americans much too slow. The Naval long-range bombardment had had excellent effect but our transports had not taken advantage of it; they should, once the enemy's forts had been silenced, have come much closer in to shore.

Our air losses had been considerable, and we had lost more aircraft shot down or damaged by our own anti-aircraft fire than by enemy action. In view of this the C-in-C Combined Operations, Lord Louis Mountbatten, recommended that, in future, air ops. should be under AOC Air until troops had actually landed, and that the GOC Troops should remain at the Tactical Air HQ until his men were ashore; and that for similar operations safety lanes should be provided for transports. Airborne troops had been misused and in future should be allotted only special tasks.

Apart from supporting Dudley Clarke's cover plan for Husky by feeding misleading information to the enemy

Operation Husky

through our own channels, we did make a contribution to its success that later became known throughout the whole world. This was Mincemeat. The idea originated with Flight Lieutenant Chumley of MI5, who, as it was a Naval job, put it up to Lieutenant-Commander the Hon. Ewen Montagu.

The idea was that the dead body of an officer should be taken in a submarine to the coast of Spain and there floated off at a time when the tide would wash it ashore. In the pocket of his tunic there would be a letter from one of our war chiefs to General Alexander, in which indications would be given that the objective of Husky was Dudley's false one. We hoped that the Spaniards would assume the body was from an aircraft which had been shot down and, as most Spanish authorities were then pro-German, that they would pass on the letter to the German Mission in Madrid.

As Deception was the special province of the LCS, Montagu had to submit the project to Johnny and we all sat in on it; but the actual job was handled by MI6. To procure the body of a man who had not obviously died of some disease or as a result of being smashed up in an accident, and who had no close relatives who would wish to attend his funeral, can have been no easy task, but somehow they got hold of a suitable corpse which had been a Captain of Royal Marines. He had, I think, died of a heart attack and we were a little worried that when the body was washed up the Spaniards would realize that he had not been drowned, so would suspect a trick. But that had to be risked.

The letter he carried was from the VCIGS, Lieutenant-General Nye, to General Alexander. Although on Cabinet Office paper, it appeared to be only a private letter sent from one friend to another; the passage that mattered being just a casual reference to coming events of which the two Generals had common knowledge, inserted between passages of gossip about mutual acquaintances. I recall noticing with pleasure that a pre-war friend of mine, Brigadier Stuart Forster, was mentioned as nominated for promotion to command of the Guards Division, given HM's approval. With this, in the dead man's tunic pocket, were put several forged hotel bills and private letters purporting to come from a girl. The body was then tinned and Montagu took it up to one of the northern ports, where he delivered it to the Commander of a submarine.

In due course the Spaniards very correctly notified the nearest British Consul that the body of one of our officers had been washed up, and handed to him all the papers that had been found on it. The Consul saw to the proper burial of the dead man and sent the papers back to London. It was disappointing to learn on their arrival that the letter from Nye to Alex had not been opened. But MI6 sent it to their laboratory for special examination, and it transpired that it *had* been skilfully opened, then re-sealed. Moreover, as we learned in due course, it had been photographed and a copy sent to Berlin.

So the trick had worked. It was a good piece of deception and we in LCS were very pleased to know that, as Montagu got an OBE for the part he played in it, Johnny succeeded in getting one for the modest, retiring Chumley as well.

It was, of course, natural that when this spectacular feat was made public it should have been hailed as one of the great deception triumphs of the war; but this is greatly to overestimate its value. It was only one of the innumerable pieces of misleading information that we conveyed to the enemy so that he might build up a false picture of our intentions. By far the greatest part of our success was due to the dreary day-to-day work carried out by Dudley's people, and in our case by Neil in faking our 'Order of Battle' and so conveying to the enemy that great forces were being mustered for attacks on areas at which we did not intend to strike.

It so happened that at the time of Mincemeat, Duff Cooper was the minister responsible for security; so he was one of the very few people outside the Chiefs of Staff organization and our immediate associates who were told about the plan. In the summer of 1950, I went to stay for the weekend with Johnny at his home, Guillards Oak, Medhurst. Joan was not with me and the Saturday proved a glorious, sunny day. Johnny, as well as being a bird-watcher, was something of a tree man, so on the Friday night we had agreed to spend Saturday hacking down old shrubs and dead wood. In consequence, we both appeared at breakfast wearing flannels. But we never did a stroke the whole of that lovely day. We

Operation Husky

lounged in deckchairs on the lawn, nattering about old friends and the war. Having gone into the house to renew our drinks, Johnny returned with them, handed me a slim volume and said, 'Dennis, what d'you think of that?'

The title of the book was *Operation Heartbreak*, and it was by Duff Cooper. Inside it was a letter (which later Johnny let me have for my collection). It read:

Dear Bevan,
I thought it might amuse you to see an advance copy of the book about which we were talking the other evening. It won't be out until the beginning of November, and if you spot any particularly foolish blunder and would let me know *soon*, there would still be time to make an alteration.
Yours ever,
Duff Cooper.

It was, of course, the story of Mincemeat. Beautifully written and charmingly told. But, oh, what a breach of security!

A few nights earlier, Duff Cooper had seen Johnny in White's, casually mentioned that he had written the book and expected soon to have advance copies of it. Johnny realized at once that, by that time, what with publishers' readers, printers' type-setters, proof-readers and so on, scores of people must have read it, so this 'most secret' operation was already blown and nothing could be done.

Duff Cooper was at that time British Ambassador in Paris and, moreover, a close friend of Churchill's. How could one possibly prosecute a man in such a position? But if I had written that story for publication I would have found myself in the Tower of London and soon after in Brixton prison, doing a three-year stretch for having infringed the Official Secrets Act.

The book, justifiably, proved a bestseller. With its publication the story was free for all. Montagu wrote his own version, *The Man Who Never Was*, out of which a film was made.

The Prime Minister, as usual, was looking ahead and sent a memo to the Chiefs concerning the war against Japan; how our commitments in it should be met after Germany's defeat and a probable demand by the public for demobilization.

During these summer months, deception in Sicily being Dudley Clarke's responsibility and no major operation against Europe definitely settled upon, the work of LCS was more or less reduced to implementing the second part of its charter – 'generally to mislead and mystify the enemy'.

For this purpose we spent most of our time (when we were not reading endless stacks of papers) thinking up rumours that would cause alarm and despondency among the German troops and civil population. I suppose that I provided my fair share of these, but it was by no means my favourite occupation as my real interests lay in the much wider fields. Moreover, Johnny began pressing me to develop closer relations with various departments in the Air Ministry, so that we might assist in providing cover for large-scale bomber raids on Germany and enter on other deceptive activities which might result from our having more detailed information about air matters generally.

From his point of view, the idea was not unreasonable, but for me it presented a difficult and unwelcome task. All my RAF friends on the Joint Planning Staff and in the Air Ministry were on the highest level. They dealt with strategy, plans in the making and the forecasting of future enemy intentions; and they talked to me about such matters with the utmost freedom. But the officers who ordered day-to-day operations and the technical side of air warfare were quite another matter. They did not know me and did not want to have anything to do with the LCS, because they had long developed their own methods for deceiving the enemy about the timing, intensity and objectives of air operations and wished to maintain the strictest secrecy about them.

On the subject of rumours for circulation to the enemy, Johnny formed three committees, although what the difference between them was I cannot for the life of me remember now. They met weekly to consider such items as we had thought up, which were termed 'themes', and the meetings were attended by representatives of MI5, SOE and PWE (my old friend, the well-known book critic Lionel Hale); it being the job of these three to put over our rumours through their respective organizations.

In August another conference, code name Quadrant,

Operation Husky

opened at Quebec. The party went by ship and General Ismay took Joan Bright, a member of his staff, with him. Joan was a truly remarkable person and enjoyed such universal popularity that she was nicknamed 'The Cabinet Offices' Sweetheart'. Her career had started as a civil servant in the British Embassy in Mexico in the early thirties. For the first year or so of the war, she was at the War Office as secretary to MI(R) which at that time handled all cloak-and-dagger doings. She was then transferred to the JPS, and soon afterwards taken on by Pug. She was in on every secret and knew everyone who had any hand in the High Direction of the War. When C-in-Cs of overseas commands, such as General Wavell, were recalled to London for consultations, their first act was to go and see Joan, so that she could put them in the picture about what was going on in other theatres of war. Then they took her out to lunch. On the trip over to Quadrant, she dined for three nights out of the five with four companions: Pug Ismay and the three Chiefs of Staff – surely an all-time high for any woman who played a part in the war.

Joan attended all the overseas VIP conferences and was responsible for allocating quarters to the British delegation. For the conference at Yalta she was sent ahead and, finding that all the Russians were rank-conscious, gave herself that of Major-General.

Roly Vintras had had her to dinner with my Joan, Peter Fleming and myself before I went into uniform, and when I did, she proved an invaluable friend to me. She ran a Special Information Centre from a room adjacent to Pug's, where she had three girls under her and was responsible for keeping the Chiefs of Staff secretariat filing section.

A few years after the war she married Philip Astley. We were delighted, as she was far from well off, and he was handsome, rich and well known. His first wife had been the film star Madeleine Carroll and during the war, as Lieutenant-Colonel, he had been in charge of press and public relations at Wavell's and then Alexander's HQ in the Middle East and Mediterranean theatres. The first we heard of their marriage was in a telegram she sent us from a yacht in the

Mediterranean. It read: 'Engaged July, married August, in the family way September.'

On their return they came for a weekend to Grove and we saw them fairly frequently in London. But, alas, the marriage lasted only nine years. Philip died of a heart attack on Christmas Eve. Joan has the consolation of a fine son. Our long friendship happily continues, and it is always a joy to have her with us.

Although no definite decision had been taken, it had now become evident that an Anglo-American army would invade France in the spring or summer of 1944. The codeword for the operation had been changed from Roundup to Overlord; and, on broad lines, we began to consider what our cover plan should be. In August we produced a paper setting out our ideas. I followed it by a memo with special reference to Norway and Sweden. This, later on, led to one of the greatest *coups* that we ever achieved in deceiving Hitler.

It was a very long paper, running to over 3500 words. Many of the paragraphs dealt with neutral countries and it stated that 'while we had to adopt a defensive attitude towards neutrals in the past . . . we should have no hesitation in asking in the future for facilities and action on their part . . .'.

In this the wish was father to the thought. Of course we dared not demand any assistance from neutrals while we were weak and at bay. All we could do was hope to keep them neutral. To have offended them might have led to their joining Germany against us. Now things were different. We could afford to wave the big stick and say, 'You will do so-and-so, or else!' But the Foreign Office never caught up with this entirely changed situation.

To give one example. The entire supply of ball bearings for the German Air Force was made by a factory in Sweden. I wrote a paper suggesting that the FO should inform the Swedish government that they must cease supplying the Germans forthwith. If they refused, we would give them three days' notice to evacuate their people from the factory area, then send our bombers to destroy it utterly

This alone could have brought the war to an end in a much shorter time. But the Foreign Office replied, 'Oh, no,

Operation Husky

we couldn't possibly do that! It would be threatening a neutral.' So the Swedes continued to send the Germans the ball bearings right up to the end of the war and the Luftwaffe was enabled to go on strafing and bombing Allied troops for another twenty-one months.

However, by devious means we did manage to wring a few minor concessions from the FO. On several occasions the wily Ronald and I teamed up to call together on Foreign Office officials. He played the part natural to him of the high-ranking ex-civil servant long practised in diplomacy and never calling a spade a spade. I played that of an ignorant and truculent ex-civilian. He put our case quietly with deference and charm. The little man on the other side of the desk said, 'No.' I simulated rising temper and eventually burst out in a torrent of indignant protest about the necessity of waging total war, and what would the public think if they knew that we were treating neutrals in such a lily-livered fashion, which led to hundreds of British soldiers being killed? Ronald, appearing horrified, endeavoured to silence me and said, 'Dennis, you really must not say such things.' But the little man had suddenly become cowed and said, 'Well, of course, of course, while we couldn't exactly, but perhaps . . .' So we usually got 'half a loaf' and went off chuckling together down the corridor.

Mussolini having gone, we hoped that Italy would soon be out of the war, but the secret negotiations for an Armistice dragged on, and the situation began to deteriorate because the Germans realized that the Italians were contemplating surrender and must have been taking urgent precautionary measures.

At last, on 3 September, the British Eighth Army crossed the Straits of Messina, and at 6 p.m. on the 8th, a cease-fire was announced. Mussolini had been a prisoner for close on seven weeks. Had we faced the issue promptly the odds are that we would have had the whole of Italy with hardly a shot fired. As it was, our procrastination had given the Germans ample time to send sufficient reinforcements into the country, with the result that we had to fight our way up the whole length of the peninsula.

Four days after the Armistice, a force of ninety parachutists led by the German air ace, Otto Skorzeny, landed on a plateau high up in the Abruzzi where Mussolini was being held a prisoner, rescued him and flew him off to Germany. It was perhaps the most spectacular and daring exploit of the war.

Chapter 14
Plan Bodyguard

In the autumn of 1943 the Churchill Club was formed.

The PM had had the excellent idea of creating a pleasant meeting place for American and Dominion officers stationed in London who were interested in history or the arts, and where they could also meet the British.

Westminster School, which lies only on the other side of Parliament Square from the Cabinet Offices, had been evacuated, so its principal building, Ashburnham House, a fine mansion constructed from the stones of the medieval monastery of Westminster, was taken over as the Club premises. Robert Lutyens, then a Squadron Leader, RAFVR, was put in charge of its decoration and furnishing. As the PM decreed that no expense was to be spared and all war-time regulations about limitations of purchases and so on were to be ignored, Robert was able to make a fine job of it. Mrs Randolph Churchill was appointed manageress of the Club, a number of her friends took on the job of hostess-assistants, and Robert's sister, then Mary Sewell, ran the bar.

No entrance fee or subscription was charged. All US and Dominion officers and other ranks were eligible for membership if they had passed through a university. It was arranged for numerous eminent politicians, travellers and authors to give lectures in the evenings; concerts were also given and a library of 5000 books assembled.

The Club proved a great success but, after a few weeks, some of the Americans said, 'Where are the British? We were told that the Club had been created to give us the opportunity of meeting some of them; but there are never any here.'

This oversight was rectified by Lutyens's being asked to nominate some British members. He consulted my friend Joe Links, who had my name put on the list.

Finding that the place was so pleasant and provided an excellent lunch at a very reasonable cost, I felt that membership might be very welcome to the less well-off members of the Joint Planning Staff. I arranged with Mrs Randolph Churchill that all officers of the JPS should be made members.

As it turned out, my lunches there cost me, on average, more than they would have done at a good restaurant because, entering into the spirit of the thing, I offered to give lunch there one day a week to any two American officers who cared to accept my hospitality. Mrs Churchill selected my guests, and I thus met quite a number of our allies who came from different parts of the United States.

It must have been about this time that we acquired three temporary additions to the staff of LCS. One was Michael Bratby, who had proved such a success as our liaison officer with the Americans in Washington. Now that they had established their main HQ for the European theatre in London, a liaison officer was no longer required in Washington, so Michael was, as one might say, returned to store and given to Harold as an assistant. Later he became an instructor at an Intelligence School in Wimbledon.

Another new arrival was a Lieutenant-Commander Alec Finter, RN. On Dudley Clarke's last visit to England, he had suggested to Johnny that it might prove helpful if, for a period of two months, we exchanged two officers so that each could gain experience of the workings of the other's staff. James Arbuthnott was the officer who was selected to go out to Dudley and Finter was sent to us. James rejoined us in due course, but Alec Finter was transferred to Eisenhower's Allied Deception Staff at Norfolk House.

Our third newcomer was Captain Gordon Waterfield, a *Times* correspondent. However, after a few months with us he was sent back at his own request to ordinary Intelligence work.

A few years after the war I met Waterfield again at our

Plan Bodyguard

annual reunion dinner, kindly arranged by Johnny at Brooks's Club. Dudley, Peter Fleming, Eddie Combe, Eric Goudie, Noel Wild and several others of our close associates were always invited and a good time was had by all. Waterfield suggested that I should write short stories for propaganda purposes to be translated into Arabic, but nothing came of this.

Early in November, Churchill, the Chiefs and their attendant entourages were to meet the Russians at the Teheran conference. We were already aware that it had been decided that an Anglo-American expeditionary force should attempt the liberation of Europe in the spring or summer of 1944; so I had been busy for some time writing a paper on the subject. I was very conscious that this must be our greatest effort and nothing left undone which might draw enemy forces away from the area we intended to invade, so I headed my paper *Essorbee* – which, being interpreted from the ancient Sanskrit, meant 'shit or bust'.

The Foreign Office could not be persuaded to adopt the plan hook, line and sinker, but we did manage to secure permission to go ahead with a few ideas which would implement our policy, particularly in Sweden – of which more later.

As usual when high-level conferences were being held abroad, we received daily reports of the deliberations. At last the eagerly awaited news came through. A definite decision had been taken. Overlord was to be launched in the first week in May (later postponed to the first week in June). At the fateful meeting, Churchill was recorded as having said, 'Our intentions must be surrounded by a bodyguard of lies.' Johnny gave the cover plan for the operation the codename Bodyguard.

Now that the date and place of the invasion had really been settled, we were able to get down to detailed planning. The latter part of November and more than half December proved the most interesting weeks during the whole of my three years in the Cabinet Offices. Hour after hour, day after day, James, Neil, Ronald and I wrestled with our problem. We submitted paper after paper to Johnny, only to have them sent back for further revision.

F

Sometimes he would join us and, haggard from sleeplessness, run his hand through his greying hair and unhappily say, 'But you cannot assume *that*, because we do not know it for a *fact*.' Again and again he would enlarge the sections of the paper, which were headed 'Considerations affecting the achievement of the object', 'Factors against the possibility of disguising the purpose of the expedition', 'Possible means by which the truth about our intentions may become known to the enemy'. In vain we weighed every word. He would not be satisfied. The paper grew and grew until it reached some twenty pages.

Gradually I came to realize that it had become a hopelessly depressing document, virtually informing the Chiefs that the chances were ten to one against the cover plan we had produced succeeding. So I decided to intervene personally, in an attempt to save the situation.

Since the 'schoolroom' days James, Ronald, Neil (after he joined us) and I had, except on very special occasions, always packed up and gone home at six o'clock; and none of us ever returned to the office after dinner. But I knew that Johnny always did, round about ten o'clock.

One night in mid-December I went back there at about nine. With me I took a novel to read, but I spread a lot of papers out on my desk and left the door ajar, so that anyone passing along the corridor would see that there was a light on in my room.

After reading for above an hour I heard footsteps approaching along the corridor of the silent, deserted basement. Slipping my novel into a drawer, I assumed the position of being hard at work. The footsteps were Johnny's and, as I had anticipated, seeing the light on, he opened the door fully to pull the cord that switched it off. At the sight of me he showed great surprise and asked, 'Dennis, what on earth are you doing here at this hour of night?'

Giving him a worried look, I replied, 'Trying to rewrite this bloody Bodyguard paper.'

'But why?' he enquired, coming into the room.

Throwing down my pencil, I sat back and said, 'Because if it goes in as it is, you are going to get the sack.'

He frowned, but sat down in the big armchair opposite my

Plan Bodyguard

desk, lit a cigarette and said quietly, 'I don't understand. Tell me what you mean.'

'It's this,' I told him. 'By your inserting paragraph after paragraph, it has become so long and complicated that no one will be able to understand it.'

'But,' he protested, 'all the arguments in it are in proper sequence and perfectly logical.'

'No doubt they are,' I retorted, 'but they give the impression that the plan has as much chance of success as you or I would have of getting round the Grand National course on an elderly cab horse. Four-fifths of it is devoted to pointing out every sort of unexpected happening that may cause it to fail.'

He shook his head. 'But, Dennis, we must put before the Chiefs the risks that will have to be run if they accept it. It would be utterly wrong to mislead them by allowing them to believe it is certain to be successful.'

'Agreed,' said I. 'But if it goes to them in its present form, they will come to the conclusion that it is bound to fail; that we have let them down and are incompetent to produce a sound cover plan. Then they'll sack the lot of us and get in a new team in the hope that it will produce something acceptable.'

For a moment he was silent, then he asked, 'Well, what do you suggest?'

'Look, Johnny,' I said, 'we've had a marvellous run of success. You have built this show up so that the Chiefs of Staff now have absolute confidence in your judgement. Give them all the reasons you can possibly think of why our plan should be shot to hell. But put them in an annexe. You know as well as I do that none of them will read it. They just haven't got the time. All that is needed is a very brief paper on the following lines: "The Controlling Officer and his section have made an intensive study of the conditions under which plan Overlord is to be carried out. Their conclusion is that the best hope of deceiving the enemy about the timing and our true objectives lies in the following steps being taken: A, B, C, D, etc. The reasons by which they have reached their conclusion are given in annexe A." It is a good plan and, believe me, they will swallow it like lambs. No one could possibly guarantee complete success and, should we have the ill-luck that something does go wrong, you will still be covered by the annexe.'

He smiled at me. 'I'll think it over, Dennis. Now let's go and have a night-cap in the mess.' We did, and then went home.

Next day, plan Bodyguard was completely redrafted. The paper itself was still longer than I would have wished and ran to three pages; but we managed to reduce the whole by at least a third and the major part of it was pushed into a five-page annexe. On 21 December it went to the Chiefs of Staff, and they accepted the whole of it without a murmur.

I was undoubtedly highly incompetent in the matter of staff duties. I took long lunches from which, at times, I returned slightly tight. I spent hours coffee-housing with my friends in the mess and the Air Ministry. I was lazy and indifferent about all minor problems to do with deception. But at least I saved dear, brilliantly capable but over-conscientious Johnny from being given a bowler hat by pushing him into redrafting plan Bodyguard.

Chapter 15
The Americans Force Anvil on Us

Christmas came and went. I forget how I spent it, but on New Year's Eve 1944, Joan and I gave another party in the basement restaurant at Chatsworth Court. As in the previous year, among our guests who sang 'Auld Lang Syne' with us, there were a score of Admirals, Generals, Air Marshals and members of the PM's entourage.

Mention of the latter reminds me that I have not yet said anything about 'Tommy' Thompson. He was a Commander, RN, and Churchill's personal ADC. I don't think Tommy was much concerned with the strategy of the war although, of course, he knew all about it because he was in constant attendance on his master; so present at innumerable conversations in which the PM chatted in private with his Cabinet colleagues, with Harry Hopkins (President Roosevelt's personal representative), Smuts, Ike, the Chiefs of Staff and many other war-time VIPs. Tommy's job was to see that the PM lacked for nothing – from new pairs of socks to the records he most enjoyed on the gramophone during weekends at Chequers.

It was on a question of supply that Tommy asked me one day to come up to his office above the PM's quarters. I had met Tommy shortly after I went into the Cabinet Offices, and on several occasions we had had meals together, so we were already good friends. Taking me into the mess next to his office, which had been established for the PM's people, he gave me a drink and told me his problem.

Tommy had come with the PM from the Admiralty where

Churchill had reigned as First Lord for the first nine months of the war. During that time Tommy had had the forethought to build up a fine cellar for him there. But when they moved to 10 Downing Street, the old man had generously insisted that its contents should all be left behind for the use of his successor. No. 10 had not been well-stocked by Chamberlain, so by now they were finding themselves very short of liquor – particularly champagne. Could I help?

I went to see my old friend, Eddie Tatham, the managing director of Justerini's, who had been far-sighted and laid in enormous stocks of wine before the war began. They were still able to supply their old customers, such as myself, with half a dozen bottles of spirits and a dozen or two of wine every month – and charged for them only the price to which the wines would have appreciated had there been no war. But Churchill had never been one of their customers. Nevertheless, Eddie agreed that it was a patriotic duty to keep Britain's champion supplied with liquor; so I was able to have some cases of champagne sent round to Tommy.

The greater part of the wine was consumed over weekends at Chequers or Chartwell. Churchill always had half a dozen guests staying to talk with him about the conduct of the war, see private cinema shows and stroll round the garden. At Chartwell there is a fine lake on which he kept a number of mandarin ducks. He enjoyed the strange belief that not only did all animals love him, but they also understood when he talked to them.

On summer evenings it was his custom to go out with his friends to the edge of the lake. With him he would take all the broken bread from the dinner table: then, cupping his hands, he would shout, 'Ahoy-ee! Ahoy-ee!' upon which all the ducks would come swimming over to be fed.

One evening Pug Ismay was in the party. As a constant visitor he knew the drill. Ill-advisedly, the PM turned to him and said, 'I bet you couldn't bring them over by just calling to them, Pug.'

Cupping his hands round his mouth, Pug shouted, 'Ahoy-ee! Ahoy-ee!' Obediently, the ducks came swimming over to receive their extra meal. Poor Churchill's face dropped.

Turning away he murmured in genuine distress, 'I do wish they hadn't done that.'

These weekends were hell for Pug. On Saturday and Sunday nights the PM would see one of the films that had been sent down for him, then sit up until two or three o'clock in the morning, nattering about the war with men of importance from many parts of the world. After a long day Pug would slump into bed. At about six o'clock his telephone would ring. Churchill, having slept throughout the afternoon, had woken fresh as a daisy, and would say:

'Pug, that was a most interesting idea that Dickie Mountbatten produced last night. Get on to the Joint Planning Staff, find out what they think, then write a short paper on it.'

So no more sleep for Pug, and he had to represent the PM at a meeting of the Chiefs of Staff at nine-thirty on the Monday morning! Yet such was his extraordinary recuperative power that, after a couple of pink gins in our little mess, he would prove the life and soul of the party at lunch.

In the Cabinet Offices we were all of the opinion that, once the Allied Expeditionary Force had firmly established a bridgehead in France, within another week or two Germany would collapse. Although that did not prove the case, it was a by no means unreasonable assumption. Our Intelligence sources suggested that Operation Point-blank (the great bombing offensive) was having a terrible effect on Berlin and Germany's other principal cities; that the German people were half-starved and utterly sick of the war; that her troops were no longer offensive-minded and, given a lead by anyone in authority, would only too gladly throw down their arms.

In consequence, the JPS turned their thoughts to a now foreseeable time when our enemy would surrender. On the assumption that by midsummer Germany would be finished, they produced a paper setting out what, as victors, our attitude should be towards the vanquished. This was just my cup of tea and I had very definite views on the subject, so I wrote a paper on it. Many historical peace treaties and the results that followed were quoted. My major contention was that, having won the war, certain conditions should be imposed on the enemy which would ensure our not losing the peace.

Just before Christmas Johnny had been in Lisbon to discuss deception measures with Henry Hopkinson (later Lord Colyton), who, for some time past, had acted as Minister of State from the Foreign Office in the Mediterranean theatre. It will be recalled that Henry had read a number of my papers written before I went into uniform and introduced me to General Brooks of PWE.

Now he suggested that, as a certain number of Portuguese clerks were employed in our Lisbon Air Attaché's office, we might pass a misleading document to the enemy, purporting it to have been stolen for them by one of these clerks.

It was a sound scheme; the only problem being the choice of a document that we might slightly alter, which would not have been too highly secret to be circulated to Air Attachés. This I succeeded in arranging with Group Captain Grierson, the Deputy Director of Plans (Air).

At the Teheran conference we had, for the first time, become on close terms with our Muscovite allies. Now that we had definitely pledged ourselves to open a Second Front – the Russians had always refused to recognize our landings in North Africa, Sicily and Italy in that light – they appeared willing really to co-operate and concert their future strategy with ours. By this time, too, the Chiefs had become so fully convinced of the value of strategic deception that they were anxious that the Russians should receive the benefit of our experience in practising it, and so decided to send Johnny on a mission to Moscow.

Johnny was most averse to this as he felt, rightly I think, that if the Russians were given knowledge of the methods we employed, the danger of their becoming known to the enemy would be greatly increased. But his objections were overruled: so, towards the end of January, off he went.

He put it to the Russians that Overlord would be greatly assisted if they could convince the enemy they intended to launch a major offensive in the summer against Finland, as this would cause the Germans to reinforce the Finnish front, drawing off reserves to the far north which, otherwise, might be sent against us in France.

The Americans Force Anvil on Us

In this the Russians did co-operate – and how! Instead of giving the sort of indications we employed in such cases – the concentration in the area of dummy tanks and aircraft, sending hundreds of empty lorries up to the front by day, then withdrawing them during the night and sending them up again, day after day, thus building up a skeleton army of 'notional' forces – they actually massed ten real divisions and launched an all-out attack against the Finns.

Naturally that served our purpose even better; but I have often wondered what lay at the bottom of the suggested threat's developing into a genuine offensive. When we learned of it, Johnny expressed quiet satisfaction and explained it by saying that the Russian interpreter had not been very good; so the General to whom he said his piece could not have understood him properly. Or was it that the wise and extremely security-minded Johnny had decided to ignore the Chiefs' orders and had not told the Russians anything worth knowing about deception?

I come now to the greatest operation of the war – the liberation of Europe. Churchill, as we know, had always been in favour of entering Hitler's Fortress Europa by way of what he termed 'the soft underbelly of the Axis'. That it was the right strategy I never doubted. Yugoslavia and Greece had far longer coastlines than northern France, Belgium and Holland, so the Germans could not possibly afford to keep strongly garrisoned all the areas where we might have landed. Moreover, they were so distant from Germany, and she had such poor communications with them, that they would have proved impossible to reinforce adequately for many weeks. By landing in the Balkans we might within quite a short time have put Germany's unwilling allies, Bulgaria, Rumania and Hungary, out of the war, then joined up with the Russians for a grand offensive from the east against the Third Reich itself.

But nothing would any longer dissuade the Americans from a head-on assault against the well-defended and easily reinforced 'Atlantic Wall', so Churchill had to accept Overlord with the best grace he could; but he still pressed for a minor operation against the Balkans, and that Alexander should be strongly reinforced in Italy, which would have enabled him to break through the Gap in the Karnische Alps and invade Austria and Hungary.

The Americans would not listen to him. Instead hey wanted Allied Forces in the Med. to be used for an invasion of southern France in the neighbourhood of the Riviera, with the object of driving north and joining up with the forces of Overlord. Again, as the forces that Britain could put into the field were not nearly as large as those of the United States, Churchill had to give way to their wishes. Overlord being the hammer, the operation against the Riviera was given the codename Anvil.

The decision to do Anvil was one of the greatest blunders that the Allies made in the war; the other was Alan Brooke's insistence that we should go into Sicily rather than Sardinia. But for them, the Allies would have been in Austria and Budapest, also possibly in Belgrade and Bucharest, before the Russians. The countries of these capitals would have been saved from Communism and the whole of post-war history altered to our immense benefit.

In the event, Anvil not only proved a waste of effort; it robbed us of great advantages that we might have gained in other areas. To create a large enough force to undertake it, Alexander's best divisions were taken away from him, with the result that he was unable to defeat the Germans in Italy until the very end of the war.

Churchill's negotiations with the Turks had reached a point at which they were seriously contemplating coming in on the side of the Allies. With the collapse of Italy, the great island of Rhodes could easily have been taken. We had not the forces in the Near East available. In vain Churchill begged the Americans to send a brigade to capture it. They refused, because they said they could not spare the troops from the build-up for Anvil. Rhodes lies off the mainland of Turkey, and the Germans swiftly took it over. The Turkish attitude changed at once. With an enemy-held base actually within sight of their shores, they would no longer consider coming in with us. So we lost an ally with a powerful army and an open door to the Balkans.

I was aware of all these discussions and that Alexander had actually declared at a C-in-Cs' meeting in London at

The Americans Force Anvil on Us

which both Churchill and Eisenhower were present: 'Leave me my present strength in Italy, and I promise you that I will be in Vienna before Monty is in Berlin.'

The following day, on returning from lunch, I happened to meet Alex crossing St James's Park. I did not then know him personally, but I gave him my smartest salute and said, 'The very best of luck in your battle, Sir,' which he acknowledged with a smile. It could not have even entered his mind that an RAF officer of my rank was referring to anything other than his campaign in Italy. But I was actually wishing him luck in his battle with the Americans. Alas, that was the one battle he lost.

To assist operations Overlord and Anvil, Dudley Clarke wrote a paper concerning deception measures to be taken in the Eastern Mediterranean theatre. It was a masterly assessment of the situation and a perfect illustration of the detailed implementation necessary to successful deception.

This immensely long and detailed plan is of particular interest because it was the product of a single brilliant mind. As the Commander of 'A' Force, Dudley had over a hundred officers under him; for, in addition to deception, he was responsible in the Mediterranean and Middle East for the work of MI9. This organization was controlled in Western Europe from London by Brigadier Norman Crockatt, whom I came to know well through his great friend, Eddie Combe. It dealt with all secret communications with our men who were prisoners of war, arranged their escape routes and so on.

A number of Dudley's officers were engaged in this work, but the majority of them were employed on tactical deception or on conveying false information by secret channels. Unlike Johnny, Dudley believed that security regarding Intelligence work came second to security about plans. So he had no opposite numbers to Ronald, James, Neil and myself. He worked without any planning staff at all, and no one was ever aware of the way his mind was working.

Chapter 16
Our Fake Army and Great *Coup* in Sweden

Now that we were well into the spring, not only were we working like demons on implementing the innumerable subsidiary plans connected with Bodyguard to deceive the enemy about the date and place of operation Overlord, we had also to think ahead to a time when the Normandy landings had taken place, and endeavour to concert measures, the object of which was to prevent the enemy from rapidly reinforcing his divisions which would be endeavouring to drive the Allies back into the sea.

The main plank in our new plan was the apparent creation of another great army in Kent making ready for a direct descent on the Pas de Calais. We had reason to think that the Germans supposed that to be the area in which our invasion force – which they were aware was being mustered – would attempt to land; so it was there that they had stationed the majority of their armoured divisions in the West.

Our task was to lead them to believe that the Normandy landings were only a feint in great strength, designed to draw their armour south, so that, when we launched a second invasion in the neighbourhood of Calais–Boulogne, it could establish itself almost unopposed north of the Seine and drive straight down on to Paris.

Neil Gordon Clark had already created many so-called 'notional' divisions, Corps HQ and so on; and, by way of Harold's secret channels, knowledge of them was being

Our Fake Army and Great *Coup* in Sweden 173

conveyed to the enemy. Actually, these fake formations consisted only of small bodies of men and vehicles, each with their own divisional signs. They, together with hundreds of dummy aircraft and gliders which were assembled on specially created airfields, were all concentrated on both sides of the Thames estuary, along the coast of which Alec Finter caused to be anchored hundreds of dummy landing craft. By these means we enabled enemy reconnaissance planes to report that a most powerful army was being mustered there in preparation for an invasion. This was further confirmed by an ever-increasing wireless traffic between these mock units. Meanwhile, every possible cover, including strict curtailment of communication by radio, was adopted to minimize the build-up in Hampshire of our real Expeditionary Force.

It had been one of the 'recommendations' in plan Bodyguard that no senior officers – other than Alex in Italy and Ike in the UK, whom the Germans already knew – should be named in connection with high commands, as this might have led to enemy Intelligence making certain correct deductions. To this there arose two exceptions.

The first was deliberate. We leaked it that George Patton had been given command of our fake First US Army Group (FUSAG) in Kent. It was highly plausible that this forceful American general had been selected by Ike to lead the invasion forces, and so would strengthen the enemy's belief that our real objective was the Pas de Calais.

The second was unforeseen and made us furious. I have been told that Ike asked for Alexander to direct the Normandy landings – this initial operation having been given the separate codename of Neptune – but as the Allied army in Italy was now being so greatly reduced in numbers to carry out Anvil, Churchill decided that Alex's brilliant generalship was needed to save us from possible calamity there. In any case Montgomery was appointed to carry out Neptune and brought back to London.

The knowledge that this had been done would be a clear indication to the Germans that the stories we were putting out about an invasion of the Balkans in the summer – to command which Monty was a natural choice – were probably a bluff; that our invasion of France would be led by him, and his having returned to England in the spring indicated that it would take place in the summer instead of not until the autumn, as we wished the enemy to believe.

Monty was, of course, asked to live quietly outside London, wear civilian clothes and be seen by as few people as possible. Yet what did this vainglorious fellow do? Ignoring the fact that he might seriously jeopardize our cover plans, he took a suite at Claridges; then in uniform, his chest a blaze of medal ribbons, went on his first night back in London to the Palladium. There, standing in the front of a box, well before the curtain went up, he remained for five minutes receiving a standing ovation from the audience.

The Joint Planning Staff of our War Cabinet had, on and off, for years examined the problem of a return to France. Then General Morgan's Allied Planning Staff at Norfolk House had done likewise for many months. Between them they embodied a high proportion of the best brains in the British and American armies. Both staffs had reached the conclusion that three divisions, with two more on the following tide, should be sufficient for the initial assault; they would be supported by further divisions landing on successive days until some twenty divisions were ashore. So there was no question of the five divisions first landed being left unsupported for more than twenty-four hours. And during that time they would have the cover of tremendous fire from the big and small guns of our warships, not to mention overwhelmingly superior air power to protect them from the Luftwaffe.

But Montgomery's victories had always depended on his having a butterfly net and sledgehammer to kill a wasp. He – and it must be said Eisenhower – flatly refused to go unless he could be given five divisions for the first landing with three more on the following tide.

People who have little knowledge of such matters cannot be expected to grasp immediately what this meant. It entailed our finding more than half as much again of everything required for landing on an enemy-held coast. Overlord had to be postponed for a month. Our strategy in the Far East was ruined, because Mountbatten's operation against Burma had to be abandoned so that his landing craft could be brought home to ship over Monty's three extra divisions. Our fishing fleets had to be denuded of seamen to get them across. A thousand seagoing tugs had to be brought over from America, and so on and so on.

Two assets only can be given to Montgomery. He was a truly dedicated soldier, with an encyclopaedic knowledge of the Army, and he was a magnificent morale-builder. In the weeks before D-Day he made a tour of the forces mustered for the invasion. At every camp he had all officers and men gather round his jeep and addressed them in the following fashion:

'We are going to France together. You are coming with me and you have nothing to fear. It is going to be a walk-over.'

His words carried complete conviction and the men cheered him to the echo. To have achieved such confidence in his leadership, and the affection of his troops, which he never lost, was a tremendous contribution to the unexpectedly long-sustained effort that had to be made before they finally defeated the enemy.

But, unlike Alexander and Slim, he never won a battle against superior forces, and he was largely responsible for at least one costly blunder – the misuse of our airborne troops which led to the disaster at Arnhem. He won his victories only by the possession of enormous fire-power. Moreover he was so arrogant that he treated our American allies with contempt; so that instead of the friendly relations which should have existed between him and their Army Group Commanders, many of them came to loathe him.

But back to our own activities. Towards the end of January, Johnny decided that it would be a good thing to get out a report on the results of strategic deception to date. As I was the oldest inhabitant of our 'village' I wrote the first draft. The final paper was sent to the Chiefs of Staff in February.

A problem that concerned us was the press. We felt that, if skilfully handled, Fleet Street could be of considerable assistance to us in misleading the enemy about our intentions. But a standing order forbade us deliberately to misinform the press. Nevertheless, many editors and leading journalists had excellent sources of information, and it was certain that they would learn a lot about Overlord before the operation actually took place. Speculative articles on the subject were most undesirable; and it seemed to us that, if we took certain editors into our confidence, far from abusing it they would give us their willing co-operation. So we got out a paper on the subject.

We now come to plan Graffham. This was a subsidiary of Bodyguard but a very important one. It will be recalled that many months before, when we had first been considering cover plans for Overlord, I had written a paper which I headed *Essorbee*; the theme of which was that no frontier of Hitler's Fortress Europa should be left unthreatened if the maximum possible number of German divisions were to be kept away from the Normandy beaches.

As the full implementation of this plan would have necessitated our threatening several neutral countries, the Foreign Office, at that time, had flatly refused to countenance our proceeding on such lines. But it is rightly said that 'water wears away a stone'. My colleagues in LCS, and many of my friends on the JPS who read the paper, realized the soundness of my arguments. And I have no doubt that numerous much more highly placed people than myself held the same views. The result was that, under pressure from many sides, the Foreign Office had gradually been pushed into giving way. A paper had been circulated early in March which had brought about this more satisfactory state of affairs.

To this paper I personally wrote a follow-up that had special reference to Norway and Sweden. It was circulated as 'Annexe II'. Apart from cover plans for new offensives by great forces, it led to one of our most successful deceptions in the whole war.

Montgomery's demand for five divisions in the initial assault meant postponing the invasion for a month, and thus threw every plan connected with Overlord completely out of gear. For cover planning, timing so that the enemy may be taken by surprise is the most vital of all factors. In this case the unforeseen delay was definitely dangerous, as we had been steadily implementing Bodyguard from the beginning of the year; and the longer enemy Intelligence was given to investigate and check the ruses we were using to deceive him, the greater chance there was of his discovering our true intentions.

Having no alternative, we readjusted all our plans.

Our minister in Stockholm, Sir Victor Mallet, was recalled to London for consultations, and he attended several meetings with us in our basement. We learned from him that, while the majority of the Swedish people were now pro-Ally and the Air Force strongly so, a great part of the Army was still pro-German. Moreover, he felt that the Swedes generally would consider it unchivalrous to jump on the bandwagon of the victors, now that Germany was being forced on to the defensive; so it was unlikely that Sweden could be persuaded to enter the war on the side of the Allies.

However, he proved most willing to help us with our deception plans and approved the idea that someone of importance should be sent on a special mission to talk to Lieutenant-General Bengt Nordenskiöld, the Commander-in-Chief of the Swedish Air Force, who, fortunately, was pro-Ally so could be counted on to give our emissary a friendly reception.

Who should be sent was the next question, and Sir Victor suggested that, as Wing Commander Thornton, our pre-war Air Attaché in Stockholm, had been on particularly good terms with Nordenskiöld, he might achieve better results than a more prominent personality.

I soon located the sometime Wing Commander and learned that he had become Air Vice-Marshal Thornton, Second in Command Bomber Command, so I feared that there was very little chance of getting him seconded from such an important post to do a job for us in Sweden. But I had underrated the enormous prestige that strategic deception, and Johnny in particular, had now achieved with the Chiefs of Staff. He asked for Thornton and the Air Vice-Marshal was promptly ordered to leave his post and take Johnny's instructions.

Thornton duly flew to Stockholm in civilian clothes and was whisked from the airport to the British Embassy in a car with the blinds down. He remained there for the rest of his stay, except for one visit to General Nordenskiöld's HQ.

into and out of which he was smuggled through a back door. These precautions to preserve secrecy were taken, not with the intention of concealing him from the Germans, but to excite their interest in the visitor. One of their agents photographed everyone who entered our Embassy; so it was a foregone conclusion that they would shortly identify Thornton as the ex-Air Attaché and realize that, as a friend of Nordenskiöld's, he had been sent over on a special mission.

The case that Thornton put to Nordenskiöld was based on my Annexe II to our paper of March. It was to the following effect:

If the Allies invade Norway, the Germans will probably decide to withdraw from it. In view of what they have done in other countries, it seems certain that, before leaving, they will murder the thousands of prominent Norwegians that they now hold prisoner in internment camps, blow up Norwegian harbours and do everything they can to wreck all those facilities without which the Norwegian people would be left in a most desperate plight. Our expeditionary force could not hope to overcome German resistance in time to prevent these horrors. But it is in Sweden's power to do so. We shall have drawn off all the Germans, so Norway's long frontier with Sweden will be wide open. We do not ask you to declare war on Germany but, on the day we invade, send your army in as a police force, to protect the rights of humanity.

General Nordenskiöld was deeply impressed. He would not, of course, commit himself; but he promised to give the matter very serious consideration and discuss it with his government.

What the Swedes eventually decided I do not know; but that was immaterial to us. What did matter was that the deception had been put over. Nordenskiöld had been led to believe that we intended to invade Norway, and he would pass on that information to ministers whom he thought he could trust. But through one or more of them it was certain that the Germans would learn of the proposal which Thornton had put to him.

They did learn of it. But not through a Swedish minister, and far more swiftly than we could possibly have expected.

Our Fake Army and Great *Coup* in Sweden

It was not until after the war that we knew the result of plan Graffham. Like other members of Hitler's staff who were captured, his Chief Staff Officer, Field Marshal Keitel, was for many days interrogated by Allied Intelligence officers. This was his account of what happened, which Johnny told me one night in 1946.

General Nordenskiöld was pro-Ally, but the Swedish chief of police was pro-German and he had 'bugged' the General's room. In consequence every word exchanged between Nordenskiöld and Thornton had been recorded. Realizing their significance, the chief of police had at once had them coded and sent to Berlin. Within three hours Keitel placed a decoded transcript on Hitler's desk at Berchtesgaden. Having read the message, Hitler brought his clenched fist down on his desk with a bang, and cried: 'I've always told you that those pig-headed British would go back to Norway. Reinforce it with two divisions at once.'

And the Führer had to be obeyed. We had another 30,000 Germans standing on their flat feet in Norway to no good purpose when we launched Overlord.

Throughout April and May our preparations for D-Day continued with ever-increasing intensity. In order to implement Bodyguard in every possible way, a dozen supplementary plans had to be formulated and put into execution. Together and individually we wrote scores of papers.

At this time Air Vice-Marshal Thornton and Derrick Morley were both in Stockholm and, on 7 April, we received a long telegram from Derrick reporting the progress of plan Graffham and difficulties that the Swedes were raising about giving us various facilities in their country that we were now demanding.

By this time Graffham was considered by Johnny to be of such importance that he nominated a committee specially to deal with it. Ronald Wingate was Chairman and the members were: Foreign Office, Anthony Nutting; Air Ministry (Policy), Wing Commander Peveler; Eisenhower's HQ, Colonel Noel Wild: Ministry of Economic Warfare, Mr Dingle Foot; and LCS, Neil Gordon Clark and myself.

The Swedes were desperately short of petrol and various

other commodities, and most anxious to acquire our latest types of fighter aircraft for their air force. These we could barter for permission to fly our reconnaissance aircraft over Sweden, use their airfields to land on in an emergency and allow the pilots to fly their machines home again, instead of being interned; and stop the supply of ball-bearings to the Germans.

All this helped to build up the picture we wanted. Johnny Bevan produced the brilliant idea of getting the Bank of England to buy up many thousands of pounds' worth of Norwegian government bonds, then at a very low price. An excellent indication that we meant to re-conquer Norway.

Finally it was decided that on D plus 2 of Overlord Sir Victor Mallet and his American colleague should present the Swedish government with a formal demand that the Swedish army should seize the Norwegian port of Trondheim – an advance of only twenty miles from the Swedish frontier – and that, should they agree, a deception plan should at once be put into operation to cause the Germans to believe that Swedish forces were being concentrated in the south for an attack on German-occupied Denmark. If they did not agree, we intended to use deception measures to persuade the Germans that they had and that a new front was about to be opened in the north.

The build-up of a great 'notional' army centred on the Thames estuary also went on apace. It was referred to as 'Third Army Group, C-in-C General George Patton'. We established in the minds of the enemy that the First US Army, including British troops, was assembling in East Anglia. Small units wore the same divisional signs as those of the divisions of our famous Eighth Army, and, through measures concerted with Dudley Clarke, it was conveyed to German Intelligence that the Eighth Army was being brought back from Italy to form part of Patton's Third Army Group – which would carry out the decisive invasion of the Continent via the Pas de Calais. This deception operation had its own codename – plan Foynes – and entailed an enormous amount of fake Order of Battle work by Neil Gordon Clark.

As further evidence for enemy reconnaissance aircraft that the main invasion was to be launched from the Kent–Essex

Our Fake Army and Great *Coup* in Sweden

area, we had hutted extensions made to the hospitals there as though we expected great numbers of casualties to be returned after our landings, cages erected to receive prisoners of war and additional airfields made. We put it across that the latter were to be used for a great fleet of helicopters that we were relying on for ferrying over much of our supplies. Our story was that, to preserve secrecy, the helicopters had been built and their pilots trained in the USA, and they would arrive only just before the invasion.

Most of this information was fed to the enemy through Lieutenant-Colonel 'Tar' Robertson, our long-invaluable collaborator in MI5, and by Major Roger Hesketh, a member of Noel Wild's staff who spent his time running between Norfolk House, Harold Peteval and the HQ of MI5 in St James's Street.

One of Hesketh's best channels was a lady, codename Theresa. She was a Russian-born refugee from France, who was said to have taken a hate against the British because on her arrival here her little dog, to which she was devoted, had been put in quarantine and died there.

Another, and undoubtedly Hesketh's best double-agent, was known as 'Garbo'. By a very skilful build-up, German Intelligence had been led to grade all the material he sent them as A1. When the collapse was near at hand he informed them that he was leaving for South America. They signalled to him, 'How are you going?' Hesketh told us with a laugh that he had had Garbo reply with the one word, 'Clandestinely.'

Towards the end of April we sent the Chiefs our final draft of Bodyguard.

The original of the paper was stamped on top with the word Bigot in letters three-quarters of an inch high. Hitherto the degrees of secrecy had been 'Confidential', 'Secret' and 'Most Secret', the latter having some months earlier been changed to 'Top Secret', so as to come into line with American procedure. But the nearer we came to D-Day, the more people had to be let into the know about our preparations for Overlord: railway and post-office officials, harbour masters, dock superintendents and scores of other civilians, not to mention the ever-increasing numbers of officers of the services who had various parts to play. In consequence, ISSB became greatly worried about security and, to limit the number of people having access to documents of the very highest secrecy, created this super-degree by which only a very limited number of officers were allowed to see papers stamped Bigot.

All of us in LCS were, of course, on the Bigot list, but in our case it made little difference as our papers always travelled to other departments in red or black boxes, or, failing that, 'by hand of officer', the envelopes being sealed with a label having on it in large red letters, 'To be opened only by ─────────', then one wrote in the name of the officer for whom it was intended.

Chapter 17
The Secret Weapon, Spies and the False Montgomery

There now arose a very serious new danger. As far back as December 1941 there had been rumours that the Germans were constructing a new type of weapon with which they would be able to bombard London. The early reports had been so vague that for fifteen months not much notice had been taken of them; but in April 1943 General Ismay had sent a memo to the PM stating that, in the opinion of the Chiefs of Staff, German experiments with long-range rockets had reached a stage when definite facts about them must be obtained. This had resulted in a committee being formed under the chairmanship of Duncan Sandys, to carry out a full investigation. During the next few months it was learned that a considerable number of Germany's leading scientists and engineers, and a very large labour force, had been concentrated at Peenemünde on the island of Usedom in the Baltic; and it was there that experiments with this secret weapon were being carried out.

By then, the War Cabinet and the Chiefs had become so concerned about this new menace that it was decided to launch a great bomber attack on Peenemünde. The raid was carried out in August, and it was so successful that photographs taken from reconnaissance aircraft on the following days showed that the experimental station had been almost entirely destroyed.

It was thought that this had put an end to the menace – at all events for a long time to come. But in the autumn reconnaissance of the French Channel coast showed a new activity.

In many places the enemy was constructing small launching sites and, in a few cases, very large ones. Later it was learned that, although the destruction of Peenemünde had proved a heavy setback, it had not forced the Germans to abandon the project. The work was being pushed forward in a new experimental station in the great caves in the Hartz mountains, which could not be destroyed by bombing, and that tests of the new weapon were being carried out in distant Poland.

In the highest circles, where alone this was known, alarm spread again, and the RAF was ordered to destroy the launching sites on the French coast. In this, although many raids were carried out, they were only partially successful. Most of the sites were well camouflaged, and no sooner were some blotted out than new ones were located. Thus by May matters had developed into a race. Would our invasion take place in time to capture the sites before the enemy could make use of them, or would he be able to launch his attack first, and perhaps destroy London?

As the representative of LCS, I attended several of the rocket committee meetings. At one, with Sir Findlater Stewart in the chair, a Home Office expert gave us an appreciation of the effect such a rocket falling on London would have. It was said to weigh seventy tons and have a twenty-ton warhead.

A boffin who was present said he had worked it out that one such rocket landing on a densely populated area would turn a square quarter of a mile of London into rubble, kill 4000 people and cause a further 10,000 casualties.

I left the meeting in no happy frame of mind; only slightly consoled by an assessment – based upon God alone knows what – that the enemy would be able to send over only one per day.

A few of us accepted this new threat philosophically. Joan had remained on in London all through the blitz; so had Bill Elliot's wife, Rosemary, and Midge, the wife of our youngest Air Vice-Marshal, the Director of Air Intelligence, Frank Inglis. She was a supervisor in a factory that made model enemy aircraft to enable our pilots to distinguish

The Secret Weapon, Spies and the False Montgomery 185

enemy from friend. Johnny Bevan's wife, Lady Barbara, had done even better. She was a marvellous mimic and, under an assumed name, took a job in a munitions factory in north London. Owing to her forceful personality, her sense of humour and her ability to talk like a born Cockney, her fellow workers made her their shop steward!

But such women were a tiny minority. By far the greater part of our Admirals, Generals and Air Marshals had, at the opening of the war – very sensibly – sent their wives and children to live in the country. As the blitz had lessened in ferocity and the danger of living in London became almost negligible, these wives and children, bored to tears by exile from their friends, had gradually drifted back to the metropolis.

Now these husbands found themselves in a most unhappy situation. On security grounds – unlike Alan Brooke, who told his wife so much – the greater part of these honest senior officers felt that they could not possibly tell their wives that within a few weeks it was on the cards that London would be reduced to a heap of rubble with them buried under it. Yet what excuse could they produce for saying to their wives: 'Darling, don't you think it would be a good idea if you went back to our lovely little cottage in Cornwall,' or, as the case might be, 'that horrid lodging in Wales, for the summer months'?

Many of my friends who held high rank did not conceal from me how intensely worried they were about the safety of their wives and children in the event of Hitler's secret weapon being brought into play.

Sir Findlater Stewart's committee recommended emergency measures which were given the highest priority. The Home Office established enormous dumps of tentage and tinned food well outside London for the relief of the thousands of refugees who would come flooding out of the metropolis. Special arrangements were made for the swift evacuation of hospitals and schools, and railway schedules re-arranged to ensure that the maximum number of trains would be available to get people away after the first missile fell.

A major anxiety was that, when it did, the population

would panic and wild disorder ensue. LCS was asked to produce a cover plan that could be broadcast to reassure the people not in the immediate vicinity of the first great bang as to its cause. Our response was to put out that a petrol barge had exploded in the Thames.

Knowledge of the menace was kept, as far as possible, from the public, although the precautions being taken necessitated a considerable number of officials' having to be told about it. But only a small circle were aware of the magnitude of the terror with which we were faced – that even half a dozen of these giant missiles might destroy the whole of central London.

Those were dark days. It was a terrible secret to have to carry about, and I was no less frightened for Joan, my family and myself than were most of my colleagues and the senior officers in the know for those dear to them.

But at least one of us treated the threat with contempt – my good friend, Eddie Combe, MC and Bar, who had fought the First World War in France from Mons to the Armistice. One night, when Joan was on leave up at Welshpool, Eddie and I cooked a lobster in brandy in the kitchen of my little flat in Chatsworth Court.

Afterwards we talked about the missile and Eddie said, 'I don't believe there is any real justification for getting the wind up. When it does come, I bet you a magnum it will be no worse than the blitz. Anyhow, when the first has fallen, I'm game to go out and wait for the second walking round Piccadilly Circus without a battle bowler.' Good old Eddie!

By this time I was becoming decidedly short of money. In consequence, I decided that, as the pay of a Wing Commander was considerably higher than that of a Squadron Leader, I must get myself promoted. Very fortunately several of my Air Ministry friends had remarked, from time to time, that I was long overdue for another ring; one of them mentioned this one day in our little mess and gave me just the excuse I needed to take the matter up with Johnny. I wrote him a letter about it. He asked me to come to see him in his room the following day and assured me that I had always given him the impression I was entirely indifferent to promotion, but he would willingly have me put up. Even then there were two or three months' delay, as my old friend, Tubby Dawson, who had recently returned to the Air Ministry as an Air Commodore and Director of Plans (Air), mislaid the memo recommending my promotion. I had, with some diffidence, to raise the matter again; then, at last, in July I became, as the French say, *'un Colonel de l'Air'*.

Unlike us civilians in uniform who made up the LCS, the other members of the Joint Planning Staff were all Regulars, so served on it for only a limited period – usually eighteen months to two years – then they were posted to a command on active service. As the STRATS and FOPS together numbered fifteen officers, this meant that every month or two one of them left, and a new man arrived to take his place. In consequence, as I worked in the fortress basement for three years, I came to know well some thirty officers of the three services who had been specially picked to become planners. I also worked closely with Dudley Clarke, Peter Fleming and several of the officers under them, the members of ISSB and with a number of the officers on the executive planning staffs in the ministries.

And plan we did, morning, noon and night, constantly racking our brains for further ideas that, if exploited, might cause the enemy to become fully convinced that plan Bodyguard indicated our true intentions.

All these schemes had, of course, to be put over to the enemy. For this LCS remained responsible. The deception section formed under Noel Wild in January at COSSAC had been given the name of 'Ops B'. In due course it went overseas and had its quarters at SHAEF. But it was never given the same status as Dudley's 'A' Force in the Med. or Peter Fleming's 'Echelon D' in the Far East. Both the latter worked directly under the Supreme Commander in their respective theatres; whereas 'Ops B' merely formed part of the SHAEF Operations Division.

In fact until they did go overseas they remained virtually a subsidiary of LCS, dealing only with tactical deception. That in itself was a very considerable work, as it entailed the implementation of plan Fortitude,* the build-up of the false invasion force centred on the Thames estuary.

Meanwhile all secret means of conveying false information to the enemy continued to be implemented by a committee of Johnny's, which met daily. Noel Wild was naturally made a member of it, but only so that he might be fully 'in the picture'. The FO, SOE, and PWE were all employed to add greater plausibility to the deceptions, but the major part in this work was carried out by a section of MI5 headed by Tar Robinson.

James, Neil and I, as planners, were not supposed to know anything about these secret Intelligence activities; but, of course, we did, and the following were the principal double agents used for the purpose.

Garbo was a Spanish liberal who had fought for Franco in the Civil War, but became disgruntled and was convinced that only Britain could lead Europe into becoming truly democratic. However, the British Embassy in Madrid had refused his services. Disgruntled again, he had moved to Lisbon and, for a while, worked for the Germans, but thought better of it and again offered his services to the British. We had then taken him on and brought him to England in April 1942 where, as cover, he was given a job in the Ministry of Information. He had a fictitious ring of twenty-four spies working under him and the information he sent to the Germans was always grade A1.

Brutus was a Polish officer who had escaped to France in 1939. He had set up a network there in the Allied cause, but was arrested by the Germans in 1941. However, he succeeded in persuading them that they had converted him to the Nazi faith and got himself sent as one of their agents to England in 1942.

Tricycle was a Yugoslav lawyer. He was recruited by the Germans in Belgrade, but got in touch with the British Embassy and was secured a passage for England in December 1940. His main source, as far as the Germans – who still believed him to be working for them – were concerned, was his friend 'Frank', who was ADC to the King of Yugoslavia.

*Fortitude North covering Scandinavia, and Fortitude South covering the Pas de Calais.

The Secret Weapon, Spies and the False Montgomery 189

Tate was a Nazi dropped by parachute in September 1940. Converted by our people, he was allowed to live under observation in Hampstead. His contact was in Hamburg and he was graded by us as high as Garbo and Brutus. But after the war we learned that the Germans had never accepted him on that level, and little of the stuff he sent was regarded as reliable by the OKW.

Treasure was a temperamental French lady of Russian origin, recruited by the Germans before the war.

The above five all had wireless and were in regular contact with the German Secret Service.

In addition to the five double agents who had wireless, there were many others who sent their communications by codes or the use of secret inks in letters via neutral countries. Among them:

Artist operated in Lisbon.

Bronx, a Peruvian diplomat.

Super, a Belgian Air Force pilot.

Mullet and Puppet, English and Austrian businessmen, worked through Dr Koessler, an Austrian Jew who had settled in Brussels before the war.

Cobweb and Beetle put stuff over from Iceland.

Pandora, whose real name was Herr Hempel, was the German Minister in Dublin. He was made use of by being sent anonymous letters containing information from people who purported to be Nazi sympathizers. In all innocence he passed on, by his Embassy wireless, the stuff sent him.

A great deal of work was required to keep these double agents going with a mass of accurate but unimportant information; and then, now and again, with some really good line of deception. Therefore, all the principal ones were managed by an officer each. Garbo was undoubtedly the most successful and his 'case officer' was Major Roger Fleetwood Hesketh, a charming and witty man, with one of the best cellars of claret in England.

Another side to the activities of LCS was concerned with security. Had the enemy learned the size of the great army being mustered in Hampshire and that FUSAG in Kent and Essex really consisted only of some 1500 officers and men carrying on ceaseless wireless traffic and other ruses, plan Bodyguard would have become a busted flush. So we constantly pressed for more rigorous censorship.

In late March we had airmail between England and Lisbon stopped.

In April travel to Ireland was banned, and certain parts of the English coast were banned to visitors.

In April, too, all service leave was stopped and censorship was imposed on diplomatic mail.

Naturally, this last measure led to the Ambassadors of neutral countries creating a tremendous fuss, as supervision of their correspondence had never before been imposed. The Foreign Office, as might be expected, gave at the knees under the storm of protest and Johnny had to fight tooth and nail to prevent Anthony Eden's restoring to the foreign Embassies their long-enjoyed diplomatic privilege immediately after D-Day. As it was still absolutely vital to prevent knowledge from reaching the enemy that General Patton's FUSAG was only a paper army, Johnny went straight to Ike, and he won. Censorship of diplomatic bags was continued until June, service leave was not restored until August, and the visitors' ban not lifted until September.

The Prime Minister also aided the deception by stating in Parliament that many raids in great strength would take place before the full-scale invasion of the Continent was launched.

On Tubby Dawson's returning to us as Director of Plans (Air), Bill Elliot had been promoted to Air Vice Marshal and sent as AOC to Gibraltar. In May I received the following letter from him, which he had found time to write in his own hand:

Air Headquarters,
Gibraltar
16 May, 1944

My dear Dennis,

It has been sadly on my mind that in the rush of leaving London I never said goodbye to you or to your wife. Gummer is going home and will tell you that I now have had the tables turned on me, and that I am diligently acting as your obedient servant – and, may I say, enjoying my new rôle.

I am asking him to take home to you a bottle of Solero '47 as

The Secret Weapon, Spies and the False Montgomery

a token of my appreciation of many good glasses of wine presented to me by you. My love to those who remember me in Plans and to John Bevan, and my kindest regards to your wife. I hope you and she have good news of your sons.
Yours ever,
William Elliot.

Gummer, who brought me the bottle of sherry, was Dudley's 'Man at Gib'. Bill refers to having the tables turned on him and being delighted to act as my obedient servant. To this there hangs a tale.

The vital importance of misleading the enemy about the date of D-Day has already been mentioned. One thing we felt certain German Intelligence would expect was that, shortly before D-Day, the Allies would launch an all-out offensive in Italy, with the object of preventing any enemy divisions there from being withdrawn and sent to France. In view of this, it was plausible that the General responsible for the Neptune landings would fly out to General Alexander's HQ to concert plans with him, and the enemy knew that Montgomery was to direct the invasion. Therefore, if Monty could be shown to have left Britain for Italy on, say, D−1, they would deduce that the invasion was definitely not going to take place during the next few days.

Obviously Monty would be far too fully occupied to take a trip to Italy the day before he was to land in France. But we might be able to find someone capable of impersonating him.

With this in mind, we went to a firm in Wardour Street which furnished us with a number of large volumes containing photographs of scores of small-part actors. In it we found one of a Mr M. E. Clifton James, who had the same long nose and in other respects a definite resemblance to our headache-making General. Enquiries revealed that Clifton James had become a Lieutenant in the Pay Corps and was stationed up in Scotland.

He was ordered down to London and interviewed at the War Office. James was told nothing about the purpose for which he was wanted, but simply asked if he was prepared to go overseas. Being middle-aged, he replied that he didn't really want to, but added very properly that if it was for some special service to his country, he would. To his astonishment it was then revealed to this very ordinary officer that he was wanted to become an understudy to the great General.

With no further information he was packed off to the north, where the General was then on leave. Monty, having been duly briefed about our plan, played up very well. On several occasions he took James out fishing with him and gave him plenty of opportunities to study his way of holding himself and his mannerisms.

They then returned to London. In great secrecy, James was fitted with a uniform ablaze with decorations and an aircraft was provided to take him to Gibraltar.

The plan was that he should arrive there fairly early in the morning, be received by the Governor, General Mason McFarlane and Bill Elliot, inspect a guard of honour, be motored off to breakfast at Government House, return to the airfield and, with due honours, be flown off to Algiers, where Dudley would take charge of him.

The airfield at Gibraltar was in clear view of Algeciras. We knew that on the top of a tall building there a powerful telescope had been mounted through which, from dawn to dusk, relays of German agents kept watch on the airfield and duly reported anything of interest that took place on it. It was therefore a certainty that within a few hours of 'Monty's' arrival, it would be known that he had passed through Gib and assumed that he was on his way to make final arrangements with Alex.

Everything seemed to be in good train when, only a couple of days before the operation was due to take place, someone asked, 'Has James ever flown? If not, he may be airsick, and it would be calamitous if our Monty staggered out of the aircraft vomiting all over the place.'

The question was put to Clifton James and his reply was, 'No. I've never travelled by air.' On hearing this, Johnny turned to me, and said, 'Dennis, this is your job. Take him up and fly him somewhere.'

Of course he did not mean literally, as I can't even drive a car. But I laid on an aircraft for next morning and arranged a flight. To my relief, James was not airsick.

The Secret Weapon, Spies and the False Montgomery 193

I never saw him again. But the ruse was 100 per cent successful. He played his part admirably. General McFarlane and Bill Elliot received him with due honours at Gibraltar. Just in case the telescope at Algeciras happened to be unmanned that morning, they had arranged for a wealthy Spaniard who was known to be pro-German to call at Government House on some cooked-up business so that he should catch sight of James as they went in to breakfast. Later we learned that, within a few hours, Berlin had been informed that Monty had passed through Gib, presumably on his way to confer with Alex. The obvious conclusion was that the invasion would not take place for several days. But it did next day.

The ending to this story is rather pathetic. James was flown on to Algiers. Dudley met him, had him taken to a small hotel where he exchanged his gorgeous plumage for an ordinary Lieutenant's battledress, gave him a bottle of whisky and told him not to leave his room until further orders.

The poor fellow had outlived his usefulness. Flying people from Algiers to England was a matter of priorities and his was now the lowest. For six weeks he remained virtually a prisoner, before he was at last flown home. Sworn to secrecy, he then saw out the remainder of the war without promotion in the Pay Corps.

A few years after the war, in an unguarded moment he told his story, and a journalist happened to be among his audience. Within a matter of days it was in all the newspapers. He could have been imprisoned under the Official Secrets Act, but I am happy to think that the authorities took no action against him and, the story having been blown, allowed him to have a 'ghost' write it for him in a book entitled *I Was Monty's Double*, which was later filmed with Clifton James playing himself.

I have always felt that he was treated shabbily in that no recognition was given to him for the considerable service he had performed very efficiently. But at least he had had one great day out in his life that no one could take from him; and that is more than many people can say.

Now that we were on the very last lap towards our tremen-

G

dous gamble, there was little more that Johnny and his team could do; but I was fortunate enough to witness the raising of the curtain.

I do not think that I have so far mentioned Air Chief Marshal Sir Richard Peck. He was Assistant Chief of Air Staff (G), the G standing for General or 'all the dirty, thankless tasks that other Assistant Chiefs had neither the time nor the inclination to do'. As I was a planner he was right off my beat, but I was introduced to him quite early on by Air Commodore Vachell.

He or his wife must have had private means, as they lived in Grosvenor House, Park Lane, and he had the same table for lunch reserved for him every day at Quaglino's. Soon after I went into uniform, he used to ask me to lunch with him there about once a month. This was, in part, returning hospitality, but I always had a shrewd suspicion that there was a bit more to it than that.

Richard Peck was, as we termed it, 'below the salt', on the principle that no officer who was not directly concerned in a plan or operation should be allowed to know about it. Peck, who had a most enquiring mind, used these occasions to pick my brains about what was going on. That suited me quite well. Inevitably, men of such high rank were in a position to know, unofficially, the state of the parties; so I did little more than confirm some of his intelligent guesses, thereby gaining his goodwill, which, on occasions, proved useful to LCS.

This usefulness was at times when for our own purposes we wanted certain items of information published in the press. Directors of Public Relations were on Brigadier level, but Peck took a special interest in such matters, greatly assisting his Air Commodore (PR) by frequently appearing at press conferences; which, in view of his high rank, largely contributed to the fact that the RAF received much greater coverage than either of the other services.

During the preparations for D-Day Richard Peck had asked me to come up to see him. When I arrived in his room, he said: 'Dennis, when Overlord takes place, the American papers will hog the whole of the operation and hardly give us a paragraph. But I am determined that the American

The Secret Weapon, Spies and the False Montgomery 195

public shall be told that the British went, too; that it was mainly the Royal Navy that covered the landings, that the RAF and our Army played just as important a part as their United States opposite numbers. There is only one way in which I can do this. I've not a hope with the dailies. But, given the names of authors who are sufficiently well known, I can get articles into the weeklies and monthlies; so I am combing the RAF for such chaps and asking for them to be assigned to me as special war correspondents for the few days needed to cover the landings. Are you prepared to play?'

'Of course, sir,' I replied. 'I'd be only too delighted.'

In consequence, he applied for me to be seconded to him, and I asked Johnny to let me go. Although there was no longer any urgent work for which I was required by LCS, he was reluctant to give his consent, and said the matter must be referred to General Ismay.

Pug, no doubt briefed by Johnny, took the view that I knew much too much to be allowed to fly over enemy-held beaches. If the aircraft happened to be shot down and I survived the crash, the Gestapo might screw my thumbs off and cause me to reveal any number of secrets they were eager to know.

Bitterly disappointed, I reported this decision to Peck; but he produced a way of getting round the difficulty. He said: 'General Ismay is right, of course. But if you did fly over the beaches, you would see nothing but dense clouds of smoke. I have a much more interesting assignment for you, to which there can be no possible objection. You shall go down to Harwell and write me a description of the 6th Airborne Division, the spearhead of the army of liberation, taking off for France.'

Permission was accordingly granted for me to become, for a few days, a war correspondent. Very early on the morning of 3 June, I left London for Harwell in an Air Ministry car.

Chapter 18
D-Day

We sped along the Great West Road, which was almost empty of traffic, to Maidenhead. In peacetime the river would have been gay with picnic parties in punts and launches; now it was still and deserted. On we went past the even lovelier upper reaches of the Thames, passing a large meadow near Goring, which brought back to my mind a scene of thirty years earlier.

On that night of 3 August 1914, I slept in a tent in that field with a Yeomanry Regiment. At one o'clock in the morning we were awakened by the order to break camp and return to London. Next day Great Britain entered the First World War against Germany. After nearly four and a half years we fought the Germans to a standstill. Since then twenty uneasy years had passed, plus another three of even more terrible conflict. Now I was on my way to see the launching of the penultimate act in the final destruction of the German armies.

More miles of England's green and pleasant land; the country lanes, the little cottages, inviolate for centuries from the brutal hand of an invader, and inviolate still, thanks to God and the Royal Air Force. Then downlands and, over the horizon, came the widely spaced buildings of the RAF station which I was to visit.

It is a peace-time aerodrome with well-designed buildings and comfortable, commodious quarters, but they are crowded now as it is also the headquarters of the 6th British Airborne Division. I see the Adjutant and am taken to the mess. I do

D-Day

not feel in any way a stranger, for never, since Nelson held the seas against all Europe and termed his Captains 'that Band of Brothers', has there been such a Band of Brothers as those who wear the Royal Air Force uniform. Within half an hour I have made a dozen new friends.

Among them is Wing Commander Macnamara, who suggests that I should go for a flight that evening in the glider that is to carry Major-General Gale, the Commander of the 6th Airborne Division, to France. Then I am introduced to the Station Commander, Group Captain Surplice. He is a tall, well-built fellow with a quiet manner, very blue eyes and white, even teeth which make his frequent smile particularly attractive. Half a dozen officers have told me already that he is the best CO they have ever served under, 'a marvellous memory, incredibly efficient and never angry'. One only has to talk to him for a few minutes to know that he is the type of man who does not have to drive his people but has at times even to restrain their eagerness for fear that they overwork in their efforts to please him.

Squadron Leader Pound, principal Administrative Officer, a veteran of the last war, with a row of decorations, fixes me up with a room and tells me something of his job – one that has little glamour but is so absolutely vital to the success of operations. Men cannot fight their best unless they are well fed and cared for, and they cannot fight at all if their equipment lets them down.

Pound takes me to the briefing room, where I meet Squadron Leader Johnson, another be-ribboned veteran. Behind a locked door with an armed sentry on guard and blacked-out windows he is already preparing the maps from which the air crews will be briefed when the signal comes through that the 'party' is definitely on. We have a most interesting chat about the forthcoming operation, but keep to tactical matters as it is still possible that there may be a postponement.

At six o'clock I go out on to the great airfield with its broad runways and scores of parked aircraft and gliders. They are wearing their war paint: special recognition signs put on only the night before, after the camp had been 'sealed'. No one who enters it may now leave it, or write or telephone from it until after the job is over.

Major Griffiths, the glider pilot who will take General Gale to France, tells me a bit about gliders, then we go up for a twenty-minute flight. There is a stiff wind so it is a bit bumpy but that does not worry me as I have never been airsick. We can hear the roar of the engines in Macnamara's aircraft which is towing us. Suddenly there is silence and, after a moment, I realize that the tow-rope has been cast off, yet we are flying smoothly on. A few minutes more and we come safely down on the airfield.

That evening I attend the preliminary briefing. It is a colour film showing a large area of France. It is just as though we were all seated in a huge aircraft flying over the country of the film. Again and again we run in over the German-held beaches to the fields in which the paratroops are to be dropped and the gliders come down. As we make our series of chair-borne flights to the different objectives the commentator points out the principal landmarks of the area by which the pilots can identify their targets.

Back in the mess I meet scores more officers: there are about equal numbers in khaki and Air Force blue, all talking and laughing together. They all look incredibly fit and their morale is terrific.

After dinner Macnamara introduces me to Major-General Richard Gale. He is a huge man with a ready laugh, shrewd eyes, a bristling moustache and a bulldog chin. He stands out from the crowd not only on account of his size but also because, instead of the conventional battledress, he is wearing beautifully cut light grey jodhpurs. We soon discover that we were both born in 1897. 'A damned good vintage,' says the General. We find, too, that we have many friends in common.

An airman asks him what weapon he is personally going to take for the battle. He roars with laughter and replies, 'Weapon! What the hell do I want with a weapon? If I have the good luck to get near any of those so-and-sos, my boots are good enough for me. I'll kick the something-somethings where it tickles most.'

A little later the station doctor, Squadron Leader Evan

Jones, tells me an amazing story. Seven days earlier one of the air-tug pilots had broken his ankle. They all knew that the job was coming fairly soon and Jones told him, 'I'm sorry, old chap, but if it is within the next three weeks it will be absolutely impossible for you to go.'

'I've been training for this job for two years,' replied the pilot seriously. 'If I can't make it I'll kill myself.' And he meant it.

Jones was so worried that he got a specialist down from London, but the break was a bad one and the specialist verified the verdict: impossible under three weeks.

There then occurred what the doctor considers one of the most remarkable examples of the triumph of mind over matter that he has ever seen. The pilot determined to make it, somehow. After six days he threw away his crutches; on the eighth he had only a slight limp and went to France. What hope have the tired, dispirited Germans against such men?

Half a dozen of us, including Richard Gale, talked on until midnight. Then the others went to bed, while the General and I stayed up alone for a further half-hour talking about the qualities which make a good leader.

He insisted at first that only one thing mattered – efficiency. If the men knew that you really knew your stuff, they would follow you blindly anywhere. I argued that was nine-tenths of the game, but the last tenth was personality, the capability of showing oneself to be independent-minded and a little out of the ruck of other men.

When we went to bed we were a bit worried about the weather, but we knew that there could not possibly be a postponement unless it became exceptionally bad. That Saturday night ships were already moving to their concentration areas, and the security of the whole operation might be jeopardized if it was put off for even a single day.

But in the morning the weather was worse. Soon after nine o'clock Wing Commander Bangay took me up for a flight in one of the paratroop-dropping aircraft. He did a practice run up to a diagonal road which had certain similarities to a road in the target area and I had the treat of seeing the air crew go through the exact drill they would follow when they dropped their human cargo in France. Then, soon after I got back, the blow fell. At 11.30 the Station Commander sent for me and told me that the operation would not take place that night.

I was utterly appalled. Even an hour earlier, in spite of the poor weather, I would have bet anyone a 100 to 1 in pounds that there would be no postponement. Richard Gale was almost certainly the only person on the station besides myself who realized the full implications. There were now over 4000 ships which had moved up in the night and many thousands of smaller craft all massed round the Isle of Wight.

The Boche had only to send over one recce plane to spot that vast concentration and he would know that the invasion was just about to start. It would give him twenty-four hours to move additional troops up to the beaches and, when our forces arrived, they would find every gun manned. Worse, he might send his whole bomber force over to the Solent that Sunday night, in which case there would be the most appalling massacre among our close-berthed, stationary shipping. Again, he knew that we had airborne forces and that they would form the spearhead of the attack. He probably knew, too, the airfields upon which the hundreds of tugs and gliders were assembled, so it was quite a possibility that he might either bomb them that night or launch his own paratroops against them to forestall our attack. In fact all operational officers on the Station had been ordered to wear their revolvers from the time that the camp was sealed, as a precaution against just such an emergency.

Fortunately, however, very few people even knew that a postponement had occurred, far less the possible use the enemy might make of it if his recce aircraft were active and alert. In consequence, that night the crowded mess was again the scene of gaiety and mirth. At about nine o'clock an impromptu sing-song started, and for over three hours we made the rafters ring with all the old choruses.

Gale had been singing with us but went off to bed at eleven o'clock. Later he told me that, just as the rest of us were breaking up, around a quarter to one, his ADC woke him. The secret code word had come over the wire from London. Tomorrow the 'do' was on.

D-Day

The morning of Monday 5 June passed quietly. Very few people as yet knew that this was now definitely D – 1. But at lunchtime the whispered word ran round among the operational officers. 'Final briefing at five o'clock!'

There were three briefings, each taking an hour, for three separate but co-ordinated operations, and I listened to them all with rapt intent. Major-General Crawford, Director of Air Operations War Office, had arrived from London to join us and, soon after, Air Vice-Marshal Hollinghurst, the AOC of the Group, came in. Both had played a great part in the preparations for the forthcoming operation and the Air Vice-Marshal was responsible for it, since under his command lay all the airfields in the area on which the aircraft and gliders that were to take the 6th Airborne Division to France were assembled.

The Station Commander, Group Captain Surplice, opened the proceedings in each case by reading orders of the day from the Supreme Commander, General Eisenhower, and the Commander-in-Chief, Air Marshal Sir Trafford Leigh Mallory. Then, having explained the general layout of the seaborne assault, he asked General Gale to describe the part that his Division was to play.

The General told us that his task was to protect the left flank of the Allied armies. To do this, three separate landings would be made to the east of the River Orne. It was imperative that a large German battery which enfiladed the assault beaches should be silenced. One of the first groups to land would storm a small *château* and seize a car in its garage. Two paratroopers, both Austrians, would get in the car and drive hell for leather towards the steel gates of the battery, shouting in German, 'Open the gate! Open the gate, the invasion has started.' The Germans would have heard the aeroplanes overhead so it was hoped that they would open up, then the paratroopers could hurl bombs through, which would render it impossible to close the gates again. It was a suicide job. This fortress battery had a twenty-foot-wide and fifteen-foot-deep concrete ditch all round it, fitted with barbed wire, and to make certain of the job the General meant to crash three gliders right across the ditch.

The two other parties were to seize the two adjacent

bridges crossing the river Orne and the Caen canal about five miles from the coast and to blow up other bridges further inland. The General then meant to establish his battle HQ between the two seized bridges, to infest with his men all the territory to the east in order to delay a German attack against the British flank and, when the attack came, as come it must, to fight with his back to the double water line.

He thought that the 21st German Panzer Division would be at him pretty soon, so he would need every anti-tank gun that he could get in. 'We shall need those guns pretty badly,' he said, and then, as though it had just occurred to him, he added, 'As a matter of fact we shall want them tomorrow.' At which a great roar of laughter went up from the packed benches of the briefing room.

The Station Commander then briefed his pilots, giving detailed instructions to each flight as to its course in and out with the navigational aids arranged to get them safely home. This may sound a simple matter, but when great numbers of aircraft are flying from many different airfields to objectives all crowded into one locality it becomes an extraordinarily complicated business, unless there is to be grave risk of losses by collision. Group Captain Surplice was followed by the signals officer, the meteorological officer and the secret devices officer. Of these, I understood only the 'Met' man, who predicted clear skies under 2000 feet and broken cloud above which would let the moonlight through so that the pilots should be able to pick out their dropping zones without difficulty.

The briefing over we returned to the mess. After dinner a few of us gathered round a very special bottle of wine that I had brought down for the occasion*. General Gale asked his ADC, General Crawford, Air Vice-Marshal Hollinghurst, Wing Commander Macnamara and myself to join him and together we drank to the success of this great venture.

While we drank the wine we talked of the coming battle. I remarked that I had never had the least doubt about the ability of the Navy to put the bulk of our main forces safely ashore, or about our troops being able to overcome the

*Rupertsberg Hoheburg Gewürtztraminer Feinste Edelbeer-Auslese 1920, the greatest Hock I have ever drunk.

D-Day

enemy's initial resistance; but the real crisis would come later when, moving more swiftly overland than we could across water, the enemy might be able to counter-attack our bridgehead with greatly superior forces.

'Yes, a lot of people are afraid of that,' replied the General, 'but they fail to take into account our immense air superiority. Think what the destruction of those bridges over the lower Seine means. Instead of the enemy being able to bring his Divisions north of the Seine cracking straight against our flank, he'll have to take them all the way round by Paris. They'll bottleneck there and, given anything like reasonable weather, General Spaatz will be able to knock merry hell out of them. As for their being able to bring a superior force against us from the centre and south of France by D plus 6, that's all right in theory. But to do so they must concentrate in a relatively small area. The sky will be all ours. Leigh Mallory will see their every move, and his boys will break up their formations wherever they become a serious menace. No, if we can secure our first objectives, I don't think you need worry.'

It was a great tribute to our airmen by a great soldier and, given even fair weather, I had no shadow of doubt about his trust being justified.

It was now ten o'clock and Group Captain Surplice had very kindly suggested that, if I accompanied him, I would see the take-off to the best advantage. First we made the complete tour of the airfield in his car; everything was in order; there was no necessity for any flap or a single last-minute instruction. Then we went to the watch tower, to within a few yards of which each aircraft would taxi up before receiving the signal to go.

The weather was still not good but it had improved a little; there were breaks between the clouds and twilight faded almost imperceptibly into moonlight. The first wave consisted of fourteen paratroop-carrying aircraft followed by four aircraft towing gliders containing special material needed as soon as possible after the paratroops had landed.

Wing Commander Bangay, in the aircraft in which he had taken me up the day before, was to lead the first wave. With him was going Air Vice-Marshal Hollinghurst or

'Holly' as this plump, dynamic, little man was known affectionately by his subordinates. There had, I think, been a certain amount of discussion as to the wisdom of his going, but he was mad keen about this highly specialized job of transporting airborne forces and insisted that the experience of seeing the actual operation would be invaluable to him in the future.

At three minutes past eleven precisely the first aircraft took off and 'Holly' led the boys he had trained so thoroughly in the assault against Hitler's Fortress Europa. The other aircraft followed at thirty-second intervals, except for the four glider tugs which took off at one-minute intervals. A Wing Commander beside me timed them with a watch. Not a single aircraft was either early or late by a split second.

We now had a period of waiting, as the second wave was not due off till 1.50 a.m. In the interval, a signal was flashed to us that the Air Commander-in-Chief, Sir Trafford Leigh Mallory, was about to arrive at the Station, and soon afterwards his plane came in. He talked for a little to the Station Commander and the two Generals, wished them luck, and took off into the night to visit other aerodromes where important operations were about to take place.

Midnight came, but somehow we did not think of it as the beginning of the long-awaited D-Day. That had already started hours ago for us. A number of us rendezvoused at General Gale's glider. There was no awkwardness in that last three-quarters of an hour. The General had just returned from a last visit to his men before they left their camp. He had drunk good English beer with them, and they were still cheering him as they came on to the airfield.

We told funny stories and laughed a lot. The General looked a more massive figure than ever, and with reason, as the innumerable pockets of his special kit were now stuffed with maps and scores of other things he would need when he landed in France. Over everything he had a light-coloured mackintosh, but he was still wearing his grey jodhpurs.

'What about your Mae West, sir?' one of his officers asked.

'Oh, I can put that on later if it's necessary,' he protested.

'Might be a bit tricky then, sir,' the officer persisted.

D-Day

The General turned to me and said good-humouredly, 'I'm supposed to be commanding this damned division, yet look how these fellows bully me. All right, I'll put it on if you like.'

About six people endeavoured to help him into it and one of them said, 'The tapes should go as high under your arms as possible, sir.'

He burbled with laughter again. 'I know what you're up to. If we fall in the water, you want my head to go under and my bottom to be left sticking up in the air.' Then, a moment later, he slapped his broad chest and exclaimed, 'Good God, look at me! I must look like Henry the Eighth.'

The comparison was not without point, and a moment earlier I had noticed that chalked on the side of the glider was the name of another English king – Richard the First. That meant, I knew, simply that Richard Gale was to be the first British General to land in France for many hours, but the unintended parallel with the Great Crusader struck me most forcibly.

The last scene before the General emplaned was one of those simple, kindly jests in which the British delight. A few mornings before, the General had exclaimed with joy on finding that there was golden syrup for breakfast. 'By Jove, I love golden syrup, and I haven't seen any for years!' Upon which he proceeded to tuck heartily into it. So now, our smiling Group Captain, who had been his official host, formally presented him with a tin to take with him to France. I contributed a pound of airtight, tinned Charbonnel & Walker chocolates.

A few minutes later the Group Captain and I were back at the watch tower. He gave the signal and the second wave – this time twenty-five gliders towed by Albemarles – began to move off. Macnamara's aircraft, S for Sugar, led the way with General Crawford in it, as he, too, was determined to learn every lesson which could be learned from the operation and, as he had told me with a smile, see that his friend Richard really went. At the end of their tow-rope was glider No. 70 carrying the GOC 6th British Airborne Division and his personal staff. Once again, at one-minute intervals, as regularly as the ticking of a clock and without a single hitch, the aircraft and their tows took off.

The job took twenty-five minutes, so having saluted the General's glider as it passed within a few feet of us, I still had plenty of time to drive over to the control room and, from its high balcony, see a panorama of the moonlit field while the last dozen gliders left it. Up there, too, I saw another thrilling sight: a great cluster of red and white lights all moving at exactly the same pace. It was a Wing of United States aircraft, carrying personnel of the American Airborne Division to the Cherbourg peninsula.

Immediately after our second wave had gone the leading aircraft of the first wave were due to return. We could hear them coming in as we went over to the briefing room, but it took the best part of a quarter of an hour from the landing of a plane to the crew's coming in, after having parked her in her allotted place and walked across. We spent some anxious moments.

At last the first pilot and his crew came in. He seemed a little surprised and very disappointed. They had dropped their parachutists right on the spot, in spite of a sudden and unexpected worsening of the weather: time $17\frac{1}{2}$ minutes past midnight, 6 June, for ever now the date-line of our opening the Second Front in Europe. 'But,' they said, 'it might have been just one of the practice night droppings we've carried out over England. It was quite dark, no flak, nothing to see, no excitement. In fact it's difficult to believe that we've had anything at all to do with opening up the Second Front.'

This may have been nothing but rather a poor party to them, but to me it was terrific news. It meant that we had achieved an almost unbelievable triumph. Security had been so good that the Germans had known neither the time nor place of assault. We had achieved the dream of all commanders for any operation: complete tactical surprise.

As other pilots came in, this fantastically good news was confirmed. Only the later-comers had seen anything. After a bit, some enemy batteries had opened up with light flak. Air Vice-Marshal 'Holly', safely returned, told us that he had seen the synchronized attack by heavy bombers on the German battery – a last attempt to put it out by pinpoint bombing. All who had seen the terrific explosions by the light of which the fort had been lit up agreed that, even if it was not totally destroyed, very few of its German garrison of 180 could still be alive and in any state to lay a gun.

Then, to offset this good news, the first bad break occurred. A little group of paratroopers came in. On being questioned, it transpired that the first of their team to jump was the Brigade Major. He had stuck in the hatch; they could not push him out or pull him back. The pilot had taken the aircraft out to sea and ran it up and down the coast for half an hour, but his comrades could not get the Major either in or out, and when he lost consciousness, they felt that the only thing to do was to return to England. After landing they got him free. Fortunately he was uninjured, but his mishap had prevented any of the rest leaving the aircraft. The pilot pleaded desperately to be allowed to make a second trip, but the Group Captain would not let him. There was too much going on.

Worse was to come. A pale-faced youngster entered the room and came up to the Group Captain. 'I'm sorry, sir. I don't know what to say, but my string broke. We lost the glider about three miles from the French coast.'

Surplice laid his hand on the boy's shoulder. 'I'm sure it wasn't your fault. Tell me what happened.'

'Well, sir, the weather let us down. Our orders were to drop the gliders off at 1600. There was cloud down to 800 and no moon coming through. It was black as pitch. I went down as low as I dared to try to get clear but in the darkness the glider must have lost our tail light and become unmanageable. With her trailing wild, the strain snapped the tow-rope and there was nothing we could do about it.'

We reckoned that the glider might have had enough height to make the beach, or at least shallow water, but our hopes were father to our thoughts and we knew that in any case that load of stores would not reach the leading paratroops in time to be used for their special operations.

A few minutes later a second tug pilot came in. The same sad story. In his case, too, he had entered low cloud several miles before he reached the coast of France, the glider had become uncontrollable and broken away. Soon after, we learned that the third and fourth pilots were back, and they too had lost their gliders.

The big briefing room was now crowded with air crews drinking tea, munching hot scones and waiting their turn to make their detailed reports to the Intelligence officers. No room full of men could have been more representative of the Empire: all the Dominions were well represented; there were a number of colonials and the rest spoke with accents ranging from Oxford to Glasgow, Dublin to Devon and Cardiff to Cockney London.

It was now about 2.45 a.m., and the next two hours were grim. If all four of the first flight of gliders had gone into the 'drink', what chance had the General and his string of twenty-five, and all the other flights now heading for the same area from the other stations in the Group, with the rest of the Airborne Division? Some of the young daredevils we had had drinks with only a few hours before were now almost certainly dead and others, weighed down by their heavy equipment, swimming desperately for their lives in the cold waters of the Channel. Hundreds more might be crashing and drowning as we stood there.

If the General and a large part of the Airborne Division were lost, their vital task would remain unaccomplished and the left flank of the British Army be left open to attack. There were hours to go yet before the first seaborne troops were due to touch down on the beaches, and the Germans must have known for two hours now that the invasion had at last started. If the airborne operation failed, the enemy might counter-attack the open beaches in the morning and hurl our troops back into the sea, rendering the whole vast plan a complete failure. The strain of waiting to hear how the second wave had fared was appalling.

During that time only one piece of good news came to cheer us. We had been misinformed about the last tug pilot back. He, too, had entered cloud but he had managed to get well over the coast before his tow-rope snapped.

At last, about 4.30, we heard the drone of aircraft. The tugs of the second wave were returning. At a quarter to five the first air crew came in. The cloud had lifted, they had cast off their gliders dead on the mark.

D-Day

Crew after crew appeared with the same glad tidings. When Macnamara and General Crawford came in we rushed towards them. They were smiling, laughing. They had put General Gale down at half past two exactly in the place he had planned to land. Of the second wave not a single glider was lost.

Douglas Warth, an official War Reporter, had gone over with the first wave of paratroopers and was thus the first reporter to witness the opening of the Second Front. He had a jeep waiting and, now that we knew the General had got in, offered me a lift back to London.

We were standing beside the telephone at the time and I heard the Chief Intelligence Officer receive a message from the control room, 'All aircraft safely landed and no wounded.'

A moment later I was saying goodbye to Group Captain Surplice, and, having thanked him for his kindness to me, I added, 'I would like to congratulate you, sir, on the wonderful show you've put up and on all your aircraft having arrived back safely.'

'What!' he exclaimed, his face lighting up. 'Are they all back? How splendid!'

'Yes,' I had the joy of answering him. 'All back without a single casualty.'

By seven o'clock I was in London. Hurrying to the Cabinet War Room I got the broader picture. Of the 286 aircraft despatched on this mission, only eight had failed to return, and the glider losses were far fewer than had been anticipated. A few hours later I learned that General Gale had landed without accident, and, achieving complete surprise, had secured the two bridges which were his principal objective.

That night I heard the King make the marvellous broadcast that he had personally prepared with such a fine understanding of his people.

D-Day was over. In champagne we drank a health to George VI and Richard 'The First' and, last but not least, to the Royal Air Force which in the dark days had saved Britain and now had safely conveyed to France the first General in the great crusade which was to bring light back to Europe.

H

Chapter 19
The Battle for France

On that morning of 6 June 1944, unshaven but unworried – owing to the great news I brought – I was just in nice time for the nine-thirty meeting of LCS. The delight that Johnny and my colleagues displayed on learning that complete surprise had been achieved can well be imagined. For half a year we had worked on plan Bodyguard, and its innumerable ramifications; and we had pulled it off.

By this time the great floating concrete harbours (Mulberrys), to make the temporary ports through which the Allied forces could be supplied, must be preparing to leave England, and Monty's men in their thousands be swarming up the beaches. They would meet with opposition, of course, but for the first few hours it could be only sporadic. We had held the great bulk of the German armour far away north of the Seine up in the Pas de Calais, and the RAF had destroyed twenty out of the twenty-two bridges over the Seine between Paris and the coast. By nightfall, before the enemy had time to bring up reinforcements, Monty would be in Caen.

But, of course, he wasn't. He threw away the wonderful advantage of surprise that we had secured for him; then it took him six weeks to get there.

Having made my report, I left the Cabinet Offices, crossed Whitehall to the Post Office and sent the following telegram to Joan, who was then on leave up at Welshpool.

'General commanding British Airborne Division spearhead of forces bringing light back to Continent landed in France by glider at 2.30 a.m. today – Love Dennis.'

The Battle for France

The degree of intimacy which can be reached in quite a short time by two strangers thrown together in exceptional circumstances is quite amazing. In the case of Richard Gale and myself it was due to the fact that, in that great sealed camp containing many hundreds of soldiers and airmen, we were the only two who knew everything that was to be known on this side of the Channel about the forthcoming operation. Surplice knew only what his pilots were required to attempt. Richard's staff knew only about the terrain and the degree of opposition which they were likely to meet in the immediate area of their landings.

But he and I knew the big picture: the numbers and quality of the German divisions stationed in France, their whereabouts and how quickly they might arrive on the scene of battle if we failed to achieve surprise; of the awful risk that if this new invention of Mulberry harbours failed to work, our troops might find themselves ashore but, within a few days, uncertain of their supplies of food or ammunition; of the immense labour that had gone into making the Atlantic Wall, and that if we failed to pierce it our army would, almost certainly, be driven back into the sea, where thousands must perish.

It was the common knowledge of this terrible gamble that must be taken so soon and must not be mentioned to anyone else that led to Richard Gale and me spending hours alone together, just walking up and down, hiding our anxiety by talking cheerfully of a score of things, yet always, now and then, returning to speculate on some aspect of the coming battle.

In the event he secured all his objectives and, although his division was to have been relieved in three days, it was not. Striking northward along the coast away from the main army, without artillery or proper transport, it fought its way for twenty-one days through town after town and village after village until it reached the mouth of the Seine. And he returned unwounded some weeks later, to split with me a magnum of champagne.

That was over thirty years ago. Our friendship ripened and we still regard each other with affection.

Only eight days after the Normandy landings, namely on

13 June, the first V1 landed on London. It arrived within hearing distance of St James's Park, and it so happened that two officers of the Joint Planning Staff were taking the well-worn route from our basement across the Park to dine at one of the service clubs in Pall Mall. They had got as far as Waterloo Steps when they heard the sound of this new weapon. Guessing what it was, they instantly threw themselves flat on the ground. Unperturbed, two civilians nearby walked on, then, as the sound of the explosion came, one remarked to the other, 'I suppose that's this new secret weapon we've heard so much about.' So much for security!

Of course, they could not know that we had expected a shell or rocket with a twenty-ton warhead. Luckily for all of us, the explosive charge carried by the V1s proved to be far smaller than that of the block-busters used in the 1940 blitz.

Personally, I did not find them particularly frightening, owing to the fact that one had warning of their approach.

The damage done by the V1s was infinitely less than that caused by the 1940 blitz and, in fact, they were little more than an unpleasant nuisance. But, whereas Londoners withstood the terrors of the blitz courageously and even cheerfully, they did not react in anything like so fine a spirit under the V1 attack. This was, no doubt, partially due to war-weariness but probably more to the fact that the weaker element who had fled to the country in 1940 had, by 1944, returned to the city to the detriment of the morale of the whole population.

Actually, we got off very lightly from Hitler's secret weapons; but it is terrible to think what might have happened had he succeeded in making them operational three months, or even one month, before he did. They would have been used to blast all our ports from the Thames estuary right round to Plymouth, thus rendering our return to the Continent next to impossible. This would inevitably have led to the war's being prolonged for another year at least and, even had we transferred our main forces to the Italian front, the odds are that, shortly after the final collapse of the Germans, it would have been the Russians who would have liberated France and arrived on our doorstep at Calais.

The Battle for France

In the Cabinet Offices War Room a big map was set up on which the place where each buzz-bomb fell was duly marked. I used to have a look at it every morning to see if I could detect any pattern to the attack. The area to suffer most was south London and I eventually came to the conclusion that the enemy's objective was to render unusable the great network of railways at Clapham Junction, as it was there that the V1s fell thickest.

Meanwhile our slow progress in France caused many of us at home bitter disappointment.

Dudley Clarke's deception plan held a considerable enemy force in the south until the Anvil invasion took place in mid-August, while our plan Bodyguard succeeded in keeping the greater part of the German Fifteenth Army in the Pas de Calais.

Nevertheless by D plus 3 the Allied Expeditionary Force was engaging nearly the whole of the German Seventh Army which was soon being reinforced from other areas.

The Germans had made Caen their major bastion on Montgomery's front, and it was not until 10 July that he could penetrate the city.

To the west of the British an American Airborne Division had the ill luck to come down in an area where a German night exercise was taking place; so, although they achieved surprise, they met with fully armed troops on the alert, and suffered severe casualties. But the American ground troops succeeded in reaching their first objectives and by 11 June the several beaches on which the Expeditionary Force landed had been fused into one continuous beach-head. By the 19th, in spite of bad weather, the Mulberry harbours had been secured in position and supplies to the Allied army assured. On the 22nd the Prime Minister paid his first visit to encourage Monty and our troops.

By 8 June, the only reinforcements so far detached from the German Fifteenth Army to assist the Seventh Army in resisting the invasion had been 1st Armoured Division. Then, early in July, OKW released the rest of its armoured reserve north of the Seine. Not wishing to weaken materially the Fifteenth Army, C-in-C West (von Rundstedt) ordered only two field divisions south from the Pas de Calais and other troops from Rommel's Army Group B in Belgium and Holland.

In my view, this could have seriously influenced the outcome of the battle and perhaps even proved disastrous. But Major Roger Hesketh came to the rescue by using Garbo.

Through interrogations after the war we learned that the message was first read by Colonel Krummacher (Chief Intelligence Officer at Hitler's HQ), passed to Colonel General Alfred Jodl (Hitler's Chief of Operations) and then to Hitler. Krummacher underlined 'attack in another place' and added 'confirms the view already held by us that a further attack is to be expected in a different area'. Jodl underlined 'in south-east and eastern England' before showing the message to Hitler.

The result was that, acting on an order sent from OKW, the Fifteenth Army was put on a maximum state of alert, the 1st and 116th Panzer Divisions were halted, ordered to converge on the Pas de Calais and all other withdrawals from that area were to be stopped.

By mid-July there were thirty Allied Divisions ashore, and, there were still twenty-two German Divisions sitting doing nothing in the Pas de Calais. At this time Montgomery held half of Caen and his front further west had penetrated some fifteen miles from the shore.

The Americans meanwhile had driven, on a wide front, right through the base of the Cotentin peninsula, held the further coast as far down as Lessey and, in their centre, penetrated in depth to St Lo. On 25 July General Omar Bradley, Commanding First US Army, launched his VII Corps southward from that city and followed it next day with his VIII Corps, his Army Group breaking through south-east in the direction of Falaise. A number of us then expected that Montgomery would break out of his confined bridgehead to join up with him and encircle the German Seventh Army. But he did no such thing.

It seemed that the British C-in-C preferred to draw the enemy down on to his front and, with superior air power, gradually destroy their army. During the first week in August, while Bradley's army was still pursuing his determined offensive, Mongtomery fought his war of attrition,

The Battle for France

with the Germans attacking him with great vigour and sustaining heavy losses.

Early in August, accompanied by Monty's patron, Alan Brooke, Churchill went to France. It was widely believed by some at the time that Churchill intended to replace the British C-in-C, but this did not prove to be the case.

By the first week in August, at long last the enemy began to realize that he had been fooled by plan Bodyguard. This was due to the fact that many actual units that we had put over as forming part of FUSAG had been sent to France and there identified by enemy Intelligence. Still more telling, our nominal Force Commander of FUSAG, General George Patton, had by then also gone to France and was known by the Germans to be C-in-C Third US Army.

Patton's Third US Army had landed at the base of the Cherbourg peninsula, not far from St Malo. By 3 August they had taken Rennes, by the 8th Le Mans, by the 13th Alençon, by the 15th Chartres, by the 20th Fontainebleau and by the 25th, on which day Paris was captured, they had reached Troyes, sixty miles nearer the Rhine than the French capital.

Meanwhile, against the advice of all his Generals, Hitler insisted on five armoured divisions and two infantry divisions – which could have ensured the German Seventh Army an orderly retreat to the Seine – being sent in as reinforcements in a counter-offensive launched in the direction of Mortain.

For the Germans the result was disastrous. Their wretched, war-weary troops, who still showed great courage in the face of terrible adversity, could not possibly stand up to the fresh, confident and well-fed Americans covered by the overwhelming air power of the Allies. The offensive petered out almost before it had begun. From three sides the enemy were driven in and all but surrounded in the Falaise pocket. Many thousands were massacred, tens of thousands more threw down their arms and surrendered. It was the end of the Battle for France. Only a remnant of the German Seventh Army and the divisions of the Fifteenth which, owing to Bodyguard, had been sent only in dribs and drabs to support it, managed to reach and cross the Seine. By the end of August several Allied spearheads were already across, while Patton's Third Army in the south was over the Meuse and driving hell for leather towards the Moselle.

During the midst of the battle for France an upheaval of the first magnitude occurred inside Germany. On 20 July, an attempt had been made to assassinate Hitler.

If any group of conspirators ever made a mess of things, surely it was this little bunch of German Generals. Von Stauffenberg stands out as the only officer who displayed real courage and decision. Crippled as he was by his many wounds, he actually did the job of planting the bomb. Owing to the fact that the conference that day took place in a flimsy wooden hut instead of the underground concrete bunker – where the air-conditioning was being repaired – the effect of the explosion was so dissipated that Hitler survived. Even so, had not von Stauffenberg's journey back to Berlin necessitated such a long flight, the plot might still have succeeded. Without him to inspire and lead them, the Generals proved to be an indecisive and cowardly lot. They shilly-shallied until it was too late to seize control of Berlin. They paid for it with their lives. The fiendish Hitler had them strung up naked from meat hooks.

His vengeance did not end with this barbarism inflicted on those who had actually been found guilty of participating in the conspiracy. During the following few months he had over 2000 people executed who were no more than vaguely suspected of being sympathetic towards the conspirators.

On 22 July, the day after we received intelligence about the attempt on Hitler's life, Johnny Bevan got out a plan to take advantage of the situation. It included the use of Aspidistra to cause the Germans to believe that there was widespread revolt in their country. But it was opposed by PWE, so not carried out.

Once the break-out from the Normandy beaches was accomplished, the British army retrieved most gloriously its reputation for determined attack. On 30 August, Twenty-first Army Group was only just across the lower Seine; by 3 September, the Guards Armoured Division entered Brussels in triumph; on the 4th, 11th Armoured seized Antwerp, and on the 5th the Canadians were in Ghent.

The Battle for France

The capture of Antwerp was an asset of the first magnitude, because the great port was practically undamaged and, up to then, the Allied armies had had to rely for their supplies entirely on the Mulberry harbours and such cargoes as could be got into the severely sabotaged ports of Normandy and Brittany – all by then several hundred miles distant.

This handicap had been most seriously increased by General de Gaulle's unauthorized liberation of Paris. Eisenhower had decreed that the French capital must be bypassed, so that he would have sufficient petrol and supplies for his armies to continue their advance on either side of it. But de Gaulle ignored this decision and, in secret, delivered a lightning stroke with his Free French divisions, which forced the German garrison in Paris to surrender. His excuse was that, had he not done so, the Communists would have seized power and, perhaps, later proved impossible to overthrow. This is not valid, because within a month or so the Allies would have done the job for him. The fact that he did prematurely liberate Paris meant that we were immediately saddled with several million more French citizens whom we had to provide with all their necessities; and this materially delayed the main Allied offensive.

On 17 September, Montgomery made his bid to cross the lower Rhine by dropping the 1st Airborne Division on Arnhem. For him to have acted so rashly was entirely contrary to his character. In view of the fact that it was already an accepted principle of war that paratroops should never be dropped in any area where they cannot with certainty be supported by ground forces within twelve hours, the operation cannot possibly be justified. The plan was that, immediately after the landing, an armoured division should drive up the road to Eindhofen. But Montgomery neglected to take into consideration that the enemy still held in strength the country on both sides of that road. So many of our tanks were destroyed by shell-fire that the attempt to break through had to be abandoned. Left to its fate, the Airborne Division fought on for some forty-eight hours with the utmost gallantry, sustaining very heavy casualties, until its survivors, having exhausted their water and ammunition, were forced to surrender.

Throughout this book I have made criticisms of General Montgomery, and I wish to state categorically that these are not inspired by personal animosity against him. I never even met him either during the war or after it. My views are based solely on the fact that, for three years, I was in a position to know in advance the plans for every major operation undertaken and follow from day to day all our campaigns as they were carried out. And, I can add, my views were shared by the majority of the regular officers who, during that time, served on the Joint Planning Staff.

Most of us who were aware of the desperate straits to which Germany had been reduced by the late summer of 1944 held the optimistic belief that the war would be over by the autumn. But shortage of supplies, and particularly petrol, seriously slowed down the advance of the Allies in the west and, although the Russians were regaining vast areas of territory in the east, the Germans were still putting up a stiff resistance against them.

Between the British and Americans there developed an unhappy divergence of opinion about future strategy. Montgomery wanted the bulk of the Allied armour to be placed under him for an all-out drive on the northern flank through Holland and so on to Berlin, while the remainder of the Allied army to the south, having in consequence been considerably weakened, should do little more than hold its ground. But Eisenhower would not agree to this. Instead of concentrating an overwhelming force behind his left flank, he preferred to keep his armour more or less equally distributed and maintain a general offensive along his whole front.

Had Montgomery's plan been adopted, there is at least a possibility that he would have been in Berlin before the Russians and the war over before the end of the year. As it was, Eisenhower's strategy got us nowhere. It is, however, interesting to speculate upon how much Montgomery's intense unpopularity with the American Generals contributed to Eisenhower's refusal to let him have his head and, perhaps, reap the major laurels of the Allied victory. Had General Alexander been C-in-C Twenty-first Army Group, it is possible that Ike would have been more willing to listen

The Battle for France

to him. So often it is upon personalities that great decisions hang.

About half-past six on the evening of 8 September the first V2 bomb fell in London. I happened to be in Trafalgar Square and heard the explosion. It was quite unlike the bang made by a buzz-bomb, so I wondered what it could be. It never occurred to me that this might be the giant rocket that we feared would cause such terrible devastation; so, unperturbed, I made my way home.

On arriving next morning at my office, I found everyone discussing the occurrence and in a highly cheerful frame of mind. Few details had yet come in, but at least it was known that, far from having a twenty-ton warhead, the bomb had done comparatively little damage.

Chapter 20
Tribute and Departure

After Eisenhower had established his Supreme Headquarters in France, with his own inter-Allied deception staff under Noel Wild, the LCS became little more than a centre for co-ordinating deception measures between Dudley Clarke in Italy, Peter Fleming in the Far East and Noel Wild on the Continent. We were no longer responsible for any battle front, so had no plans to formulate and were virtually reduced to an Intelligence section, passing information to the enemy by our already established 'Most Secret' channels; and I had never played any part in this.

In consequence, I became hopelessly bored, and spent most of my time compiling numerous groups of postage stamps – Queen Victoria heads in different frames, a collection representative of the Empire, another of low (so not too unreasonable in price) denominations of all foreign first issues, and yet others of beasts, birds, Rajahs, gods and goddesses, all of which I later arranged on occasional tables, under glass. But I was really wasting my time, so I decided to make an attempt to get out of uniform and on 5 August 1944 I sent a letter to the Secretary of State for Air asking, with Johnny's approval, to be allowed to relinquish my commission in the RAFVR.

As is so often the case in government offices where non-urgent matters are concerned, my application doubtless drifted from tray to tray without reply, while I suffered further weeks of boredom. My friends in the operational departments of the Air Ministry had no power to deal with

Tribute and Departure

such matters and I was in no position to press for my release because a rota for priority of demobilization had been got out and circulated. This was based on a combination of age and length of service and, although I was by then forty-seven, I had been in uniform for only two and three-quarter years. In consequence, out of the fifty-odd categories, I ranked only in the seventeenth – and no one at all was normally eligible for release until the war ended.

At long last, however, circumstances provided me with the chance I needed. In response to a recommendation from Johnny, we received the following, of which I have a photostat:

TOP SECRET

Copy of a Minute OS1716(4) dated 11 October 1944 from Secretary, Chiefs of Staff Committee to London Controlling Officer.

The Chiefs of Staff today approved your paper proposing certain reductions in the Staff of the London Controlling Section consequent upon the closing stages of the war against Germany having been reached.

2 The Chiefs of Staff instructed me to inform you that they wished to take this opportunity to place on record their warm appreciation of the outstanding contribution which the London Controlling Section, and its subsidiary sections in the operational theatres, have made to the success of the various major operations which have been carried out during the last two years. In their view the record of success has been unique.

3 The Chiefs of Staff went so far as to record the opinion that, in at least once instance, 'the Section' made a decisive contribution to the success of a major operation, namely, 'the Allies return to the Continent in June 1944'.

4 The Chiefs of Staff instructed me to request that you would convey their appreciation to all those within your organization who have contributed to its outstanding success.

L. C. Hollis
Major-General and Deputy Chief Staff Officer to the
Prime Minister

The above document is unquestionably an exhibition piece, because during my three years in the War Cabinet Offices, during which no minutes of a Chiefs of Staff meeting remained unread by me, there was no single instance of their congratulating any other section of the Joint Planning Staff or formation of any kind; and this, following that concerning the success of Torch, was our second bouquet.

The phrases *'outstanding* contribution to the success of various major operations', 'record of success of the cover and deception plans has been *unique*', and 'made a *decisive* contribution to the success of . . . Overlord' are tributes that it would be impossible to surpass. It was, of course, Johnny Bevan, by his tireless concentration on the work with which he had been charged, who had earned and deserved them. We others were truly happy for him, and bathed in his reflected glory.

Our contribution to victory having been so great, it might well have been supposed that Johnny would have left with a Grand Cross of the Bath and Ronald, Harold, James, Neil, Derrick and myself with CBs or, at least, CBEs

But no. Johnny put all six of us up for decorations, and dear General Pug Ismay backed his recommendations. But Sir Edward Bridges, the all-powerful Secretary of the War Cabinet, decreed that a CB for Johnny and an OBE for one of us was an adequate reward for our whole section.

Naturally, we congratulated Johnny on receiving the distinction which had gone in 1914–18 to every Lieutenant-Colonel who had managed to survive for a year on the Western Front. Harold Peteval, presumably because he had served so long and faithfully, had been Johnny's top recommendation, so got the OBE.

Bridges's refusal to agree to all of our team's receiving honours was partly, perhaps, a reflection of the PM's attitude. Very rightly he was himself endowed with every honour his Sovereign could bestow; yet he is reported once to have said, 'The greater the services a man can render to his country the more fortunate he is, so to honour him publicly is redundant.'

It is related of him that, after the war, when he was no longer Prime Minister, having occasion to visit the Cabinet

Tribute and Departure

Offices, he ran into Pug Ismay, who was still Chief Staff Officer to the Minister of Defence; the new Prime Minister, Clement Attlee, had just rewarded Pug for his great services in the war by giving him a peerage.

Churchill said, 'Hullo, Pug. Where are you off to?'

Pug replied, 'To the House of Lords, sir. Alan Brooke and Peter Portal are about to present me as a new Peer.'

'Oh!' replied Churchill. 'So they're about to make you a Lord, Pug, are they? Why didn't you tell me you'd like to be a Lord? I'd have made you a Duke.'

That is all very well, but one does not *ask* one's chief to make one anything.

Some eighteen months later, I was decorated with the US Bronze Star. When I received it at the hands of the then senior American General stationed in Britain, the citation given with it was the very ordinary one of 'valuable co-operation'; but as the General pinned it on my chest, he leaned forward and whispered, 'We can't put it in writing, but I know the really big things you did.'

At the time I formed the cynical impression that he probably said the same thing to every British officer he decorated, and that the only reason for my receiving the Bronze Star was because, during the war, I had taken so many Americans out to lunch!

To my surprise, a quarter of a century later, I learned that was not the case. Pug died in 1966 and his old friend, Ronald Wingate, took on the job of going through his papers in order to write his biography. At our annual LCS Reunion Dinner at Brooks's in 1967, Ronald told me what had actually happened.

When Bridges had slaughtered the decorations of the section to two, Pug had said to Ronald, 'I don't mind who has the OBE, but the Americans have allocated a Bronze Star to LCS, and that must go to Dennis.'

Anyhow, this 'strawberry' of 11 October from the Chiefs of Staff – as opposed to a 'raspberry' indicating grave displeasure – gave me my chance to renew my application to be relieved of my commission.

James Arbuthnott, too, was extremely anxious to get out and, as the Colonial Office applied for his release on the grounds that he was urgently needed to reassume the direction of tea planting in Ceylon, he was the first of us to be released.

I had to soldier on for another month or more and, in November, I wrote one last paper. Why I should have been asked to draft a declaration by the Prime Minister and the President, I have no idea. It was to be used as a broadcast, stating the true situation to the German soldier, pointing out that further resistance was utterly useless, and proposing that for the future good of his own country he and his comrades should refuse to continue killing and being killed. Presumably one of my old friends in the Air Ministry, recalling my original efforts, had asked for me to do this. In any case, it was a pleasant change from killing time by stamp-collecting.

When I wrote the paper I had still had no information about if and when I was to be released, but I ran into my old acquaintance of 1940, Air Commodore John Vachell. On learning that he was in close touch with the Assistant Chief of Air Staff for Personnel, I asked his help, with the result that, early in December, I was officially notified that my commission was to be terminated on the 22nd.

During my last weeks with LCS I paid forty-six calls on officers with whom I was working in the Cabinet Offices and the three service ministries to say farewell and wrote over twenty letters to others who, by then, were serving abroad.

Some of my letters were formal thanks for their kind reception of me when, as a very junior officer, I had first met them; but the great majority were long and personal. The replies I received were truly heart-warming.

Among them from my earliest sponsor was a long screed from Johnny Darvall, then C-in-C Transport Command, recalling 1941 and the fool's paradise in which the JPS then lived, anticipating an early German collapse.

A charming few lines from Louis Greig; and from Oliver Stanley: '... you must go with a very happy heart, as I hear on all sides what really great work Johnny Bevan and his team have done.'

From Roly Vintras: '... I shall always remember our

friendship during the war with the very greatest pleasure. It has done so very much to make my long spells as a Whitehall Warrior tolerable.'

From Dallas Brooks: '. . . It seems to me that war has only one virtue. It brings people together who might not otherwise have met. Blessings upon you.'

From Eddie Combe, writing on behalf of ISSB: ' . . . During the long period when we worked together, the solution of many problems, difficult and in some cases contentious, was made easier by the cordial personal relationship which always existed between you and ISSB. I am very happy to have this opportunity of thanking you for your so effective co-operation.'

From Dudley Clarke: '. . . Nobody has appreciated more than I have how much happy relations between "A" Force and LCS have meant in making our work smooth and far easier than it might well have been. I know very well that much of the kindness and consideration which I have invariably received from LCS has been due to yourself. . . .'

Dear James having left before me, I also wrote to him. In his reply, a passage ran: '. . . I wish you and Joan could realize how much Chatsworth and the Hungaria have meant to me these past two years. I don't think I've ever had so much kindness before from any family. . . .'

But James had already written to me shortly after he left. I feel very self-conscious in quoting his letter, but it touched me deeply.

> The Cottage,
> Instow,
> North Devon
> 12/XI

My dear Dennis,
I can't let our very happy two years together end with a bare 'goodbye'. . . . You see I am doubtful, Dennis, whether I should have been able to use the word "happy" about the last two years, if it had not been for you. We have often discussed my advent to the Old Schoolroom, so I will not repeat that – but from that very day I have regarded you with much affection & much respect. I have the advantage of knowing a Service from inside as well as the other side & I can assure you that any of the

Services would have gained by your strong independent & intelligent attitude, had your career gone that way. You did save us in LCS from so much of the unnecessary tedium & inefficiency of the military staff mind! I think your background of 'Worcester', last war service, business & literature which incidentally gave you a wide knowledge of Europe, a perfect one for the job we had to do & with the chaps we had to do it with. What I'm trying to say is that it was not only because I like and found you absolutely congenial that you made so much difference to my career in LCS, but also because of the influence your character & experience had on the whole party. It's hard to express but I mean we should have lost a great deal in humour, kindliness, breadth of vision & imagination had you not been there. I feel it would have been narrower, more staff-duty ruled in fact all the opposites of what I have written above, had you not been there – in short the old schoolroom atmosphere would have persisted to the end.

You will be interested to hear that I had a perfectly delightful letter from Johnny a day or two ago. It was a most generous tribute to the small part I played & what will interest you more is that a great deal of it might have been copied almost word for word from your History of LCS. And knowing as I do that you wrote what you did for that very purpose – at least to guide J's thoughts into what you so generously thought were the right channels apropos of my work – I cannot tell you how much I appreciate this kindness.

Dennis, I apologise for this most un-British letter – it's only because I'm fond of you & one can't *always* be incoherent!
Yours affect'ly
James.

It was my good fortune to leave with the spotlight focussed on me. My old friend Dickie Dickson, later as a Marshal of the Royal Air Force to occupy the highest pinnacle of any service career, namely the first ever independent Chairman of the Chiefs of Staff Committee, had returned from a tour of duty as C-in-C Air, Middle East, to become Assistant Chief of Air Staff (Policy). To introduce him to the officers who would be working under him, Air Marshal Colyer, who was handing over to him, gave a cocktail party.

As Regular Air Staff officers were normally given new postings every eighteen months or two years, after three years I was the oldest member not only of LCS but also of

Tribute and Departure

the Operational Air Staff, so I knew nearly everybody present. As my departure had been noised abroad, they made a most kindly fuss of me and showered upon me congratulations on the wonderful success of the deception plans to which I had contributed.

Then, the very night before I was due to leave, another Christmas party was given in the ground floor Joint Planning Staff mess for the officers, clerks and typists who worked in the Cabinet offices. Again I was the centre of attention by scores of well-wishers drinking to my successful career as an author.

Early in January 1945 I wrote Johnny a long letter, expressing my admiration for his resolution, tireless efforts and magnificent achievements. He replied in an equally long letter recalling many of our early difficulties, thanking me for my unfailing support and stating that without my enthusiasm he would have thrown his hand in. Our happy friendship has now continued for over thirty years.

I have omitted to mention my last act as a deception planner. Curious to relate, although I had seen the Chief of Air Staff, Sir Charles Portal, many times striding along the corridors of the Air Ministry, and twice at big parties given by Pug Ismay, I had never been introduced to him. It was not until twenty years later that I was to meet him when lunching with our friends Tommy and Phyl Sopwith.

However, having been his sole representative for three years on LCS, when I made my farewells I felt it only proper that I should present myself to him. To my annoyance his personal assistant (as I learned later without consulting him) told me that he was too busy to see me. So I left it at that.

What I had hoped to do was to submit to him my ideas about deception in the future. Dear Johnny had always been hypnotized by his powerful acquaintances in the Army. He disliked the other two services and definitely distrusted all civilians, so it would have been useless for me to leave my brain-child to him.

It was that in peace-time, after the great reduction of our forces, military deception would be almost valueless in persuading our potential enemies (the Russians) that Britain was to be feared. But that it could be done by *scientific* deception. I envisaged, at a comparatively small cost, a considerable area of the South Downs being enclosed in barbed wire and electric fences. Within it a company of Engineers would be stationed, their personnel hand-picked and subject to the strictest security measures. All they would do was to dig a jigsaw of trenches and several great pits, the chalk from which would be easily visible in photographs taken by the reconnaissance aircraft of other powers. We would then let it leak out that, although our fighting services had become almost negligible, we possessed a new scientific weapon of great power – perhaps one which would enable us to bombard Moscow with atom bombs – then not considered possible – or something of that kind.

As I was unable to see Portal, I put my idea to Dickie Dickson, who thought it sound. But I don't think he ever did anything about it.

Some time during 1943 Johnny asked me to write a history of our section. This I started to do and got as far as the time when Harold, Ronald and James had joined Johnny and myself. I endeavoured to make it a really living document, describing the difficulties with which we had been faced in our early days and giving word portraits of everyone concerned. One night, long before I had brought it up to date, it was shown to Johnny without my knowledge.

The following day Johnny returned it to me, remarking coldly, 'This won't do at all, Dennis. No one will want to read all this nonsense about the sort of people we are. What I require for our files is a simple, straightforward record of the operations we have carried out.'

How wrong he was, seeing that the document was intended for posterity. But it was OK by me. I was delighted to be relieved of the job; although later, as I kept the original copy, it has proved of considerable value in writing this book.

No other history of LCS was attempted until some time after the war was over. Germany having been defeated, Ronald was sent out to the Far East to relieve Peter Fleming and, for his services there, awarded the OBE. On the collapse of Japan he came back to London and took over from Johnny as Controlling Officer, so that Johnny might return

Tribute and Departure

to civilian life. Having little to occupy him, Ronald then proceeded to write the official history of LCS.

His final conclusion was that, during the last two years of the war, by threats and ruses we had kept 400,000 German troops standing idle, in readiness to repel attacks that never matured. Not a bad performance for seven civilians.

Glossary of Codenames

OPERATIONS

Anvil (later Dragoon) Allied invasion of South of France, 1944
Bolero Despatch of US forces to Britain, 1942
Husky Allied invasion of Sicily, 1943
Ironclad Capture of Madagascar, 1942
Neptune Normandy landings. Part of Overlord, 1944
Overlord Allied invasion of France, 1944
Point-blank Intensive bombing of German cities, 1944
Roundup Plan for Allied invasion of Europe, 1943. Superseded by Overlord
Sea-lion German plan for projected invasion of England, 1940
Torch Allied invasion of North Africa, 1943

DECEPTION PLANS

Bodyguard (formerly Jael) Overall cover plan for Overlord
Fortitude (South) Part of Bodyguard: notional invasion of Pas de Calais, 1944
Foynes Part of Bodyguard: notional transfer of Eighth Army to England
Graffham Part of Bodyguard: notional invasion of Norway, 1944
Hardboiled Notional invasion of southern Norway, 1942
Mincemeat Part of cover plan for Husky ('The Man Who Never Was')
Passover (later Steppingstone and finally Overthrow) Part of cover plan for Torch: notional invasion of Pas de Calais, 1943
Solo One Part of cover plan for Torch: notional invasion of Norway, 1943

Index

Compiled by Gordon Robinson

Aerial Warfare (D.W. war paper), 12
After the Battle (D.W. war paper), 12, 44–5, 149–50
Air Ministry 'Star Fish' organization, Shepperton, 17–18
Airborne Divisions: 6th on D-Day, 195–209, 210; 1st at Arnhem, 217
Alençon, 215
Alexander, Field Marshal Sir Harold (later 1st Earl), 61, 86, 105–6, 108, 109, 119, 124–5, 126, 151, 152, 155, 169–71, 173, 175, 191, 192, 193, 218
Algiers, 126, 193; landings, 101, 102, 104, 105
Allenby, General Sir Edmund (later Field Marshal 1st Viscount), 19
Allied Planning Staff HQ, Norfolk House, St James's Square, 95, 131, 141, 148, 160, 174
Amery, Leopold Stennett, 54
Anderson, General, 104, 119
Andrade, Professor H. A. de C., 132–3
Anfa, 116–18
Antrim, Lieutenant the Earl of, 18
Antwerp, liberation of, 216, 217
Anzio landings, 124

Arbuthnott, Commander James, 30, 89–92, 93, 99, 102, 128, 129, 132, 133, 148, 160, 161, 162, 171, 188, 222, 223–4, 225–6, 228
Army Camouflage Development Centre, Farnham, 18
Arnhem, 175, 217
Arnhem, General von, 104
Art of War, The (D.W. war paper), 73
Artist (agent), 189
Aspidistra radio transmitter, 147–8
Astley, Philip, 155–6
Atlantic Wall, 211
Attlee, Clement (later 1st Earl), 24, 30, 66, 114, 223
Auchinleck, General Sir Claude (later Field Marshal), 105
Azores air base, 68–9

Baddington, Lieutenant-Colonel, 18
Baker, Mr (office messenger), 31
Balkan deception plan, 41–2, 173
Bangay, Wing Commander, 199, 203
Basic Principles of Enemy Deception, The (D.W. war paper), 33–6
Baumer, Colonel William H., 143
Beatty, Charles, 96
Beaverbrook, 1st Baron Sir William, 24, 30, 66

Index

Bell, Tommy, 30
Bergen, 55
Berlin, 216, 218; bombing of, 167
Bevan, Lady Barbara, 59, 185
Bevan, Lieutenant-Colonel J. H. (later Colonel), 11, 71, 80, 105, 114, 127, 128, 130, 133, 136, 137, 139, 141, 143, 146, 148, 151, 152–4, 171, 175, 179, 180, 186–7, 190, 191, 194, 195, 216, 220, 221, 224, 226, 227, 228–9; appointed London Controlling Officer, 35–6, 53, 57; qualities, 57; background, 58; temperament, 59, 110–11; service in 1914–18, 59–60; meetings in Paris with Churchill, 60; active service in Norway (1940), 61; lecturing Home Guard, 61; charm, 62; reorganizes LCS, 62–5; obsession with security, 63–4, 95–7; paper on *Strategic Deception – Sweden*, 64; move to basement, 66–7; proposals for new establishment, 67–8; liaison with Americans, 69–70, 95–7; paper on *Deception – Return to the Continent*, 72–3; cover plan for North Africa landings, 75–7, 82, 84, 92–3, 94, 98, 100; staff reinforcements, 78–9, 88, 89, 132; relationship with staff, 90; powers of persuasion, 111, 177; circulation of rumours, 154, 188; drafting cover plan for Overlord, 161–4; visits Lisbon and Moscow, 168–9; made a CB, 222
Beveridge plan, 138
Bevin, Ernest, 24, 31, 66
Birkin, Charles, 109
bombing of German cities, intensive (Operation Pointblank), 167
Bracken, Brendan, 24
Bradley, General Omar, 214
Bratby, Major Michael, 70–1, 85, 96, 160

Brest, 43
Bridges, Sir Edward, 24, 25, 66, 114, 222
Bright, Joan, 18, 36–7, 155–6
Bronx (agent), 189
Brooke, General Sir Alan (later Field Marshal 1st Viscount Alanbrooke), 24, 60, 106, 114, 116, 123–4, 170, 185, 215, 223
Brooks, General Dallas, 51, 55–6, 134, 147–8, 168, 225
Brunyate, Major, 29
Brussels liberation, 216
Brutus (agent), 188, 189
Bryant, Sir Arthur, 123
Buckley, Mr (Home Office), 29
Burges, Lawrence, 128
Burma deception, 42
Business of War (Kennedy), 123
Buzzard, Captain, 31, 92
Byron, Wing Commander, 29

Caen, 210, 213, 214
Cairo, 105, 106, 126
Camberley Staff College, Minley Manor, 107–8, 109
camouflage and dummies, use of, 17–18, 87, 173
Capel-Dunn, Lieutenant-Colonel Denis, 127–8
Carroll, Madeleine, 155
Casablanca: landings, 83, 103–4; security arrangements for Conference 1943 (Operation Symbol), 110, 112–25, 147
Casey, Richard (later 1st Baron), 86
Cass, Major, 29
Cassino battle, 124
censorship of diplomatic bags, 190
Cessation of Hostilities (D.W. war paper), 51–2
Chamberlain, Neville, 166
Chambers, Colonel, 56
Chartres, 215
Chartwell, 166
Chatsworth Court flat, Earls Court, 12, 22, 68, 75, 109, 128,

Index

131, 134, 137, 143, 165, 186, 225
Chiang Kai-shek, 149
Chumley, Flight Lieutenant, 151, 152
Churchill, Clementine (later Lady), 74
Churchill, Mrs Randolph, 159, 160
Churchill, Winston (later Sir), 25, 27, 66, 67, 69, 75, 81, 102–3, 105, 153, 161, 165, 171, 173, 183, 221, 224; choice of code names, 37–8; fears another German war, 49; suggests Madagascar deception, 55; discussions with Col. Bevan in Paris, 60; headquarters, 21, 23–4, 74, 126; paper on expeditions to Continent, 71–2; resolve to liberate Europe, 108; Casablanca Conference, 110, 112–23; persuades Americans to occupy North Africa and strike through Italy, 121–3; at the White House, 144–6; plans for postwar, 149–50; creates Churchill Club, 159; wine supply, 166; entertains at Chartwell, 166–7; recuperative powers, 167; accepts Overlord, 169–70; aids Bodyguard deception, 190; visits troops in France, 213, 215; attitude to honours, 222–3
Churchill Club, Ashburnham House, 159
Clapham Junction, 213
Clark, Major Neil Gordon, 29, 128, 129, 132, 133, 137, 148, 152, 161, 162, 171, 172, 179, 180, 188, 222
Clarke, Lieutenant-Colonel Dudley, 19–20, 34, 54, 85, 86–7, 89, 95, 96, 97, 100, 126, 140, 142, 148, 150–1, 154, 160, 161, 171, 180, 187, 192, 193, 213, 225

Clemenceau, Georges, 60
Cobweb and Beetle (agents), 189
codewords, 37–8
Codrington, 116, 118
Colyer, Air Marshal, 226
Combe, Major Eddie (later Lieutenant-Colonel), 27–8, 29–30, 47, 81, 135, 161, 171, 186, 225
Combined Operations HQ, 18
commissioned into RAFVR to a post on the Joint Planning Staff, 21–2, 109; release (D.W.'s), 226–7
Cooke, Lieutenant-Colonel Peter, 96
Cooper, Alfred Duff (later 1st Viscount Norwich), 152–3
Corsica, 123
cover planning, general principles of, 34–6
Crawford, Major-General, 201, 202, 205, 209
Crockatt, Brigadier Norman, 18, 20, 171
Cruikshank, Dr Charles, 12 fn.
Crusade in Europe (Eisenhower), 123
Cunningham, Admiral Sir Andrew (later 1st Viscount), 89, 123
Cuthbert, Captain, 89

D-Day: deception regarding time and place, 172–3, 191–3; landings, 204–9
Daluege, General, 55
Darlan, Admiral, 103
Darvall, Air Marshal Sir Lawrence, 26, 224
Davey, Charles Balfour, 95, 107, 108
Dawson, Air Commodore Tubby, 187, 190
Deception and Attrition in the Pacific (war paper), 52, 54
Deception – Return to the Continent (war paper), 73

Index

Deception in World War II (Cruikshank), 12
Deception on the Highest Plane (D.W. war paper), 50, 56
decorated with US Bronze Star, 223
Delgado, Umberto, 68, 69
Dickson, Group Captain William 'Dickie' (later Marshal of the RAF Sir William), 12–13, 21, 22, 25, 26, 106, 226, 228
Diego-Suarez, 45–6, 47, 48, 55
Dill, Field Marshal Sir John, 107, 108
double agents, 181, 188–9, 214
Dublin, 189

Eden, Anthony (later Lord Avon), 24, 41–2, 66, 190
Eden, Joan, 37, 63, 66
Eindhofen, 217
Eisenhower, General Dwight, 93, 95, 121, 123, 131, 133, 143, 160, 165, 171, 173, 174, 179, 190, 201, 217, 218
El Alamein, 105–6
Elliot, Air Chief Marshal Sir William, 68–9, 78, 103–4, 184, 190, 192, 193
Elliot, Rosemary, 184
entertaining: at Chatsworth Court, 62, 75, 109–10, 128, 143–4, 165; at the Churchill Club, 160
Europe, plan for Allied invasion of, 1943 (Operation Roundup), 84, 121–2
European theatre, deception in ('Ops B'), 187–8
Executive Planning Section (EPS), 38

fake invasion force on Thames estuary, First US Army Group (FUSAG) (plan Fortitude), 172–3, 180–1, 188, 189–90
Falaise, massacre of Germans at, 215
Falkenhausen, 56

false information to enemy, conveying, 35, 82–3, 180–1, 188–9, 214
Far East, deception in ('Echelon D'), 36, 42, 54–5, 187
Finland, Russian offensive against, 168–9
Finter, Lieutenant-Commander Alec, 160, 173
Fleming, Major Peter, 36, 42, 48, 54, 96, 97–8, 148, 155, 161, 187, 228
Foch, Marshal Ferdinand, 60
Fontainebleau, 215
Foot, Dingle (later Sir), 179
Foreign Office and neutrals, dealings with, 64, 74, 75, 156–7
Forster, Brigadier Stuart, 151
France, Allied invasion 1944 (Operation Overlord), 168–9, 194–209; cover plans: Bodyguard, 156, 161–4, 172, 173, 176, 179, 181, 187, 190, 210, 213, 215; Fortitude (South), notional invasion of Pas de Calais, 172–3, 180–1, 188, 189–90, 213; plan Foynes, notional transfer of Eighth Army, 180; Graffham, notional invasion of Norway, 176–80; Normandy landings (Operation Neptune), 38, 173, 191, 204–11; battle for France, 210–19; Third US army advance, 215, 216
Franco, General, 73–4, 112, 118, 188
Future Operations Planning Staff (FOPS), 13, 20, 25, 26, 27, 30–1, 49, 52, 57, 121, 187

Gale, General Sir Richard, 107–9, 197–206, 208–9, 210–11
Garbo (agent), 181, 188, 189, 214
Gaulle, General Charles de, 80, 120, 121, 217
Gelis, General, 55
George VI, 12, 80, 137, 150, 209, 222

Index

George, David Lloyd (1st Earl Lloyd-George), 60
German plan for projected invasion of England, 1940 (Sea Lion), 38
Ghent, 216
Gibraltar, 84–5, 86, 88, 93, 120, 190–1, 192, 193
Giraud, General, 120–1
Goldbranson, Lieutenant-Colonel, 95
Gort, General (later Field Marshal 1st Viscount), 85, 86
Gott, General, 105, 106
Goudie, Major Eric, 29, 81, 137, 161
Graham, Colonel, 28, 81
Green, Tom, 135–6
Green, Mrs, 135–6
Greig, Sir Louis, 22, 26, 224
Grierson, Group Captain, 168
Griffiths, Major, 198
Groom, Group Captain Victor, 26, 28, 31, 40
Gubbins, Major-General Colin (later Sir), 18, 134–5
Guingand, General Freddy de, 106
Gummer ('Man at Gib'), 190, 191

Haig, Field Marshal 1st Earl, 60
Hale, Lionel, 154
Hallorhan, Captain, 20
Hambro, Sir Charles, 61
Hamburg contact, 189
Hare, Robertson, 144
Harvey, Wing Commander, 31
Harwell RAF station, 195–209
Hesketh, Major Roger Fleetwood, 59, 181, 189, 214
Hitler, Adolf, 46, 50, 51, 52, 56, 71, 72, 73, 74, 112, 118, 119, 124, 132, 147, 156, 169, 176, 179, 204, 212, 214, 215; assassination attempt, 216
Hoare, Sir Reginald, 128, 131–2, 133

Holland, Major-General Joe, 18
Hollinghurst, Air Vice-Marshal, 201, 202, 203–4, 206
Hollis, Brigadier (later General) Sir Leslie, 24, 25, 66, 91, 113, 136, 138, 144–6, 221
Hopkins, Harry, 165
Hopkinson, Henry (later Lord Colyton), 86, 168
How to Keep Turkey Out of the War (D.W. war paper), 12
Hughes-Hallett, Captain Charles (later Admiral Sir Charles), 92
Hungaria restaurant, 137, 143, 225
Hutchinson, Commander, 91

I Was Monty's Double, 193
Implementation of Military Deception, The (war paper), 36
Information to the Press (war paper), 94
Inglis, Air Vice-Marshal Frank, 184
Inglis, Midge, 184
Inter-Services Security Board (ISSB), 38, 67, 69, 71, 81, 82, 225; codeword register, 37; composition of, 28–9; cover planning, 18–19, 34, 46; security, 18–19, 98, 182
Ismay, General Sir Hastings, (later 1st Baron) 18, 24, 25, 28, 36, 66, 78, 79, 91, 102, 109, 113, 123, 128–9, 136, 144, 155, 166–7, 183, 195, 222, 223, 227
Italy: armistice plans, 147, 157; Allied invasion, 157

Jacob, Colonel Ian (later General), 24, 25, 113, 136
James, M. E. Clifton, 191–3
Jean Bart wreck, 117–18
Jodl, Colonel General Alfred, 214
Johnson, Squadron Leader, 197
Joint Planning Staff of the War Cabinet (JPS), 56, 66, 75, 109, 131, 136, 137, 143, 154; officers,

Joint Planning Staff—*contd*
12–13, 61–2, 139, 160, 187;
creates deception section, 20–1;
fortress HQ, 24; Joint Intelligence Committee, 45, 51, 55,
127, 133, 136; original Torch
plan, 104; preference for
Sardinia invasion, 123–4;
papers, 133; post-war plans,
167; planning for a return to
France, 174; congratulates
London Controlling Section,
221–2
Jones, Mr (civilian PA), 144–6
Jones, Squadron Leader Evan,
198–9

Keitel, Field Marshal, 179
Kennedy, Major-General Sir
John, 123
Kershaw, Wing Commander, 136
Kesselring, Field Marshal, 100–1
Khartoum, 113
Knight, Maxwell, 74
Koessler, Dr, 189
Krummacher, Colonel, 214

Le Mans, 215
Leigh Mallory, Air Marshal Sir
Trafford, 201, 203, 204
Lennox, Lieutenant-Colonel
Gilbert, 29
Lessey, 214
Lewis, Commander 'Ginger', 28–9
Lindemann, Professor, 23, 74
Links, Joe, 160
Lisbon, 168, 190; German agents
in, 113, 188
London Controlling Section
(LCS): established as Deception
Section of FOPS, 20; composition, 20–1, 32; headquarters, 26;
detached from FOPS on Col.
Bevan's appointment, 57–65;
move to fortress basement,
66–7; liaison with US,
69–70, 95–7; deception plans:
Bodyguard (1944), 156, 161–4,
172, 173, 176, 179, 181, 187,
190, 210, 213, 215; Fortitude
(1944), 172–3, 180–1, 188,
189–90, 213; Foynes (1944),
180; Graffham (1944), 176–80;
Hardboiled (1942), 36–40, 45,
46, 48, 54, 55; Mincemeat
(1943), 151–3; Passover (1943),
77–8, 82, 84, 93, 94; Solo One,
77–8, 82, 83, 93, 94; cover for
Casablanca Conference, 112–15;
cover for Husky, 140–2, 151–3;
completion of section, 128–32;
tribute from Chiefs of Staff, 57,
221–2; Reunion Dinner, 161,
223; history of, 228–9
Lumby, Lieutenant-Colonel
A. F. R., 20, 26–7, 28, 32–3,
35, 36, 37, 38, 39, 40, 44, 47,
48, 49, 50, 52–3, 62, 63, 64,
70, 79–80, 81, 92
Lutyens, Squadron Leader
Robert, 159, 160
Lyttelton, Oliver (Lord Chandos),
27

MacFarlane, General Mason, 85,
86, 192, 193
Macnamara, Wing Commander,
197, 198, 202, 205, 209
Madagascar, capture of (Operation Ironclad), 45–8, 55
Maisky, Ivan, 42
Mallet, Sir Victor, 177, 180
Mann, Major, 31
Martin (Churchill secretary), 23
Medhurst, Air Chief Marshal Sir
Charles, 91, 143
Mediterranean and Middle East
deception ('A' Force), 19–20,
34, 86–7, 89, 171, 187, 225
Mersa Matruh, 105
Messerschmitt, Willi, 56
Military Intelligence (Research),
MI(R), 18
Military Intelligence (Secret
Intelligence Service) (MI6),
19, 29, 51, 151, 152

Index

Military Intelligence (Security Service) (MI5), 12, 19, 29, 51, 61, 82, 115, 188
Military Intelligence (War Office branch responsible for escape and evasion of POWs) (MI9), 20, 171
Ministry of Information, 12, 188
Mockler-Ferryman, Brigadier, 95
Moffat, Major John, 29
Montagu, Lieutenant-Commander the Hon. Ewen, 29, 88, 151-2, 153
Montgomery, General Bernard (later Field Marshal 1st Viscount), 87, 104, 125; at El Alamein, 105-6; morale-builder, 105, 175; criticized, 105-7, 109, 174-5, 217-18; bogged down in Sicily, 124; directing Normandy operations, 173, 174-5, 176, 210, 213, 214-15; security risk, 174; his double, 191-3; Arnhem drop, 217; unpopularity with Americans, 218
Morgan, General Freddy, 130-1, 141, 148, 174
Morley, Major Derrick, 129-31, 133, 137, 148, 179, 222
Mortain, 215
Morton, Major Sir Desmond, 23, 66, 74, 75, 110
Moscow mission to co-ordinate deception strategy (1944), 168-9
Mountbatten, Lord Louis (later Admiral of the Fleet 1st Earl), 25, 116, 117, 123, 150, 167, 174
Mulberry harbours, 210, 211, 213, 217
Mullet and Puppet (agents), 189
Mussolini, Benito, 157-8
mystic German leader ruse, 50-1, 56

neutrals, dealings with, 64, 73-5, 156-7
Niemoller, Pastor, 56

Nogues, General, 103
Nordenskiöld, Lieutenant-General Bengt, 177-9
Normandy landings 1944 (Operation Neptune), 38, 173, 191, 206-11
North Africa, Allied invasion of (Operation Torch), 101-5; cover plans: 75-8, 83-6, 88, 92-101; Passover (later Steppingstone and Overthrow), notional invasion of Pas de Calais, 1943, 77-8, 82, 84, 93, 94; Solo One: notional invasion of Norway, 1943, 77-8, 82, 83, 93, 94
Northern Ireland, US troops in, 69
Norway, notional invasions of: Hardboiled (1942), 36-40, 45, 46, 48, 54, 55; Solo One (1943), 77-8, 82, 83, 93, 94; Graffham (1944), 176-80
Nutting, Anthony, 179
Nye, Lieutenant-General, 114, 151, 152

Oberkommando der Wehrmacht (OKW), 189, 213, 214
Odessa, 41
oil supplies, German, 51, 52
Operation Heartbreak (Duff Cooper), 153
Oran, 103, 104

Paget, General Sir Bernard, 126
Pandora (Herr Hempel) agent, 189
Paris, liberation of, 215, 217
Pas de Calais, notional invasions of: Passover (1943), 77-8, 82, 84, 93, 94; Fortitude (South) (1944), 172-3, 180-1, 188, 189-90, 213
Patton, General George, 103-4, 173, 180, 190, 215, 216
peace, planning ahead for, 44-5, 49, 149-50, 167

Peck (Churchill secretary), 23
Peck, Air Chief Marshal Sir
  Richard, 194–5
Peenemünde raid on rocket
  establishment, 183–4
Percival, General, 43
Pershing, General John, 60
Pétain, Marshal, 46, 103, 112,
  120, 121
Peteval, Major Harold (later
  Lieutenant-Colonel), 78–9, 91,
  92, 93, 127, 128, 129, 130, 133,
  148, 160, 172, 181, 222, 228
Peveler, Wing Commander, 179
Philippeville, 104, 105
Pim, Captain, 23
Political Warfare Executive
  (PWE), 19, 35, 56, 134, 188,
  216
Portal, Air Chief Marshal Sir
  Charles (later 1st Viscount),
  25, 116, 118–19, 123, 223, 227,
  228
Pound, Admiral Sir Dudley, 25
Pound, Squadron Leader, 197
press relations and coverage,
  175–6, 194
prisoners of war, assisting escaping,
  20, 171
promoted Wing Commander,
  186–7

Quaglino's restaurant, 194
Quebec conference (Quadrant),
  154–5

Rance, Mr (Office of Works), 67
Rennes, 215
Resistance to Invasion (D.W. war
  paper), 12
revolution plan for Germany
  (Aspidistra), 216
Rhodes, 170
Ritchie, General, 105
Robertshaw, Commander, 26, 31
Robertson, Lieutenant-Colonel
  'Tar', 58, 181, 188
rockets: V1, 212–13; V2, 219

Rodeise, General, 55
Rome, Allied capture of, 124
Rommel, General Erwin, 105,
  214
Roosevelt, Franklin D., 24, 95,
  110, 112–13, 117, 118, 145–6,
  165, 224
Rowan (Churchill secretary), 23
Rules restaurant, 29, 30, 135
Rundstedt, General Karl von, 213
Russia: co-ordination of deception
  strategy, 168–9; plan to
  deceive with bogus scientific
  weapon, 227–8

Sacht, 56
St Lo, 214
Salazar, President, 69
Sanders, General Leman von, 19
Sandys, Duncan, 183
Sardinia, 123–4, 125, 170
Scharnhorst, Gneisenau and *Prinz
  Eugen* break-out from Brest, 43
Scott, Peter, 71
secret weapon threat, 183–6
security work, 18–19, 98, 189–90
Seven Assignments (Clarke), 19
Sewell, Mary, 159
Sfax, occupation by Allies, 119
Sicily, Allied invasion of: cover
  plan, 125–6, 140–2, 146–7,
  Mincemeat (The Man Who
  Never Was), 151–3; landings,
  150–4
Singapore surrender to Japanese,
  43
Skorzeny, Otto, 158
Slessor, Air Marshal Sir John, 109
Slim, Field Marshal William
  Joseph (later 1st Viscount), 175
Smuts, General Jan Christian
  (later Field Marshal), 48, 113,
  165
Somerville, Admiral Sir James, 89
Sopwith, Phyl, 227
Sopwith, Tommy, 227
South of France, Allied invasion
  of (Anvil), 170, 173, 213

Index

Spaatz, General, 203
Spain, plans to occupy, 73–5; shelter for U-boats, 73
Special Operations Executive (SOE), 18, 19, 35, 135, 188
Stanley, Maureen, 53
Stanley, Colonel Oliver, 13, 20, 21, 22, 27, 29, 30–1, 33, 36, 37, 38, 39, 41, 44, 49, 51, 52, 53, 54, 56, 57, 224
Stauffenberg, General von, 216
Stavanger, 36, 39
Stewart, Sir Findlater, 184, 185
Stockholm, 177, 179
Stranger than Fiction (Wheatley), 12
Strangeways, Major David, 85–7, 88
Strategic Deception – Sweden (Col Bevan), war paper, 64
Strategical Planning Staff (STRATS), 26, 27, 52, 71, 74–5, 82, 187
Sturges, Major-General, 47, 48
Super (agent), 189
Supreme Headquarters Allied Expeditionary Force (SHAEF), 187
Surplice, Group Captain, 197, 200–5, 207, 209, 211
Sweden, Allied strategic deception plans, 64, 177–80; supplying ball bearings to Germans, 156–7

Tate (agent), 189
Tatham, Eddie, 166
Tedder, Air Chief Marshal Sir Arthur (later Marshal of the Royal Air Force 1st Baron), 119
Teheran conference (1943), 161, 168
Templer, General Sir Gerald (later Field Marshal), 130
Tennant, Flight Lieutenant, 29
Theresa (agent), 181
Thompson, Commander 'Tommy', 23, 74, 110, 114, 165–6

Thornton, Air Vice-Marshal, 177–9
Tito, President, 122
Total War (D.W. war paper), 12
Treasure (agent), 189
tributes to D.W.'s contribution, 221–2, 224–7
Tricycle (agent), 188
Trondheim, 180
Troyes, 215
Tunis, Allied occupation of, 87, 125
Turkish attitudes, 170
Turner, Colonel Sir John, 18, 141
Twenty Committee, 19, 148

United States, establishing deception links with, 70–1; forces despatched to Britain (Operation Bolero), 69–70, 121
Uxbridge Intake Course, 21–2, 26

Vachell, Air Commodore John, 194, 224
Village Defence (D.W. war paper), 12
Vintras, Group Captain Roland, 21, 25–6, 28, 33, 36, 68, 91, 147, 155, 224–5

war correspondents, 195, 209
War Diaries (Alanbrooke), 123–4
war papers to Joint Planning Staff of War Cabinet, 12, 33–6, 44–5, 50–2, 54, 55, 56, 61–4, 73–5, 94, 142–3, 147, 149–50, 156, 161–4, 167, 176, 224
Warth, Douglas, 209
Washington conferences, 122, 144–6, 149
Waterfield, Captain Gordon, 160–1
Wavell, General Sir Archibald (later Field Marshal 1st Earl), 19, 20, 42, 54, 55, 105, 155
Weber-Brown, Lieutenant-Colonel, 136, 137–9

Wheatley, Joan (wife), 22, 31, 36, 96, 135–6, 152, 155, 186, 190, 191, 210, 225; member of MI5, 12; entertaining at Chatsworth Court, 62, 109–10, 128, 143–4, 165; remains in London throughout the blitz, 184
White, Lieutenant-Colonel, 31
Wild, Colonel Noel, 161, 179, 181, 187, 188
Wilson, Sir Charles (later Lord Moran), 114–15
Wilson, Field Marshal Sir Henry, 60
Wilson, General 'Jumbo', 126
wine supplier for Churchill, 166
Wingate, Sir Reginald, 80
Wingate, Major Ronald (later Colonel), 79–82, 91, 92, 93, 110–11, 112, 128, 129, 133, 137, 148, 157, 161, 162, 171, 179, 222, 223, 228–9
Wyatt, Harvey, 24

Yalta conference (1945), 155
Younger, Diana (stepdaughter), 12, 62
Younger, Jack (stepson), 12
Younger, William (stepson), 12